Nepotism
in
Organizations

The Organizational Frontier Series

SIOP Organizational Frontiers Series

SERIES EDITOR

Eduardo Salas
University of Central Florida

Jones: (2012) *Nepotism in Organizations*

Hofmann/Frese: (2011) *Errors in Organizations*

Outtz: (2009) *Adverse Impact: Implications for Organizational Staffing and High-Stakes Selection*

Kozlowski/Salas: (2009) *Learning, Training, and Development in Organizations*

Klein/Becker/Meyer: (2009) *Commitment in Organizations: Accumulated Wisdom and New Directions*

Salas/Goodwin/Burke: (2009) *Team Effectiveness in Complex Organizations*

Kanfer/Chen/Pritchard: (2008) *Work Motivation: Past, Present, and Future*

De Dreu/Gelfand: (2008) *The Psychology of Conflict and Conflict Management in Organizations*

Ostroff/Judge: (2007) *Perspectives on Organizational Fit*

Baum/Frese/Baron: (2007) *The Psychology of Entrepreneurship*

Weekley/Ployhart: (2006) *Situational Judgment Tests: Theory, Measurement, and Application*

Dipboye/Colella: (2005) *Discrimination at Work: The Psychological and Organizational Bases*

Griffin/O'Leary-Kelly: (2004) *The Dark Side of Organizational Behavior*

Hofmann/Tetrick: (2003) *Health and Safety in Organizations*

Jackson/Hitt/DeNisi: (2003) *Managing Knowledge for Sustained Competitive Knowledge*

Barrick/Ryan: (2003) *Personality and Work*

Lord/Klimoski/Kanfer: (2002) *Emotions in the Workplace*

Drasgow/Schmitt: (2002) *Measuring and Analyzing Behavior in Organizations*

Feldman: (2002) *Work Careers*

Zaccaro/Klimoski: (2001) *The Nature of Organizational Leadership*

Rynes/Gerhart: (2000) *Compensation in Organizations*

Klein/Kozlowski: (2000) *Multilevel Theory, Research, and Methods in Organizations*

Ilgen/Pulakos: (1999) *The Changing Nature of Performance*

Earley/Erez: (1997) *New Perspectives on International I–O Psychology*

Murphy: (1996) *Individual Differences and Behavior in Organizations*

Guzzo/Salas: (1995) *Team Effectiveness and Decision Making*

Howard: (1995) *The Changing Nature of Work*

Schmitt/Borman: (1993) *Personnel Selection in Organizations*

Zedeck: (1991) *Work, Families, and Organizations*

Schneider: (1990) *Organizational Culture and Climate*

Goldstein: (1989) *Training and Development in Organizations*

Campbell/Campbell: (1988) *Productivity in Organizations*

Hall: (1987) *Career Development in Organizations*

Nepotism
in
Organizations

Edited by

Robert G. Jones
Missouri State University

Routledge
Taylor & Francis Group
New York   London

Routledge
Taylor & Francis Group
711 Third Avenue
New York, NY 10017

Routledge
Taylor & Francis Group
27 Church Road
Hove, East Sussex BN3 2FA

© 2012 by Taylor & Francis Group, LLC
Routledge is an imprint of Taylor & Francis Group, an Informa business

Printed in the United States of America on acid-free paper
Version Date: 20110808

International Standard Book Number: 978-0-415-88276-7 (Hardback)

Library of Congress Cataloging-in-Publication Data

Nepotism in organizations / editor, Robert G. Jones.
　　p. cm. -- (SIOP Organizational frontiers series)
　　Summary: "Preface: Nepotism is a pervasive phenomenon in human organizations (Bellow, 2003). The Family Firm Institute (FFI, 2009), a group of practitioners and academics with about 1,500 members, is designed to provide "education and networking services" to consultants of family firms. The Web page for FFI (www.ffi.org) states that family firms are "the dominant form of business organization worldwide." Although this statement appears to be unsubstantiated by research evidence, it would be easy to argue that family connections are a major determinant of behavior in organizations. For example, major stockholders of one of the most successful business enterprises in the last century, Walmart, are relatives of its founder. It is not hard to find other examples of the integration of familial and organizational relationships (Bellow, 2003). Given that a primary purpose of industrial-organizational (I-O) psychology is to study behavior in work organizations from the perspective of scientific psychology, it is remarkable how little descriptive research exists on this topic. A PsychInfo search using the search phrase "nepotism and organizations" yielded 27 articles, and included several about animal behavior (with notable exceptions in the I-O psychology literature by Werbel and Hames, 1996, and Kets de Vries, 1993). Apologists might argue that broader organizational studies have dealt with this under such umbrellas as social capital. However, research in ethological journals suggests that there is a meaningful set of psychological phenomena related specifically to nepotism that has not been explored in organizations. The titles found in this search ("In Praise of Nepotism," "Anti-Nepotism Reconsidered," "Nepotism: Boon or Bane") suggest another possible explanation for this lack of."--Provided by publisher.
　　Includes bibliographical references and index.
　　ISBN 978-0-415-88276-7 (hardback)
　　1. Family corporations. 2. Nepotism. I. Jones, Robert G. Dr.

HD62.25.N47 2011
338.6--dc23
　　　　　　　　　　　　　　　　　　　　　　　　　　　　　　　　　　　2011031243

Visit the Taylor & Francis Web site at
http://www.taylorandfrancis.com

and the Psychology Press Web site at
http://www.psypress.com

Contents

Series Foreword

And now for something new in our science. Yes, the elephant is in the room, but most people simply were not aware—organizational nepotism. This is a refreshing and welcome volume. A topic that probably is talked about but not researched enough despite its prevalence in organizations. A quick perusal of our journals and textbooks will lead us to conclude that this topic is not really "mainstream" industrial–organizational (I–O) psychology. Hopefully, the research discussed in this volume will engage more scholars and practitioners to deal with this topic.

Robert (Bob) Jones has assembled an outstanding group of scholars looking with fresh eyes at this problem. This group of scientists provides us with definitions, theories, constructs, and approaches to think about nepotism. These are different views from different disciplines. This volume is full of interesting and insightful suggestions about what might matter in nepotism. The authors lay out a potential research stream and also creates a path for applications and practices.

On behalf of SIOP's Organizational Frontier Book Series, thank you Bob! And thanks to all the authors! This is a wonderful contribution to our science. I hope this volume generates the much needed research on the topic.

Eduardo Salas
University of Central Florida
Organizational Frontier Book Series Editor

Series Foreword

Preface

Nepotism is a pervasive phenomenon in human organizations (Bellow, 2003). The Family Firm Institute (FFI, 2009), a group of practitioners and academics with about 1,500 members, is designed to provide "education and networking services" to consultants of family firms. The Web page for FFI (www.ffi.org) states that family firms are "the dominant form of business organization worldwide." Although this statement appears to be unsubstantiated by research evidence, it would be easy to argue that family connections are a major determinant of behavior in organizations. For example, major stockholders of one of the most successful business enterprises in the last century, Walmart, are relatives of its founder. It is not hard to find other examples of the integration of familial and organizational relationships (Bellow, 2003).

Given that a primary purpose of industrial–organizational (I–O) psychology is to study behavior in work organizations from the perspective of scientific psychology, it is remarkable how little descriptive research exists on this topic. A PsychInfo search using the search phrase "nepotism and organizations" yielded 27 articles, and included several about animal behavior (with notable exceptions in the I–O psychology literature by Werbel and Hames, 1996, and Kets de Vries, 1993). Apologists might argue that broader organizational studies have dealt with this under such umbrellas as social capital. However, research in ethological journals suggests that there is a meaningful set of psychological phenomena related specifically to nepotism that has not been explored in organizations.

The titles found in this search ("In Praise of Nepotism," "Anti-Nepotism Reconsidered," "Nepotism: Boon or Bane") suggest another possible explanation for this lack of research. Specifically, given the fundamental importance of "job-related" decision making in organizations, it is possible that there is an implicit prejudice with respect to nepotism. Specifically, much of the work of human resources professionals is aimed at avoiding decisions based on things that are not demonstrably job related and rational. Decisions that appear to be influenced by family relationships seem not to conform to these "job-related and rational" standards for decision making. Although there are very good practical reasons for basing decisions on apparently rational and job-related factors, there may also be good reasons for understanding the assumptions underlying apparently non-rational decisions, as well. There may even be important things to learn by exploring our own professional prejudice against nepotism. Therefore, it is the premise of this book that defining a psychology of nepotism from various descriptive perspectives will contribute substantially to our effectiveness as scientist–practitioners.

We will rely on two main assumptions. Perhaps the most important question we can ask is whether nepotism is adaptive to an organization. To address this, the first assumption we will follow is what Mulder (this volume, Chapter 10) refers to as the "neutrality principle." We will attempt to define nepotism through the *descriptive* lens of human behaviors and psychological characteristics, rather than as a *good* or *bad* phenomenon. *Prescriptive* arguments certainly will arise as authors explore the definition of the phenomenon from their topical perspectives. At the very least, the negative connotation sometimes accorded the term (Bellow, 2003) makes it hard to avoid passing judgment. Nevertheless, the final chapter will draw on previous chapters to construct a general set of "frontier" issues regarding the relationships between nepotism constructs and *actual* (as opposed to supposed or assumed) organizational effectiveness. If the success across cultures of organizations with nested familial relationships is an indication, nepotism does in fact have some effect on effectiveness. And the ability of I–O psychology and its relatives to adapt to (or eradicate) this pervasive phenomenon is likely to prove important to our own continued effectiveness. Put simply, if we do not understand the phenomenon descriptively, we cannot do much about it.

Our second assumption is that scientific definitions evolve, often to the extent of abandoning the original conceptualization. This evolution is a result of the social and paradigmatic structures around empirical science, and our strategy relies on, and follows from these (assumed) structures. Specifically, the book is structured around common topical headings from I–O psychology textbooks. These conventional topics have evolved substantial empirical literatures, providing convenient structures for framing our exploration into the prevalent but underresearched problems of nepotism.

Applying the lenses of topical constructs to nepotism may merely put old wine into new bottles. The "new bottle" here is a different way of viewing conventional topical areas in our field (for example, selection, recruitment, commitment, culture) by reference to existing phenomena, without changing prescriptions for practice. But even this modest "new bottle" outcome may prove important, given the context of organizational practice, where scientists commonly deal with the "folk theories" and jargon around such things as nepotism. The close relationship between science and practice in I–O psychology makes understanding such folk theories particularly important, since it allows us to address them through existing scientific lenses.

But it is also possible that given recent innovations in areas such as evolutionary psychology, the authors will arrive at meaningful new constructs. Additionally, if nepotism is actually multiple phenomena, the development and integration of constructs across topical areas is a potentially valuable contribution to both scientific practice and practical science.

Integrating topical areas is also one of the major problems with an edited volume. Two factors are likely to provide advantages to integrating this volume. First, ironically, the newness of the topic as an area for empirical development suggests that the definition problem will consume a considerable portion of the chapters. This will likely show very explicitly the similarities and differences in perspectives, making it easier for readers to construct their own integrating schemata. Second, the structuring of the book will highlight the integration of I–O psychology as a whole. The strategy of ordering of chapters according to I–O psychology textbook topics will have the added advantage of integrating discussions using convention. Thus, themes are likely to emerge relating to such things as culture, ethics, organizational change and development, and underlying factors influencing both perceptions and realities of nepotism. These will be explicitly highlighted in the two final chapters—one aimed at theoretical construction and the other at practice and effectiveness.

The chapter authors are from two general groups. The first is a group of leading thinkers and experts regarding the I–O "headings" of each chapter. Unique to this group is the fact that most of its authors have considerable practitioner experience, in addition to their prominent scholarly work. These authors will therefore bring many examples and phenomenological insights to their chapters. Questioning assumptions is a demonstrable part of their background, as well. The second group includes relatively new scholars who have begun the arduous task of constructing meaningful empirical structures to support future research and practice relating to nepotism. A potentially valuable component of this volume is the interaction between these two groups as chapter draft contents are shared among authors. The final chapter will attempt to summarize these interactions.

The authors in the book will carry the primary responsibility for delineating content in their chapters. This is a result of the lack of empirical and conceptual development of the topic of inquiry, and is a large part of the reason for arranging things in terms of "conventional" I–O textbook topics. As mentioned earlier, a large part of each chapter will be the developing of definitions of nepotism from the perspective of I–O topical areas. Authors are able to do this definition and its consequent construct development as a result of their considerable expertise or, in the cases where there is nascent research literature, from their particular research base.

REFERENCES

Bellow, A. (2004). *In praise of nepotism*. New York: Doubleday.

Kets de Vries, M. F. (1993). The dynamics of family controlled firms: The good and the bad news. *Organizational Dynamics, 21*(3), 59–71.

Stich, S. (1993) The future of folk psychology. In S. M. Christensen & D. R. Turner (Eds.), *Folk psychology and the philosophy of mind* (pp. 93–117). Hillsdale, NJ: Lawrence Erlbaum.

Werbel, J. D., & Hames, D. S. (1996). Anti-nepotism reconsidered: The case of husband and wife employment. *Group & Organization Management, 21*(3), 365–379.

Acknowledgments

Contrary to the popular myth, attempts at exploring frontiers are not usually accomplished through rugged individualism. Risk taking under conditions of uncertainty typically relies on mutual support. Perhaps the most famous explorations in history and science are identified with a single name (for example, Darwin, Erikson, Columbus, Curie), but closer scrutiny almost always shows this use of a single name to be at least an oversimplification, and often excludes major contributors. Perhaps the use of a single name has developed as a heuristic device to aid history students in remembering important events. Regardless, when we take risks, we usually rely on one another.

This Frontiers book is no different. The authors, editors, and Society for Industrial and Organizational Psychology Frontiers board members all took part in developing this volume. We all owe debts of gratitude to our academic and professional colleagues, mentors, and students. We also owe a debt to Adam Bellow for pioneering the book that inspired this one.

Perhaps most relevant to our efforts, and to this particular book, are the family members who supported our risk taking. Thanks to all who contributed.

About the Editor

Robert G. Jones, PhD, is professor of psychology and department head at Missouri State University. After a first career in music and banking, he returned to school to obtain his PhD in industrial–organizational psychology from The Ohio State University in 1992. In this second career, Dr. Jones and his students, colleagues, and clients have dealt with a broad range of issues in selection and assessment. Most of this work has focused on understanding and managing the bases for applied, person perception–based assessments, including emotive perception and prejudices. He has addressed these issues in various publications, numerous applied settings, and classrooms in the United States, Australia, and The Netherlands. As book review editor of *Personnel Psychology* (1999–2004), Dr. Jones had the pleasant task of reading lots of books, including the ones that inspired this one.

About the Contributors

Thomas E. Becker, PhD, is a professor of management in the Lerner College of Business and Economics at the University of Delaware. He received his PhD in industrial–organizational psychology from The Ohio State University in 1990. His research interests are employee commitment, integrity, motivation, job performance, and research methods. He has published in leading journals in psychology and management, and in 2009, coedited a book, *Commitment in Organizations* (SIOP Organizational Frontiers Series, Routledge/Psychology Press), with John Meyer and Howard Klein. Dr. Becker is an associate editor at *Human Performance*, and a member of the editorial board at *Organizational Behavior and Human Decision Processes*. He has held the Belgian International Franqui Chair in the Human Sciences and a Mercator professorship at Johann Wolfgang Goethe University in Frankfurt, Germany. He is a member of the Association for Psychological Science and the Society for Industrial and Organizational Psychology.

Benjamin Biermeier-Hanson is a doctoral student in industrial–organizational psychology at Wayne State University (Detroit, Michigan). He received his BA from the University of Minnesota (2005) in psychology. His primary research interests include leadership, organizational culture, and biases in performance ratings. Biermeier-Hanson's teaching interests focus on methodological and quantitative issues.

Marcus W. Dickson is professor of organizational psychology and associate department chair at Wayne State University (Detroit, Michigan). His research has focused on issues of leadership, particularly in a cross-cultural context, and he was coprincipal investigator of Project GLOBE, the largest study of leadership and culture conducted to date. Dickson is currently focusing on the organizational effects of leader betrayal of trust, and on a variety of projects related to assessing and promoting classroom excellence.

Arthur Gutman is a professor of psychology and past chair of the industrial–organizational (I–O) graduate program at Florida Institute of

Technology. He is lead author of *EEO Law and Personnel Practices*, 3rd Edition (Taylor & Francis, 2010) and the originator of "On the Legal Front," a column on workplace discrimination issues that appears quarterly in the *Industrial–Organizational Psychologist*. He has authored or coauthored book chapters on legal issues such as adverse impact, job analysis, age discrimination, Equal Employment Opportunity Commission (EEOC) statistics, as well as written summaries of major issues in personnel selection. He has consulted with private and public employers, creating and validating tests, doing program evaluations, and working on legal issues relating to workplace discrimination, including functioning as an expert witness. Gutman's main teaching interests are personnel law, personnel selection, and statistics and research design.

Aline Masuda, PhD, is a professor and codirector of the Department of People Management at Escucla de Alta Direction y Administración (EADA) Business School in Barcelona, Spain. She holds a PhD in industrial and organizational psychology from the State University of New York–Albany and a master's from Missouri State University. Previously, she was a senior project manager for International Survey Research, currently part of Towers Watson. Dr. Masuda also worked at the workforce research and marketing intelligence departments at IBM and was a postdoctoral researcher at the Instituto de Estudios Superior de la Empresa (IESE) Business School (Barcelona). She conducts research in motivation and leadership, employee attitudes, the work–family interface, and flexible working arrangements across cultures.

Ketan H. Mhatre, PhD, is a visiting assistant professor of psychology at Claremont McKenna College (Claremont, California). He earned his master of management studies from Mumbai University and his PhD in organizational behavior and leadership from the University of Nebraska. He did his postdoctoral work at Kravis Leadership Institute at Claremont McKenna College for a year and a half before assuming the visiting assistant professor's position there. Dr. Mhatre's research interests include authentic leadership and authentic leadership development, positive psychological capital, trust, nepotism in leadership contexts, leadership influence tactics, and time perception in leadership. His publications include research articles in several peer-reviewed journals as well as book chapters in edited books on leadership-related topics.

Paul M. Muchinsky, PhD, is the Joseph M. Bryan Distinguished Professor at the University of North Carolina at Greensboro. He received his PhD in industrial–organizational psychology from Purdue University (W. Lafayette, Indiana). Dr. Muchinsky is a Fellow of four divisions of the American Psychological Association (Teaching, Industrial/Organizational, Consulting, Counseling). He was the inaugural recipient of the Distinguished Teaching Contributions Award from the Society for Industrial and Organizational Psychology. In 2008, Dr. Muchinsky received an honorary doctorate (doctor of science) from Gettysburg College (Pennsylvania), his alma mater. He is the author of the textbook *Psychology Applied to Work.*

Bridgette K. Mulder, PhD, is an organizational psychologist who has worked as both an internal and external consultant specializing in the areas of leadership development, talent management, change management, and organizational effectiveness. She has practiced in a variety of industries including health care, manufacturing, and nonprofit environments. Her primary areas of research have centered on nepotism and personnel selection decisions. Dr. Mulder earned her doctorate in industrial–organizational psychology at DePaul University (Chicago, Illinois) in 2008, and has taught several undergraduate and graduate psychology courses as a part-time faculty member at the same university.

Levi R. G. Nieminen is a member of the research and development group at Denison Consulting in Ann Arbor, Michigan, where his research focuses on the intersection of organizational culture, leadership, and organizational effectiveness. Nieminen's role at Denison, which includes conducting research and translating research-based solutions for clients and the larger scientific community, is a unique example of the scientist–practitioner tradition. At the time of this book's publication, Nieminen is also a doctoral candidate at Wayne State University (Detroit, Michigan), with PhD completion anticipated in 2011. His research and teaching interests at Wayne State have a strong foundation in statistics and measurement, with a special concentration in research methodology related to employee selection and hiring practices. His methodological work is published in the recent *Handbook of Employee Selection* (2010) as well as the *Journal of Business and Psychology* (2010). In addition, Nieminen is an active early-career member of the organizational sciences community, both nationally, as a frequent presenter at the Society for Industrial and Organizational Psychology (SIOP) and the Academy of Management, and regionally in the metropolitan Detroit area (for example, the Michigan Association of Industrial and Organizational Psychologists).

Heidi R. Riggio is a social psychologist and associate professor in the Department of Psychology at California State University, Los Angeles. She has published empirical research articles in the areas of family relationships (including adult sibling relationships) and relationship attitudes. Riggio has also published teaching materials in critical thinking and organizational psychology.

Ronald E. Riggio, PhD, is the Henry R. Kravis Professor of Leadership and Organizational Psychology and former director of the Kravis Leadership Institute at Claremont McKenna College (California). Dr. Riggio is the author of over a dozen books, and 100 book chapters and research articles in the areas of leadership, assessment centers, organizational psychology, and social psychology. Recent books include *The Art of Followership* (Jossey-Bass, 2008); *The Practice of Leadership* (Jossey-Bass, 2007); and *Transformational Leadership*, 2nd Edition, coauthored with Bernard M. Bass (Erlbaum, 2006).

Juan I. Sanchez, PhD, is professor of management and international business, and Knight-Ridder Byron Harless Eminent Chair of Management at Florida International University (Miami). He earned his master's and PhD in industrial and organizational psychology from the University of South Florida, Tampa. His research has received awards from the International Personnel Management Association and the National Society for Performance and Instruction. Dr. Sanchez has published more than 70 articles in refereed journals including the *Academy of Management Journal*; *Academy of Management Executive*; *Journal of Applied Psychology*; *Journal of Organizational Behavior*; *Personnel Psychology*; *Journal of Occupational and Organizational Psychology*; *Group and Organization Management*; *Journal of Vocational Behavior*; *Journal of Applied Social Psychology*; *International Journal of Human Resource Management*; *Journal of Business and Psychology, Educational and Psychological Measurement*; *Human*

Resource Management; and *Human Resources Management Review*. A Fellow of the Society for Industrial and Organizational Psychology and the American Psychological Association, he has served on the editorial boards of the *Journal of Applied Psychology, Personnel Psychology, Group and Organization Management*, and the *International Journal of Selection and Assessment*. Dr. Sanchez currently serves as associate editor for the *Journal of Occupational and Organizational Psychology*. He has served on three National Academy of Sciences panels, the State Department's Board of Examiners, and has consulted with multiple organizations in Europe, Latin America, and the United States, including projects for the Federal Aviation Administration, the U.S. Army, the Social Security Administration, the Department of Labor, and the Veterans Administration.

Tracy Stout is an assistant professor at Missouri State University and currently holds the position of information literacy librarian. She earned dual master's degrees in industrial–organizational psychology from Missouri State University (Springfield), and information resources and library science from the University of Arizona (Tucson). Stout is currently earning a PhD in information science and learning technologies from the University of Missouri (Columbia). Her research on nepotism and job choice has been presented at the Society for Industrial and Organizational Psychology annual conference. In addition to nepotism, her current research interests include information literacy, student success and retention, and diversity. Stout is presently involved in a recruitment program for the American Library Association to increase diversity within the profession.

Edwin A. J. van Hooft, PhD, is an associate professor in work and organizational psychology at the Department of Psychology, University of Amsterdam. He received his PhD from the Vrije Universiteit, Amsterdam, in 2004. His research interests include job-search behavior, unemployment, recruitment and organizational attraction, and motivation and self-regulation in individuals and groups. Dr. van Hooft's work has appeared in journals, including the *Journal of Applied Psychology, Personnel Psychology, Journal of Vocational Behavior, Journal of Occupational and Organizational Psychology*, and the *Academy of Management Journal*.

Michelle Visio, PhD, is associate professor of psychology at Missouri State University (Springfield). She has published articles on work–family conflict, eldercare issues, and same-sex sexual harassment. Prior to her academic career, she worked as operations manager for her family's business. She received her PhD in applied experimental psychology from Southern Illinois University of Carbondale. Dr. Visio's research interests include work and family linkages, employee eldercare issues, gender and forensic interviewing, and gender stereotype violations in the workplace.

Guillermo Wated, PhD, received his PhD (2002) in industrial and organizational psychology from Florida International University (Miami), and his MBA (1994) from the University of Miami. He is now assistant professor of psychology at Barry University (Miami Shores, Florida). His research has been published in journals such as the *Journal of Business Ethics, Group and Organization Management,* and the *International Journal of Stress Management.* His research interests include the nature, antecedents, and consequences of counterproductive behaviors in organizations and the impact of work-related stressors on organizational outcomes. Dr. Wated's consulting experience consists of both private and public organizations in the areas of test development, work-related attitude and consumer opinion surveys, job analysis, key performance indicators (KPIs), and data collection and analysis.

1

Defining a Psychology of Nepotism

Robert G. Jones
Missouri State University

There is an irony to one of the ultimate scenes in the movie *Good Night, and Good Luck* (Clooney, 2005), in which Jeff Daniels, playing a character similar to CBS executive Frank Stanton, has a candid, private conversation with two members of the CBS news team. The two are a closeted couple who have been hiding their marital relationship in the interest of preserving their jobs in an organization (CBS) with an anti-nepotism policy. Stanton was an industrial–organizational (I–O) psychologist, and this scene was based on true events from the 1950s McCarthy era. Here's the irony: Although I–O psychologists like Stanton have been dealing with the issue of nepotism in practice for a long time, our field has not yet defined this pervasive phenomenon or developed workable, empirically based approaches for managing it.

In this chapter, I will put forward the case for such a systematic study of nepotism. As a starting place, I will conceive a cautious, initial definition of the phenomenon from which future work can draw. A very brief description of associated historical themes and human resource practices will also be provided to establish a context for both research and practice. This will lead to an exploration of the larger question of the common "engineering approach" taken in I–O psychology and juxtapose it to descriptive scientific inquiry. Throughout the chapter, I hope to provide both reasons and means for scientist–practitioners to integrate an understanding of this phenomenon into their work. In particular, while framing a new research area has importance for descriptive science, this book will also try to direct research toward a frontier that serves people in the workplace from the start—by asking important questions. Finally, the chapters in the volume will be described.

TOWARD A WORKING DEFINITION

This book will define nepotism (variously) as a set of psychological and social processes associated with observed phenomena with respect to family membership (broadly defined) in and around organizations. More specific definitions require attention to several issues, including the conflating of vernacular terms (Stich, 1993), the need to communicate with organizational clients (Klimoski & Jones, 2008), and providing too constricting a preliminary definition. Although the lion's share of the definition process will rely on chapter authors, I also will define nepotism in this chapter, and review the definitions offered throughout the book in the final chapter.

As a starting place, nepotism can be defined in terms of both observed phenomena and potential underlying social and psychological processes. Regarding the observed phenomena, common understandings and popular definitions are a good place to start. The *Oxford English Dictionary* (2011) lists four definitions for the term, all of which are derived from the word *nepos* and the practice by early Christian bishops of conferring status on their nephews. The first definition is: "a. The showing of special favour or unfair preference to a relative in conferring a position, job, privilege, etc.; *spec.* such favour or preference shown to an illegitimate son by a pope or other high-ranking ecclesiastic." The "obsolete" definition under this heading is "b. In extended use: unfair preferment of or favouritism shown to friends, protégés, or others within a person's sphere of influence. Also (occasionally), the exploitation for one's personal advantage of one's influential status." Ironically, it is this latter, supposedly obsolete definition that appears to be the common use of the term, at least by reference to anti-nepotism policies that deal with more than just the relationship between managers and their nephews (Bellow, 2003). Following from the neutrality principle (see Mulder, this volume, Chapter 10), I will drop the "unfair" component of this definition in order to direct discourse toward understanding the phenomenon descriptively.

There are several other general definitions of nepotism. A putatively traditional definition is "the bestowal of patronage by reason of relationship regardless of merit" (Simon, Clark, & Tifft, 1966). Bellow's (2003) initial definition of nepotism is "favoritism based on kinship" (p. 11). But he also defines a "new nepotism," which involves deliberate occupational choice by offspring. Jones and colleagues (2008) go further, suggesting that nepotism be defined by distinguishing "nepotism as a hiring decision based solely on family ties (kinship)" versus a career choice "that leads to hiring based on merit." Stout, Levesque, and Jones (2007) encompass both this deliberate career choice and meritorious hiring of family members, but further broaden the definition in terms of familial coercion. The obvious conclusion here is that the common definition of nepotism based on observer perceptions of favoritism actually belies several underlying processes.

In order to define underlying psychological variables associated with observed phenomena, a short foray into research on animal behavior is informative. This research suggests that nepotism is defined narrowly in terms of preferential treatment on the basis of closer versus more distant genetic relationships (Park, Schaller, & Van Vugt, 2008). One problem with this definition is that it is based entirely on inferences from behavioral tendencies rather than from any notion of precursor constructs or effectiveness criteria. It also appears to differ between species (Park et al., 2008; Zinck, Châline, & Jaisson, 2009), making it difficult to identify a strictly human definition of any psychological phenomenon. Further, the effects of apparently nepotistic relationships tend to vary depending on other social organizing structures in higher mammals (Wittemyer & Getz, 2007). All this is to say that underlying variables are likely to be complex and multifaceted.

On the other hand, there appears to be a shared notion of nepotism as an organizing tendency. One way of approaching this is to understand what nepotism is not. Specifically, where physical systems tend toward disorganization (the law of entropy), human systems tend to organize. One of the bases for this organization is familial relationships. Extending Cialdini's (2001) principle of a "fixed action pattern" for explaining decision-making heuristics, we might conceive of psychology of nepotism in terms of an underlying, heuristic organizing principle, based on and perpetuating shared motives and common interests (Park et al., 2008). Thus, nepotism could be thought of as "commitment," as this term is defined by Klein, Becker, and Meyer (2009).

At the individual level, people make decisions based on both conscious and more automatic reference to what is "normal" or expected in their family group (Cialdini, 2001). By extension, personal decisions about careers as well as practical decisions about who to hire, contract with, listen to for advice, develop, and otherwise place in positions of trust may be based on familial ties. At the broader, organizational level, this "binding" organizing force may be manifest in the actual structures and processes of organizations, as well as in the perceptions of both internal and external stakeholders.

One evidential basis for inferring a natural (versus "nurtural") basis of nepotism as an organizing system is its apparent prevalence across cultures. This will be left to explore in the final chapter. On the other hand, it is also worth noting that ethical and legal perspectives vary across cultures (Sackett et al., 2010). This complicates the task of defining nepotism as well. An understanding of cultural norms and economic necessities will help explain more about the context of nepotism and to manage it. Such cultural norms and other boundary conditions will also be revisited in the final chapters.

A LITTLE HISTORY AND CURRENT CONTEXT

A quick look at examples of the power of familial ties will help to bolster the case for studying nepotism. In addition to Bellow's extensive, recent historical examples of familial ties in politics, the arts, and other areas, Jones et al. (2008) give examples particularly relevant to I–O psychology, relating to testing, selection, and succession practices. More relevant to practice, efforts to root out nepotism continue. Many organizations currently have anti-nepotism policies. One practical question is whether these policies have their desired effect of reducing undue influence of familial relationships in organizations. If the introductory example from CBS in this chapter is an indication, there are those who find ways around such policies, and it would not be too great a leap to ask whether such policies make sense in an increasingly "family-friendly" world. It is perhaps noteworthy, as well, that a lack of legal status for gay and lesbian couples means that they may fall outside the purview of marital anti-nepotism policies.

A second practical question is whether nepotism policies (or their absence) have salubrious effects. Related to this, does nepotism itself lead to more, less, or equally effective organizational functions? What are the conditions under which such relationships might hold? Without an understanding of variables associated with the organizing presence of families in organizations, the answers to these questions remain conjectural, and these practices open to challenge.

ENGINEERING AND SCIENCE

At the risk of stating the obvious, let us consider a simple analogy that demonstrates the need for a value-neutral description of nepotism. Most people would agree that bridges are good if we are trying to get across a river and stay dry. However, poorly constructed bridges can be highly hazardous and exact unacceptable costs in exchange for the good they provide. The same can be said of blind adherence to the idea that "nepotism is bad" when fashioning anti-nepotism policies. In both cases (bridges and nepotism), knowing how to create a positive good without exacting unacceptable costs is one way of defining the success of the engineering we do (with bridges and anti-nepotism policies).

For both bridges and anti-nepotism policies, a fundamental truism is that we usually need to understand a phenomenon before trying to operate on it. This is reflected in the conventional process of first doing descriptive research to empirically define a phenomenon of interest. From this, more differentiated models, frameworks, taxonomies, and eventually theories grow, sometimes altering the initial concepts beyond recognition. Just as basic descriptions of physical phenomena make bridges better, so too a more complete and accurate description of nepotism should inform and enhance the effectiveness of organizational practices.

Certainly I–O psychology and related fields have done this quite well in many domains, by applying scientific rigor and definitions to common terms like those in the chapters of this book. In fact, the chapters of the book are designed to follow the common topic headings in introductory I–O psychology textbooks in order to apply some of our best-developed and defined conceptual frameworks to understanding the phenomenon called nepotism.

OVERVIEW OF THE CHAPTERS

In order, phenomena associated with the legal system; decision making of managers (and family in managerial roles); career and job choice decisions of family members; the values and commitments of family versus other stakeholders; and the conflicts associated with cultures, principles, and other individuals (including family members) will be covered. The book will conclude with an integrating framework, followed by a chapter summarizing definitions and future directions. Implications for practice will be drawn tentatively throughout the book, given the paucity of research in this topical area. Nevertheless, the research questions posed should provide places to start for practitioners. Also, organizational change and development issues will receive consideration in several key chapters.

In the chapter following this one, Arthur Gutman will review legal and policy issues related to nepotism. Starting with consideration of the implications of traditional equal employment opportunity (EEO) and affirmative action for nepotism, this chapter will evolve our understanding of the legal status of nepotism policies and processes in organizations. Issues of job relatedness, spousal hiring policies, and anti-nepotism policies will be considered in the frame of EEO law. The underlying question is whether existing precedent suggests that nepotism leads to unfair hiring in the legal sense. A review of case law dealing with nepotism will help to answer this question of its legal definition and provide some important context for later chapters.

In Chapter 3, Paul Muchinsky will tackle core questions about organizational decisions in nepotistic circumstances. The chapter will explore the potential influences of familial relationships in the development, implementation, and success or failure of procedures for hiring, placement, compensation, succession, and other core organizational decisions. Questions about the "invasion" of family relationships into decision making will be explored, particularly as they pertain to staffing and the problems of organizational development and change. The underserved topics of placement and promotion will also be discussed through the lens of familial relationships. For example, descriptively, to what extent are promotion decisions in family organizations predicated on family relationships? Might placement decisions follow closely from shared interests and career development experiences common among family members? Can placement decisions be more easily managed in the change process from family to nonfamily organizations? This is a very challenging set of issues, core to any discussion of nepotism.

Career choice and job search research have a long history as ancillary topics in I–O psychology. In Chapter 4, Edwin van Hooft and Tracy Stout will bring them to center stage in the discussion of nepotism. These authors have both completed recent research related to job search and career choice behaviors as they relate to nepotism. These topics take the perspective of the person who chooses to seek and accept a privileged career or job. The chapter will provide some fresh insights based on empirically based definitions of nepotistic choice constructs.

Implications for organizational culture will be developed further in Chapter 5 (by Marcus Dickson, Levi Nieminen, and Benjamin Biermeier-Hanson), and framed in terms of the attraction–selection–attrition approach. Conflict between family culture and broader external cultures, and the assimilation of organization stakeholders through acculturation to dominant organizational (family) values will be discussed. Practical issues of cultural change will also be introduced and considered in this chapter, helping provide a thread to these topics in later chapters.

Tom Becker will compare some likely differences in bases and foci of commitment for familial versus nonfamilial organizational relationships in Chapter 6. He will deal with the core psychological issues underlying the organizing nature of nepotism. Through rational self-interest and the balancing of commitments to various stakeholders, Becker will describe some variables that may help to explain ongoing human decisions about choosing to join and to remain with a firm. This chapter will also deal with the extent to which organizational change may be affected by shared commitments and familial values.

In Chapter 7, Aline Masuda and Michelle Visio deal with difficult questions around nepotism and the interface between work and family. Work–family border theory will be used to frame the positive and not-so-positive aspects of integration of work and family. Cultural and personality differences will help to frame practical implications, which will provide an essential anchoring context for other discussions.

Ketan Mhatre, Ron Riggio, and Heidi Riggio's Chapter 8 on leadership emergence is framed in terms of heuristics, relationships, and contexts that may influence leadership emergence and effectiveness. In particular, others' perceptions of leadership nepotism, organizational type and culture, procedural justice, and leader characteristics will be considered. This chapter will conclude with considerations of factors from existing leadership literatures that may affect perceptions of nepotism.

Guillermo Wated and Juan Sanchez (Chapter 9) discuss the ethics of nepotism across cultures. Their focus is on the culture of corruption that exists in certain organizations, and how broader cultural differences may make a difference in prevalence and management of nepotism. Stakeholder theory is also discussed, leading to questions about organizational effectiveness "according to whom" in the final chapter.

In the penultimate chapter, Bridgette Mulder presents an integrating framework that posits variables explaining nepotistic relationships and how these may affect organizational policies and behavior. Her previous empirical work developing a model of perceptions of nepotism will provide some helpful integration of the constructs and relationships posited in the previous chapters. The main task of this chapter will be to provide Frontiers Series readers with future directions for research into nepotism.

An enduring question in evolutionary perspectives is whether nepotistic relationships are adaptive. The final chapter will explore reasons behind the relative (in)effectiveness of important examples of family firms, such as Walmart, the Limited Stores, Ford Motors, Lehman Brothers, and other organizations with substantial familial relationships among top decision makers. The primary purpose of this chapter is to provide ideas from the frontier of this area of inquiry to help scientist–practitioners and managers to better manage nepotism in the present. This chapter provides a definitional framework derived from the previous chapters that points toward questions of effective adaptation to and management of nepotistic constructs. The intention here is to integrate from the start the engineering aspect of inquiry (organizational effectiveness focus) with the nascent descriptive research agenda arising from the book.

SUMMARY

Psychology needs to develop an understanding of the binding forces of nepotism in organizations. Its prevalence as a phenomenon, our lack of understanding of its associated variables and effects, and the complexity of practices associated with it make this a daunting task. But organizational practices, in particular those aimed at changing both systems and perceptions, are likely improved by accounting for what we will refer to, for now, as nepotism.

REFERENCES

Bellow, A. (2003). *In praise of nepotism: A natural history.* New York: Doubleday.

Cialdini, R. B. (2001). *Influence: Science and practice* (4th ed.). Boston: Allyn & Bacon.

Clooney, G. (Director). (2005). *Good night, and good luck* [Motion picture]. United States: Warner Brothers Pictures Inc.

Jones, R. G., Stout, T., Harder, B., Levine, E., Levine, J., & Sanchez, J. I. (2008). Personnel psychology and nepotism: Should we support anti-nepotism policies? *The Industrial/Organizational Psychologist, 45*(3), 17–20.

Klein, H. J., Becker, T. E., and Meyer, J. P. (2009). *Commitment in organizations: Accumulated wisdom and new directions.* New York: Routledge/Taylor & Francis.

Klimoski, R. J., & Jones, R. G. (2008). Intuiting the selection context. *Industrial and Organizational Psychology, 1*(3), 352–354.

OED Online (March 2011). "nepotism, n." Oxford University Press. http://www.oed.com/view/Entry/126151?redirectedFrom=nepotism.

Park, J. H., Schaller, M., & Van Vugt, M. (2008). Psychology of human kin recognition: Heuristic cues, erroneous inferences, and their implications. *Review of General Psychology, 12*(3), 215–235.

Sackett, P. R., Shen, W., Myors, B., Lievens, F., Schollaert, E., Van Hoye, G., ... and Aguinis, H. (2010). Perspectives from twenty-two countries on the legal environment for selection. In J. L. Farr & N. T. Tippins (Eds.), *Handbook of employee selection* (pp. 651–676). New York: Routledge/Taylor & Francis.

Simon, R. J., Clark, S. M., & Tifft, L. L. (1966). Of nepotism, marriage, and the pursuit of an academic career. *Sociology of Education, 39*, 344–358.

Stich, S. (1993). The future of folk psychology. In S. M. Christensen & D. R. Turner (Eds.), *Folk psychology and the philosophy of mind* (pp. 93–117). Hillsdale, NJ: Lawrence Erlbaum.

Stout, T., Levesque, C., & Jones, R. G. (2007). *Nepotism, self determination, and career choice.* Paper presented at the meeting of the Society for Industrial and Organizational Psychology (SIOP), New York.

Wittemyer, G., & Getz, W. M. (2007). Hierarchical dominance structure and social organization in African elephants, *Loxodonta africana. Animal Behaviour, 73*(4), 671–681.

Zinck, L., Châline, N., & Jaisson, P. (2009). Absence of nepotism in worker–queen care in polygynous colonies of the ant *Ectatomma tuberculatum. Journal of Insect Behavior, 22*, 196–204.

2

Nepotism and Employment Law

Arthur Gutman
Florida Institute of Technology

This chapter addresses legal issues associated with nepotism in the workplace. Most of the relevant case law addresses policies that oppose nepotism, or anti-nepotism policies. Such policies are common in federal, state, and municipal agencies, and, in more recent times, private entities. Anti-nepotism policies address relatives of existing employees, with broad targets. For example, Section 310.102 of the Code of Federal Regulations defines *relative* as follows:

> *Relative* means father, mother, son, daughter, brother, sister, uncle, aunt, first cousin, nephew, niece, husband, wife, father-in-law, mother-in-law, son-in-law, daughter-in-law, brother-in-law, sister-in-law, stepfather, stepmother, stepson, stepdaughter, stepbrother, stepsister, half brother, or half sister.

Additionally, some employers extend this definition to unrelated significant others of existing employees.

Although not as prevalent as anti-nepotism policies, there is also case law relating to policies that facilitate the selection of relatives. For lack of a better term, I will call these pro-nepotism policies. For example, in *EEOC v. Steamship* (1995), the Equal Employment Opportunity Commission (EEOC) challenged a union policy requiring that new members must be sponsored by existing members. The policy was defeated via Title VII of the Civil Rights Act of 1964, which prohibits discrimination based on race, color, religion, sex, or national origin. As it turned out, all existing union members were White, as were 30 new members inducted between 1980 and 1986. As a result, each inductee was a blood relative of an existing member, usually a son or brother. The 1st Circuit Court rejected the policy under adverse impact rules to be discussed in greater detail later.

The example in *EEOC v. Steamship* is somewhat extreme. A more common example of a pro-nepotism policy is when employers use word-of-mouth recruitment coupled with walk-in hiring. For example, in 1991, the EEOC settled a lawsuit with World's Finest Chocolate in which the company agreed to pay $2 million to a class of minorities and females (CA #86 C 0237). The company was located in the middle of Chicago, the pay was good, and the jobs required no technical skills. Nevertheless, as a result of its word-of-mouth recruitment policy, the company was more than 98% White male, and an overwhelming majority of the new recruits were friends and relatives of existing workers.

For purposes of exposition, this chapter is divided into five sections. The first section briefly discusses preliminary considerations and the second overviews laws applicable to anti-nepotism and pro-nepotism policies. The third section then focuses on anti-nepotism policies, the fourth section focuses on proscriptions related to freedom of association in relation to sexual liaisons, and the last section focuses on pro-nepotism policies.

PRELIMINARY CONSIDERATIONS

As noted in Chapter 1, it is not the purpose of this book to treat nepotism as being either good or bad. Nevertheless, it is difficult to consider legal issues in this domain absent associated moral and ethical considerations. In general, the view of industrial–organizational (I–O) psychologists is that any policy relating to recruitment, hiring, or promotion of individuals should be based on qualifications to perform the job. Therefore, by default, it is a bad thing when, because of favoritism (of any kind), a less qualified individual is hired or promoted. That said, after reviewing case law on nepotism, I am left with the impression that anti-nepotism laws can easily overkill if they do more than prevent favoritism and conflicts of interest. A poorly thought out, overly broad anti-nepotism policy can just as easily discriminate against individuals who have the qualifications to perform a job. This, too, is bad.

To illustrate, consider the case of Earl and Theresa Stadtman. Both were PhD biochemists seeking university teaching jobs in 1950. At the time, most colleges and universities had anti-nepotism policies. Earl received a concrete offer of $5,000 per year at the Institute of Radiobiology and Biophysics at the University of Chicago. He wrote to the director of the institute that he could not take the job unless a suitable position was available for his wife. The director responded as follows:

> If your decision is to be based upon simultaneous academic staff appointments for both you and Mrs. Stadtman, it may mean that you are closing your opportunities for an academic career, since I believe that the policy of the University of Chicago in this regard is no different from that of most other universities.

Earl Stadtman did not accept the offer. Instead, both Earl and Theresa Stadtman went on to legendary 50-year careers at the National Institutes of Health (NIH) for which they were bestowed many honors.[1] The fact that the Stadtman story occurred in the context of academia is ironic, because universities have long favored the offspring of alumni in their admission processes. Furthermore, the pendulum has swung with respect to faculty, and it is now common for husbands and wives to work not only within the same university, but also within the same department. Indeed, it is not unheard of for a university to hire one spouse to attract the other spouse.

Consider, for example, *Siler-Khodr v. University of Texas, San Antonio* (2002), a case decided under the Equal Pay Act of 1963 (or EPA). The EPA prohibits unequal pay between males and females for jobs deemed equal in skill, effort, responsibility, and working conditions, unless pay differentials can be justified by other factors (e.g., merit). In this case, a university paid the husband of a female professor more than the female plaintiff for the same job, arguing that it needed to pay him more in order to recruit his wife. The university's policy was to base salary primarily on grant funding, a area in which the plaintiff's performance was as good (if not better) than the male spouse. The university lost.

On a more general level, case law is disposed to "bad" things. Plaintiffs never challenge workplace policies because they are too good or overly fair. Rather, they go to court because they believe they are being harmed. Therefore, despite the disclaimer that this book casts no opinion on the goodness or badness of nepotism, the overwhelming majority of challenges to anti- and pro-nepotism policies occur because someone believes the challenged policy is bad.

OVERVIEW OF APPLICABLE LAWS

The laws most frequently applied in nepotism cases are amendments to the United States Constitution and Title VII. Also relevant are state and municipal laws and ordinances that prohibit practices not addressed in federal laws. Detailed discussions of how constitutional amendments, Title VII, and other federal laws apply to workplace discrimination are provided by Gutman, Koppes, and Vodanovich (2010). The purpose of the present discussion is to broadly overview how the law applies to challenges of anti-nepotism and pro-nepotism policies.

Constitutional Claims

Constitutional claims feature the three levels of scrutiny depicted in Table 2.1. Strict scrutiny is the most exacting standard, and applies to fundamental rights and "suspect classifications" (e.g., race, color, religion, national origin). The most important fundamental rights are captured in the first 10 amendments to the Constitution (also known as the Bill of Rights). These rights include freedom of speech, freedom of association, and privacy, among others. The 5th Amendment obligates the federal government to protect these fundamental rights. Similarly, the Equal Protection Clause of the 14th Amendment obligates state and local governments to protect what is guaranteed in the Bill of Rights and other amendments.

No right is absolute. However, to restrict a fundamental right, there must be *compelling government interest* matched by a restriction that is *narrowly tailored* (or minimally restrictive) to that interest. For example, in *Rowe v. Wade* (1973), the landmark abortion case, the Supreme Court ruled that the right to abortion is fundamental under the 9th Amendment

TABLE 2.1

Levels of Scrutiny in Constitutional Claims

Rational basis	There must be a reasonable relationship between a restrictive law or policy and a legitimate governmental interest.
Moderate scrutiny	There must be an important government objective for a restrictive law or policy and a solution substantially related to that objective.
Strict scrutiny	There must be a compelling government interest for a restrictive law or policy and a solution narrowly tailored to that interest.

guarantee of privacy. Therefore, restrictions on abortions must pass the strict scrutiny test.[2]

In comparison, restrictions via moderate scrutiny (also called intermediate scrutiny) require proof of an *important government interest* and a *substantially related* solution to that interest. Moderate scrutiny applies to "quasi-suspect" classifications, most notably, sex and illegitimacy. For example, the U.S. Supreme Court applied moderate scrutiny in *United States v. Virginia* (1996) to strike down an all-male admissions policy to Virginia Military Institute, a state-funded university.

Last, rational basis, the least exacting standard, requires that restrictions merely serve a *legitimate government interest*. In general, it is a default standard applicable to rights not protected by the two more heightened standards. It also applies to "nonsuspect" classifications (e.g., age and disability). For example, driving as a privilege, and most laws restricting that privilege (e.g., license, registration fees, speed limits, etc.) generally pass the rational basis test. Returning to *Rowe v. Wade*, prior to this landmark ruling, abortion was, in essence, a privilege that was almost as easy for states and municipalities to restrict as the privilege of driving.[3]

For present purposes, it is important to note that most constitutional challenges feature 14th Amendment claims against state and local agencies in which plaintiffs argue that no-spouse rules restrict the fundamental right to marry or freely associate. As we will witness later in this chapter, the most common ruling in such cases is that no-spouse rules, and other anti-nepotism policies, do not restrict fundamental rights, leaving defendants with the much easier task of proving that anti-nepotism policies serve legitimate government interests.

Title VII

The Title VII classifications (race, color, religion, sex, and national origin) are "suspect" under constitutional law. However, unlike constitutional law, which also protects fundamental rights and privileges, Title VII claimants must prove discrimination based on one or more of the classifications. On the other hand, Title VII permits claims against private entities as well as government agencies, whereas most constitutional challenges feature only government agencies.[4] Two major theories in Title VII have been applied to nepotism policies: adverse impact and disparate treatment.

TABLE 2.2

The Adverse Impact Judicial Scenario

Phase 1	Plaintiffs present statistical applicant flow or demographic disparities that an identified practice disproportionately excludes protected group members.
Phase 2	Defendants prove that the challenged practice is job related and consistent with business necessity.
Phase 3	Plaintiffs prove that alternative practices exist that are equally as valid as the challenged practice but produce less or no adverse impact.

Adverse Impact Theory

Adverse impact theory is unique to Title VII,[5] and does not apply in constitutional claims.[6] The adverse impact judicial scenario, depicted in Table 2.2, has three phases, each with a burden of proof. In Phase 1 (the prima facie phase), the plaintiff must prove statistically that a selection practice disproportionately excludes members of one protected group as compared to another. If the plaintiff succeeds, the defendant must prove in Phase 2 that the challenged practice is job related and consistent with business necessity. If the defendant succeeds, the plaintiff must prove in Phase 3 that there are other selection practices that are as valid as the challenged practice, but produce less or no adverse impact. For present purposes, only the first two phases are important.

For example, in the Supreme Court's landmark ruling in *Griggs v. Duke Power* (1971), two selection criteria disproportionately excluded Blacks (a high school diploma requirement and passing scores on two cognitive tests). Duke Power had no evidence that these criteria were job related and lost. Analogously, in the aforementioned case of *EEOC v. Steamship* (1995), featuring recruitment of new members only if sponsored by existing members, the union argued that its membership sponsorship policy (MSP) was necessary to preserve "family traditions" as well as "necessary adjuncts in carrying on the business of steamship clerks." However, the 1st Circuit struck down the MSP, ruling:

> We will not tarry. Here, the Union has not shown even the glimmerings of a business necessity defense. Instead, it asks us to undertake a leap of faith. It makes absolutely no effort to explain, logically, why family tradition, and, thus, the MSP, are necessary adjuncts to carrying on the business of steamship clerks; and we, like the district court, can discern no essential

connection. ... If courts were to accept an employer's arbitrary *ipse dixit* as a satisfactory justification for retaining a policy that produces an invidiously discriminatory impact, Title VII would be reduced to no more than a toothless tiger.

EEOC v. Steamship was a pro-nepotism case. There are also adverse impact challenges to anti-nepotism rules. These are challenges in the private sector that parallel constitutional challenges in the public sector. For example, there are several cases in which females have argued that no-spouse rules adversely impact women. As we will discuss later, there are in fact instances in which no-spouse rules have illegally adversely impacted women.

Disparate Treatment Theory

In adverse impact theory, the motive (or intention) to discriminate is irrelevant. Not so in disparate treatment theory. Here, plaintiffs must prove that they suffered an adverse employment consequence because of class membership. Most claims of disparate treatment are made by individual plaintiffs (as opposed to class-action claims), and these claims are decided using the three-phase judicial scenario depicted in Table 2.3.

Unlike adverse impact claims, where there is a burden of proof in all three phases, there are much lighter burdens on the plaintiff in Phase 1 and the defendant in Phase 2, and the only burden of proof is on the plaintiff in Phase 3. More specifically, in Phase 1, plaintiffs need only show that they are a protected class member, they are qualified for the at-issue job or promotion, and that they suffered an adverse employment decision. In Phase 2, the defendant need only articulate (or explain), without proof,

TABLE 2.3

The Disparate Treatment Judicial Scenario

Phase 1	Plaintiff is protected by the statute, qualified for the job or promotion in question, and suffers an adverse employment decision (e.g., failure to hire, failure to promote or train, termination, etc.).
Phase 2	Defendant must articulate a legitimate reason for the selection decision made in Phase 1; proof is unnecessary.
Phase 3	Plaintiff must provide direct or indirect evidence that the articulation by defendant in Phase 2 is a pretext for discrimination.

why the adverse employment decision was made. Then, in Phase 3, the plaintiff must provide direct evidence (e.g., eyewitness or documents) or indirect evidence (e.g., that similarly situated individuals were better treated) that the explanation offered in Phase 2 is a pretext designed to mask the motive to discriminate.

For example, in the Supreme Court's landmark ruling in *McDonald Douglass v. Green* (1973), Green, a Black male, was laid off in a reduction-in-force (or RIF) and later reapplied for his former position when the company was rehiring. Green easily passed the Phase 1 burden (he was Black, qualified based on prior service, and he was not rehired) and the company easily passed the Phase 2 burden (explaining that Green was not rehired because of illegal acts he committed against the company during the layoff period). Ultimately, Green lost in Phase 3 because similarly situated White employees involved in illegal actions against the company were not rehired.

For present purposes, compare *Holder v. City of Raleigh* (1989), a pro-nepotism case, to *Yancey v. Weyerhaeuser* (2002), an anti-nepotism case. Holder, a Black applicant, claimed race discrimination after he was passed over for two recreation department maintenance jobs in favor of White applicants who were related to existing higher-level employees. Holder satisfied the Phase 1 burden under Title VII disparate treatment rules, and the defendant provided several explanations in Phase 2. Holder proved that these explanations were pretext for discrimination based on nepotism in Phase 3, but the 4th Circuit ruled that nepotism, by itself, is not a valid claim in Title VII, and that it is a race-neutral policy.

On the other hand, in *Yancey v. Weyerhaeuser*, Yancey was told that he or his son must resign their jobs at a railroad yard. Yancey, who was offered a severance package, claimed age discrimination under the Age Discrimination in Employment Act (ADEA). Using disparate treatment rules paralleling those in Title VII, Yancey satisfied the Phase 1 burden, and in Phase 2, the defendant appealed to its anti-nepotism policy as the explanation. However, in Phase 3, Yancey proved that the anti-nepotism explanation was a pretext for age discrimination because the company had not uniformly enforced the policy in the past, and it knew that Yancey and his son worked for the railroad for 5 years. A jury found that Weyerhaeuser willfully violated the ADEA, and Yancey was awarded $169,625. The 8th Circuit then supported the award on appeal.

Other Relevant Issues

There are two other major forms of discrimination; the pattern or practice of discrimination and retaliation. Pattern or practice claims apply broadly to Title VII, constitutional claims, and most other anti-discrimination laws. The lone exception is the Equal Pay Act, which has a unique judicial scenario for determining equal pay for equal work. Retaliation claims, on the other hand, apply to constitutional claims and any anti-discrimination law, including the Equal Pay Act.

Pattern or Practice Theory

The pattern or practice of discrimination constitutes disparate treatment against entire groups or classes of people. The rules in such cases are beyond the scope of this chapter.[7] For present purposes, consider the case of *Local 53 v. Vogler* (1969), in which a union attempted to preserve its pre-Title VII history of all-White membership by imposing pro-nepotism policies similar to the ones seen in *EEOC v. Steamship* (1996).[8] The union required that applicants be recommended by three existing members and obtain approval by members in a secret ballot. Membership was also open to apprentices who were "sons or close relatives living in the households of members." The 5th Circuit rejected the policy ruling:

> In pursuing its exclusionary and nepotistic policies, Local 53 engaged in a pattern and practice of discrimination on the basis of race and national origin both in membership and referrals. It was found to be Local 53's practice to refer white persons of limited experience and white journeymen of other trade unions as mechanic asbestos workers. It was also found to be its practice to refuse to consider negroes or Mexican-Americans for membership and to refuse to refer negroes for employment or to accept negroes for referral for employment.

The court also ruled "while the nepotism requirement is applicable to black and white alike and is not on its face discriminatory, in a completely white union the present effect of its continued application is to forever deny to [Blacks] and Mexican-Americans any real opportunity for membership." In short, as in individual disparate treatment theory, the pro-nepotism policy was deemed a pretext for discrimination based on race and national origin in pattern or practice theory. This case will be discussed again later.

Retaliation Theory

The rules in retaliation theory are the same as in disparate treatment theory. If an employee opposes an employer policy, or sues the employer, and the employer reacts by imposing adverse consequences against the employee (e.g., demotion, termination, and so forth), the employer may be liable even if the original challenge is disallowed.[9] For present purposes, consider the case of *Sowards v. Loudon County* (2000). Sowards, a jailer, supported her husband's failed campaign for sheriff. She was terminated a year later for cause, the explanation being that she missed an outstanding warrant on a person brought into the jail. The 6th Circuit ruled that Sowards had a valid retaliation claim on grounds that she was terminated not for the reason offered, but instead for exercising her 1st Amendment right to engage in intimate and political activity.

State Laws

Finally, there are no federal laws that expressly prohibit anti-nepotism policies. However, as this chapter was going to press, there were laws prohibiting discrimination based on marriage in the District of Columbia and at least 21 states.[10] For purposes of exposition, sample cases will be discussed in the next section. For present purposes, it is sufficient to know that such laws are occasionally effective in opposing anti-nepotism policies, but the circumstances under which they are effective are case specific.

CHALLENGES TO ANTI-NEPOTISM POLICIES

This section focuses on constitutional and Title VII challenges to anti-nepotism policies. The plaintiffs in most of these cases are female spouses. Therefore, no-spouse rules are emphasized. Also discussed are claims by state laws that prohibit discrimination against married couples.

Constitutional Claims

The common ruling in constitutional claims is that anti-nepotism policies do not violate fundamental rights, and they are constitutional under the rational basis test. Although these claims generally feature no-spouse rules, the main infringement is usually not so much against marriage per se but rather against conflicts of interest associated with being married and working together.

For example, in *Keckeisen v. Independent School District 612* (1975), a school district's anti-nepotism policy prohibited married couples from being in administrator–teacher relationships or from working in the same building. It also prohibited "all other situations where a conflict of interest occurs." A principal's contract was not renewed after he married a teacher under his supervision, and he sued, claiming infringement on his fundamental right to marry. The school district argued that it had a legitimate interest to enforce the policy to avoid conflicts of interest and favoritism. Applying the rational basis test, the 8th Circuit agreed, ruling:

> Although the freedom to marry was recognized as a personal right, the school district's policy did not deny people the right to marry; it only prohibited the employment of married couples in administrator–teacher relationships.

However, the 8th Circuit indicated it might have ruled differently if the no-spouse policy bore more directly on marriage per se. Accordingly:

> Were the right to marriage claim not so attenuated by the fact that marriage itself is not the subject of the School Board's policy—i.e., were the right more directly involved—then we should perhaps, reach a different result.

Then, in *Espinoza v. Thomas* (1978), the 8th Circuit extended its ruling in *Keckeisen* to a no-cohabitation rule. In *Thomas*, a female applicant was excluded from a transit authority job because she lived with an existing employee, a violation of transit authority policy. The 8th Circuit ruled that the transit authority's no-spouse policy also applied to an "espoused relationship." The court also ruled that the policy was a "reasonable classification that bore a fair and substantial relationship to the objectives of the policy," and that it was "neither arbitrary nor capricious."

In *Montgomery v. Carr* (1996), a no-spouse rule was applied to married couples working at the same school, but unlike *Keckeisen*, where the husband lost his job, the wife in this case was transferred to a different school after the marriage. The policy was challenged, and the 6th Circuit ruled that it did not "constitute a direct and substantial burden on the right to marry" and that it was a rational policy because married couples working at the same facility had caused problems at other schools in the past.

In *Parks v. Warner Robbins, GA* (1994), the anti-nepotism policy prohibited relatives of city employees from working in the same department, but only if both were supervisors. An engaged couple, both supervisors in a police department, was informed that their marriage would violate the city's policy, and that the spouse with less seniority would be terminated. The couple delayed their marriage for 4 years, during which time they challenged the policy. Unfortunately for them, the 11th Circuit ruled that the policy was "rationally related" to the city's "legitimate interest in preventing conflicts of interest and reducing favoritism and sexual harassment."

In *Waters v. Gaston County, NC* (1995), a case involving paramedics, a county ordinance permitted employees to marry as long as they did not work in the same division or union, and neither spouse supervised the other. The main challenge in this case related to exemptions granted to married couples in the past that were not granted to the plaintiffs. Applying the rational basis test, the 6th Circuit ruled there was insufficient evidence to support the claim that the policy "had applied the ordinance arbitrary and irrationally by selectively exempting other couples from its regulatory scheme."

The 6th Circuit then extended its ruling in *Waters* in *Wright v. MetroHealth Medical Center* (1995). The male and female in this case worked on a four-person helicopter crew at a public medical hospital, she as a registered nurse and he as a pilot. Prior to the wedding, the female was offered a transfer to another unit within the same locale. After the wedding, the male was transferred from Ohio to Louisiana, effectively costing a loss of employment for both spouses unless they moved. The plaintiffs challenged the policy on grounds that its enforcement was "sporadic and selective." However, the court ruled that selective application, by itself, is insufficient to defeat the policy. Accordingly:

A claim of selective application of a facially lawful state regulation requires a showing that … the selective treatment was motivated by an intention to discriminate on the basis of impermissible considerations, such as race or religion, to punish or inhibit the exercise of constitutional rights, or by a malicious or bad faith intent to injure the person.

The court also ruled that the hospital's policy did not "directly and substantially interfere with plaintiffs' fundamental right to marry," and that it was "rationally related to a legitimate interest of avoiding potential conflicts and low morale of other crew members."

It is arguable that the Wrights had a legitimate retaliation claim. However, that claim was never made. In comparison, in *Vaughn v. Lawrenceburg Power System* (2001), a couple was informed that if they married, the lower paid employee (the female) would be terminated. However, the male was terminated after he formally objected to the company policy during an interview. The policy itself passed the rational basis test on grounds that "a government employer may have a legitimate concern about the inherent loyalty that one spouse will show to another, making discipline more difficult." However, the 6th Circuit ruled that the male had a valid case of retaliation on grounds that he was terminated for opposing a company policy, which is a protected activity based on the 1st Amendment right to "compelled speech."

A final point to note is that although the focus is on spouses, the general ruling in no-spouse cases has been applied to other relatives. For example, in *Roche v. Town of Waream* (1998), the daughter of a selectman and five other applicants were excluded from employment as seasonal police officers based on an unwritten anti-nepotism policy. The District Court for the District of Massachusetts ruled that the policy was rationally related to a legitimate government interest of avoiding the "appearance of conflict of interest and/or nepotism."

In short, under constitutional law, anti-nepotism policies are generally deemed rationally related to legitimate government interests primarily on the basis of conflicts of interest. Furthermore, claims that anti-nepotism policies are selectively enforced are difficult to prove because they do not generally implicate fundamental rights or suspect classifications such as race or national origin. That said, employees have a right to challenge anti-nepotism policies both internally and in court, and employers should avoid adverse consequences for employees that do so.

Title VII: Adverse Impact Claims

The most common adverse impact claim is that no-spouse rules adversely impact married women. Recall that in any adverse impact challenge, the plaintiffs must first prove adverse impact statistically, and if successful, the defendant must prove that the policy is job related. The courts have addressed both issues.

The problem in proving adverse impact based on no-spouse rules is small sample size (or small N). This is not a problem for other causes of adverse impact. For example, adverse impact based on height and weight has been inferred from population data showing that mean heights and weights are significantly lower for females than males (for example, *Dothard v. Rawlinson*, 1977). Similarly, adverse impact based on diploma requirements has been inferred from population data showing significantly lower graduation rates for Blacks than Whites (for example, *Griggs v. Duke Power*, 1971). However, courts have forced plaintiffs to prove adverse impact for no-spouse rules on a case-by-case basis, and this can serve as a major barrier.

For example, in both *Harper v. TWA* (1975) and *Thomas v. Metroflight* (1987), the no-spouse rule dictated that, if an employee married a departmental coworker and one spouse did not transfer or resign, the spouse with less seniority would be terminated. In *Harper*, the plaintiff could only document five prior instances in which the rule was applied (resulting in termination of the female in four instances), and the 8th Circuit ruled that "statistical evidence derived from an extremely small universe, as in the present case, has little predictive value and must be disregarded." In *Thomas*, the plaintiff could only document one prior instance in which the rule was applied (resulting in termination of the female) and the 10th Circuit ruled "a sample of two is too small to make even a 100% impact rate significant."

Interestingly, in *Thomas*, the 10th Circuit credited prior studies suggesting that no-spouse rules generally do adversely impact females, and that such polices are unjustified.[11] Accordingly:

> We affirm on this issue *reluctantly* [emphasis added] because we suspect, as others have claimed, that "no-spouse" rules in practice often result in discrimination against women, and are generally unjustified. But we cannot accept our own speculations or others' conclusions as a substitute for plaintiff's required proof, nor may we take judicial notice of evidence that might have been but was not presented.

The implication of this ruling is that if adverse impact were proven with a larger N, the ruling would have favored the plaintiffs.

Indeed, there are at least three cases in which adverse impact has been proven with larger N, and the plaintiffs won in two of them, and arguably, should have won in the third case. One of the plaintiff victories is an EEOC decision [EEOC Dec. 75-239, 2 Empl. Prac. Guide (CCH) P 6492, at 4260-61 (Mar. 2, 1976)] in which the no-spouse rule led to exclusion of the female in 65 of 66 applications, and the EEOC declared that the rule was not job related. The other two cases involved circuit court rulings.

In *Yuhas v. Libbey-Owens-Ford Co.* (1977), there was substantial statistical evidence of adverse impact, but the rulings on job relatedness differed at the district and circuit court levels. Here, the no-spouse rule applied to job applicants with spouses already employed in the same capacity as the at-issue job, but it did not apply to existing employees married prior to implementation of the rule or to posthire marriages. The adverse impact claim was based on a sample of 74 cases in which a wife was the excluded applicant in 71 of them. Libbey-Owens-Ford argued that the rule was job related because it was needed to prevent excessive absenteeism, tardiness, scheduling of work assignments and vacation, and morale problems. The District Court for the Northern District of Illinois rejected the employer's job-relatedness defense, but the 7th Circuit overturned this part of the ruling.

The district court ruling made sense if only because the concerns offered by Libbey-Owens-Ford would seemingly apply regardless of when two employees are married. Additionally, Libbey-Owens-Ford presented no evidence, statistical or otherwise, that the policy affected job performance. The 7th Circuit conceded that adverse impact was proven, but overturned the decision for reasons relating more so to historical factors than to whether the policy was job related. Accordingly:

> The no-spouse rule ... does not place women at a disadvantage because they failed to develop certain personal characteristics as a consequence of their environmental or genetic backgrounds. Rather, the rule's discriminatory impact is the result of the historical fact that in the past far more men than women chose to work in defendant's Ottawa plants, with the result that substantially more than half of the employees in those plants are now men. Defendant asserts, and there is nothing in the record contradicting its assertion, that in some of its other plants historical circumstances operated

differently and there is a majority of female workers. In those plants, the no-spouse rule, which is in effect on a company-wide basis, has a discriminatory impact on men.

The more recent run of cases in adverse impact theory suggest that the 7th Circuit ruling is questionable because Libbey-Owens-Ford merely asserted there was adverse impact on men in plants in other regions of the country, implying a burden to prove otherwise on the plaintiff. More important, even if that assertion was true, motive is irrelevant in adverse impact theory, meaning the men in those other plants would have the same opportunity to claim adverse impact based on sex as *Yuhas* claimed.

The ruling in the third case (*EEOC v. Rath Packing Company*, 1986) is more consistent with the run of cases in adverse impact theory. Here, the EEOC proved adverse impact and, ultimately, that the policy (exclusion of spouses in hiring) was not job related. However, as in *Yuhas*, there was disagreement between the district court and circuit court.

The District Court for the Southern District of Iowa ruled that adverse impact was proven, but that Rath's policy was job related. Nevertheless, the court ruled for the three plaintiffs based on disparate treatment theory, and three plaintiffs were entitled to a $1 million award. The EEOC then appealed the adverse impact ruling on grounds that "Rath failed to establish that the subjective hiring procedures were necessary or essential and that there were no alternative practices with less discriminatory effect." Rath argued that this case was *Yuhas* revisited, but the 8th Circuit, though not rejecting *Yuhas*, distinguished between the two cases because Rath had only one plant. The court ruled that the Rath's defense was weak because it "perceived" problems associated with married couples, but did not prove them. Accordingly:

> Rath argues that its no-spouse rule was directed at problems which had occurred when married couples worked at Rath; these problems were dual absenteeism, vacation scheduling, supervision, and employee pressure to hire spouses. ... We hold that the district court applied the wrong legal standard in determining whether the no-spouse rule was justified by business necessity. The district court did not consider whether there was a compelling need for the no-spouse rule. In order for Rath to prevail, *the problem to be addressed by the no-spouse rule must be concrete and demonstrable, not just "perceived"* [emphasis added]; and the rule must be

essential to eliminating the problem, not simply reasonable or designed to improve conditions.

In short, there is more evidence of success in adverse impact challenges to anti-nepotism policies in Title VII adverse impact theory than in constitutional claims, but only if adverse impact on women can be proven statistically. However, it must be noted that all three of the major cases in which adverse impact was proven with larger *N* are dated. That said, the author believes that the facts in both *Yuhas* and *Rath* would constitute illegal adverse impact based on sex, should those facts reemerge.

Title VII: Disparate Treatment Claims

Disparate treatment challenges to anti-nepotism policies require proof that adverse employment decisions based on such policies are a pretext for discrimination. The defendant prevails in such cases if the policy is enforced equally based on race, color, religion, sex, and/or national origin. For example, in *Amey v. Delta Airlines* (1980) several Black applicants were excluded from employment based on an anti-nepotism policy, but the plaintiffs lost because Delta had a history of enforcing the policy for Black and White applicants alike. However, there are cases in which female spouses have proven that anti-nepotism policies were more strictly applied to females than males.

For example, in *McDowell v. Mississippi Power and Light* (MP&L) (1986), McDowell, who was married to an existing MP&L employee in violation of a no-spouse rule, presented evidence that MP&L had a history of discrimination against females, and that derogatory sex-based remarks were made by company officials in close temporal proximity relation to her application. McDowell, also presented 14 prior instances in which the anti-nepotism policy was not enforced for males, that questions related to familial ties were not raised in 13 of these instances, and that males were previously given the opportunity to show how they would avoid family conflicts, whereas McDowell was not. The judge ruled "the defendant's anti-nepotism policy was applied to foreclose plaintiff's employment, utilizing stricter standards to assess plaintiff's situation than those applied to similarly situated men who generally were not subjected to any consideration under the policy." McDowell was awarded approximately $50,000, most of it in back pay.

Similarly, in *Kilgo v. Bowman Transportation* (1983), Kilgo initiated a class-action pattern or practice suit alleging that Bowman had a history of hiring only males as truck drivers. The company offered different explanations for excluding various females, and in one of the refusals (Rita Hart) used the anti-nepotism policy as the reason for exclusion. However, the judge ruled that the policy had not been enforced in the past, and therefore the exclusion of Hart was a pretext for sex discrimination.

More recently, in *Fuller v. Architect of the Capitol* (2002), the female spouse of a male employee was initially accepted for employment as a laborer, but the offer was rescinded when the company learned her husband was employed elsewhere in the company. The company moved for summary judgment,[12] but the judge denied the motion because Fuller presented evidence that a similarly situated male who applied at the same time as Fuller was not excluded. Fuller also had evidence that the policy was not enforced in 10 other cases, both before and after her application. The case did not go to trial, an indication that the company and Fuller likely settled.

In short, careless employers have lost disparate claims by enforcing their anti-nepotism policies for females but not males. Furthermore, it would appear that when the selective enforcement practice is provable, it is easier for plaintiffs to prevail under Title VII as compared to 14th amendment claims as in the aforementioned cases of *Waters v. Gaston County, NC* (1995) and *Wright v. MetroHealth Medical Center* (1995).

State Law Claims

There are cases in which plaintiffs who were likely losers under federal law have prevailed under state laws prohibiting discrimination based on marital status. For example, in *Ross v. Stouffer Hotel* (1991), a male employee was fired after he married a female coworker. The company's no-spouse rule permitted one of the spouses to transfer, but neither one complied and the less senior was terminated. However, the Supreme Court of Hawaii favored Ross based on the state law.

In *River Bend v. Illinois Human Rights Commission* (1992), a female teacher successfully challenged a school district policy prohibiting her from working at a school at which her husband was the principal. Recall that such policies have been supported under the 14th Amendment (for example, *Keckeisen v. Independent School District 612*, 1975, and

Montgomery v. Carr, 1996). However, in this case, the plaintiff sued based on an Illinois state law prohibiting discrimination based on marital status, and the Appellate Court of Illinois (3rd District) ruled in her favor because the school district failed to prove that the husband could not effectively supervise the wife.

In a more recent case (*Taylor v. LSI*, 2010), a Minnesota Court of Appeals ruled in favor of LeAnn Taylor, whose husband was terminated for valid reasons but who refused to answer questions relating to his wife's employment at the company. The company subsequently terminated the wife. Taylor worked for LSI for 18 years, and had received good performance appraisals and a major promotion. As a result, the court ruled that her termination was in violation of the Minnesota Human Rights Act.

These aforementioned cases were relatively straightforward, as there were no reasons other than marriage for enforcing the anti-spouse rules. However, in other cases, employers have prevailed under state laws on marriage discrimination given legitimate conflicts of interest. This occurred, for example in *Sioux City Police Officers Association v. City of Sioux City* (1993), where the policy was applied to married police officers working in the same department and in *Boaden v. Illinois* (1994) for married state troopers who wanted to work with each other.

In short, it is possible for plaintiffs to prevail under state law proscriptions against marital discrimination in cases that are much more difficult to make under federal laws. Therefore, employers need to determine if such laws apply in their own states or municipalities before enforcing no-spouse rules.

POLICIES RELATING TO PRIVACY AND FREEDOM OF ASSOCIATION

The previous section focused primarily on cases in which one spouse is excluded because both spouses work for the same employer. The focus in this section is on exclusions based on presumed illicit liaisons between existing employees and others either inside or outside the company. The main issues in these cases are privacy and freedom of association. The rulings in this domain are mixed depending up the nature of the alliance and the manner in which information about these alliances is obtained.

For example, in *Shuman v. Philadelphia* (1979), a police officer separated from his wife was terminated on grounds of "moral turpitude" for engaging in a sexual affair with an 18-year-old college student. The critical issue here, however, was not so much the affair, but rather how it was investigated. The police department was informed of the affair by the student's mother and confirmed it by conducting a 1-month surveillance of the officer. The District Court for the Eastern District of Pennsylvania conceded that the police department has "an interest in regulating, and concomitantly, investing such activities." However, by conducting the surveillance, the court ruled that the department "trampled on constitutionally protected zones of privacy" and that the sexual liaison had no bearing on the officer's ability to perform his job.

Similarly, in *Thorne v. City of El Segundo* (1983), a female typist in a police department applied for and ranked highly in an exam for entry-level police officers but was excluded after revealing on a polygraph test that she had a miscarriage. The main issue here was that the polygraph investigator followed up discovery of the miscarriage with questions relating to her sexual practices and abortion. During the course of the questioning, Thorne told the investigator that she had a relationship with a police officer in the department and was excluded. The department argued that the questions by the investigator related to sexual history related to her ability to perform the job, and the district court judge in this case favored the police department, ruling that

> Sexual relations among officers in a paramilitary organization such as a police department are an appropriate matter of inquiry with respect to employment in light of their possible adverse effect on morale, assignments, and the command–subordinate relationship.

However, the 9th Circuit overturned the ruling on grounds that the investigator violated the plaintiff's privacy rights, and the questions asked were unrelated to job performance. Also of note, Thorne won on the Title VII disparate treatment theory on grounds that various explanations offered for her exclusion were a pretext for sex discrimination based on stereotypical views related to females as police officers, and that females were held to higher moral standards than men.

Plaintiffs have won in other cases as well. For example, in *Reuter v. Skipper* (1993), a female correctional officer was terminated for violating a conflict-of-interest policy by engaging in a relationship with an ex-inmate. The policy dictated that employees not engage in relationships with a person that "has been imprisoned or convicted of a felony within the last 10 years." The District Court for the District of Oregon tried the case under moderate scrutiny and ruled that the policy infringed on the constitutional right of free association, and it "was not reasonably tailored to the state's interest in securing and protecting the jail." The court also ruled the policy could not survive even the rational basis test, as there was "no rational connection between the rule and the promotion of safety of persons and property."

More recently, in *Pucci v. Ninth District Court* (2008), Pucci, a state court administrator, claimed she was wrongfully terminated by the chief judge of the court for engaging in a domestic relationship with a rival judge. Pucci argued that she was terminated based on the chief judge's religious views on domestic relationships without benefit of marriage. The District Court for the Easter District of Michigan, Southern Division rejected the religious discrimination claim but permitted her claim of sex discrimination to proceed to trial on grounds that Pucci was replaced by a male whose qualifications "were demonstrably inferior to hers."

On the other hand, female plaintiffs have lost cases in which the policies have involved adultery. For example, in *Mercure v. Van Buren Township* (2000), Mercure was terminated from the police force for engaging in a sexual relationship with the wife of a fellow police officer, even though the wife and his fellow officer were estranged at the time of the affair. Marcum claimed infringement on his fundamental rights of association and privacy. However, the District Court for the Eastern District in Michigan ruled that "no liberty interest protected by the Constitution was implicated in a plaintiff's termination from the police force because adultery was not a protected interest." This ruling was based in large part on *Bowers v. Attorney General of Georgia* (1966), in which the Supreme Court rejected the "proposition that any kind of private sexual conduct between consenting adults is constitutionally insulated from state proscription."

Similar rulings were subsequently rendered in *Marcum v. McWhorter* (2002) and *Beecham v. Henderson County* (2005). In *Marcum*, a police officer was terminated for having an intimate relationship and cohabitating with a married woman. Marcum was separated from his wife but not yet divorced when the relationship began. His paramour was also married when the relationship began. Based on the prior ruling in *Mercure* and the

Supreme Court precedent in *Bowers*, the 3rd Circuit ruled that Marcum's termination "did not infringe his right of association as guaranteed by the First and Fourteenth Amendments."

Similarly, in *Beecham*, a deputy clerk for the Henderson County Court was terminated for engaging in a sexual relationship with an attorney practicing before the court who was then married. At the time, the attorney was married to another court employee who worked in close proximity to the plaintiff. Following the 3rd Circuit's ruling in *Marcum*, the 6th Circuit ruled that no constitutional rights were violated because "it was unacceptably disruptive to the workplace for a woman employed in the office of one of the county's court to be openly and deeply involved in a romantic relationship with a man still married to a woman employed in the other county court down the hall."

In short, it would appear to be legal for state and local agencies to exclude applicants or employees who are engaged in adulterous or presumably illicit relationships as long as the information obtained regarding these relationships is not done in a way that infringes on the constitutional right of privacy. At the same time, it must be recognized as in the *Pucci* case, that not all sexual relationships are excluded from constitutional protection.

CHALLENGES TO PRO-NEPOTISM POLICIES

Pro-nepotism policies are generally legal unless prohibited by state or federal law. They are illegal, however, under Title VII if they adversely impact a protected class, or preserve a pattern or practice of discrimination that existed in the pre-Title VII era. There are three major types of cases in which pro-nepotism policies have been addressed: (a) admission policies requiring applicants for union membership to be related to existing members; (b) word-of-mouth recruitment in homogeneous workforces; and (c) policies relating to spouses and paramours in sexual harassment claims.

Union Membership

The challenge to pro-nepotism policies first emerged in *Kotch v. Board of River Port Pilot Commissioners* (1947), a 14th Amendment case. In order to serve as licensed state river pilots, otherwise qualified individuals had to serve a 6-month apprenticeship under incumbent pilots. The plaintiffs alleged that incumbent pilots selected only their relatives and friends for apprenticeship. In a close 5-4 Supreme Court ruling, Justice Black, speaking for the majority, supported the policy, ruling:

> This selective application of a regulation is discrimination in the broad sense, but it may or may not deny equal protection of the laws. Clearly, it might offend that constitutional safeguard if it rested on grounds wholly irrelevant to achievement of the regulation's objectives. An example would be a law applied to deny a person a right to earn a living or hold any job because of hostility to his particular race, religion, beliefs, or because of any other reason having no rational relation to the regulated activities.

Justice Black also ruled that the policy was not arbitrary, and that it provided the "safest and most efficiently operated pilotage system practicable." Justice Rutledge, speaking for the dissent, opined that "blood" was the "crux of selection," and therefore is "forbidden by the Fourteenth Amendment's guaranty against denial of the equal protection of the laws."

The issue of favoritism for relatives emerged again two decades later in *Local 53 v. Volger* (1969), another Louisiana case. Unlike *Kotch*, *Volger* involved a charge of pattern or practice of racial discrimination under Title VII. Local 53 was an exclusive bargaining agent operating a referral system for journeymen and helpers for asbestos contractors. The union required that applicants for membership obtain recommendations from existing members, after which a favorable vote by existing members was required. In effect, the policy perpetuated an all-White union membership that existed in the pre-Title VII era. The 5th Circuit struck down the union policy, ruling:

> While the nepotism requirement is applicable to black and white alike and is not on its face discriminatory, in a completely white union the present effect of its continued application is to forever deny to negroes and Mexican-Americans any real opportunity for membership.

A similar ruling was rendered for union seniority in *Robinson v. Lorillard* (1971). Citing the Volger ruling, the 4th Circuit ruled:

> The controlling difference between the hypothetical typing requirement and the nepotism rule rejected in *Vogler* is *business necessity*. When an

employer or union has discriminated in the past and when its present policies renew or exaggerate discriminatory effects, those policies must yield, unless there is an overriding legitimate, non-racial business purpose.

A similar ruling was rendered by the 9th Circuit in relation to shipping clerks in *Gibson v. Local 40* (1976). Additionally, as noted in the Introduction, a similar ruling was subsequently rendered by the 1st Circuit in *EEOC v. Steamship* (1996).

In short, union policies requiring familial association with existing members is not illegal if the membership is heterogeneous (i.e., diverse), but is illegal under Title VII disparate treatment and adverse impact theory when the membership is homogeneous and includes little or no minority representation.

Word-of-Mouth Recruitment

The implications of policies that explicitly favor familial relationships are relatively obvious and straightforward. However, similar implications derive from more subtle causes of discrimination such as word-of-mouth recruitment. Based on the rulings in *Volger, Steamship*, and related cases on homogeneous workshops, the EEOC issued the following guidance on word-of-mouth recruitment on May 9, 2006:

> Title VII may be violated if an inquiry as to an applicant's friends and relatives employed by the employer is used to give preferential treatment to friends and relatives of employees when the work force is made up of *predominately one race or ethnic group* [emphasis added]. A policy or practice of according such a preference would reduce or eliminate opportunities for members of other protected groups and as such would violate Title VII, unless it is job related and consistent with business necessity. See, e.g., *Thomas v. Washington County School Board*, 915 F.2d 922, 925 (4th Cir. 1990) (in a predominately white workforce, nepotism and word-of-mouth hiring practices may operate to exclude African-Americans as effectively as any intentionally discriminatory policy).

The case cited (*Thomas v. Washington County School Board*, 1990) presents a textbook illustration of how word-of-mouth recruitment can lead to illegal racial discrimination. Thomas, a Black woman, was educated in Washington County and later graduated cum laude from college and was certified to teach in Virginia. Thomas applied for job openings on three separate occasions over a 2-year period, and each one was filled by a White teacher. Although Thomas kept her application current, she was never notified of any openings. Thomas proved that at least 46 relatives of school employees were hired between 1981 and 1988 and that teaching vacancies were never advertised. Other Black applicants testified to the same effect. As a result, the 4th Circuit ruled that Washington County's "policies and practices amount to nepotism and word-of-mouth hiring, which, in the context of a predominantly white work force, serve to freeze the effects of past discrimination."

Similar rulings were rendered in several other cases. For example, in *Bonilla v. Oakland Scavenger Company* (1982), the 9th Circuit struck down a collectively bargained policy in which ownership of company shares was restricted to family members, all of whom were of Italian ancestry. The court ruled:

> We reject the Company's argument that its legitimate interest in protecting its family members overrides the countervailing national interest in eliminating employment discrimination based on race and national origin. To the extent that preferential wages, hours, and job assignments are tied to ownership of the Company's stock, the shareholder preference plan violates Title VII because the plan's effect is to discriminate against [plaintiffs] with respect to [their] compensation, terms, conditions, or privileges of employment because of [their] race, color, … or national origin.

Similar rulings were rendered by the 2nd Circuit in *Grant v. Bethlehem Steel* (1980) in relation to a word-of-mouth hiring system in which superintendents referred only their White friends and relatives for jobs as construction foremen; by the 9th Circuit in *Domingo v. New England Fish* (1984), in which Eskimos and Filipinos were frozen out of technical and professional jobs at a salmon cannery; and more recently by the District Court of the Southern District of New York in *United States v. New York* (2010), in which a word-of-mouth recruitment policy by the New York City Department of Transportation preserved an all-male bridge-painting crew.

Two additional points are worth noting. First, word-of-mouth policies have been defeated under disparate treatment and adverse impact theory. Second, not all instances of word-of-mouth recruitment in homogeneous workforces amount to illegal discrimination. For example, in *EEOC v. Consolidated* (1993), an employer's word-of-mouth recruitment resulted in exclusive hiring of Korean immigrants. However, Consolidated pre-vailed because there was evidence many non-Koreans were offered work and declined because the jobs were undesirable.

In short, the use of word-of-mouth recruitment in homogeneous workforces has the same implications as explicit policies that favor friends and relatives, and is illegal under Title VII, except, of course, if the jobs are undesirable.

Favoritism and Sexual Harassment

A final point to note in regard to pro-nepotism policies is that it is gener-ally legal to grant preferences to spouses and paramours. Or as noted by the EEOC in Policy Guidance N-915.048, issued on January 12, 1990:

> Not all types of sexual favoritism violate Title VII. It is the Commission's position that Title VII does not prohibit isolated instances of preferen-tial treatment based upon consensual romantic relationships. An isolated instance of favoritism toward a "paramour" (or a spouse, or a friend) may be unfair, but it does not discriminate against women or men in viola-tion of Title VII, since both are disadvantaged for reasons other than their genders. A female charging party who is denied an employment benefit because of such sexual favoritism would not have been treated more favor-ably had she been a man nor, conversely, was she treated less favorably because she was a woman.

There are several cases in which female plaintiffs have challenged this policy and lost, both before (*DeCinto v. Westchester County Medical Center*, 1986) and after the EEOC guidance (see *Herman v. Western Financial*, 1994; *Thompson v. Olson*, 1994; *Ellert v. University of Texas*, 1995; *Taken v. Oklahoma*, 1997).

That said, it is illegal under quid pro quo[15] sexual harassment theory for an employer to coerce an employee into becoming a paramour under threats to terms and conditions of employment. Or as noted by the EEOC:

> If a female employee is coerced into submitting to unwelcome sexual advances in return for a job benefit, other female employees who were qualified for but were denied the benefit may be able to establish that sex was generally made a condition for receiving the benefit.[7] Thus, in order for a woman to have obtained the job benefit at issue, it would have been

necessary to grant sexual favors, a condition that would not have been imposed on men. This is substantially the same as a traditional sexual harassment charge alleging that sexual favors were implicitly demanded as a "quid pro quo" in return for job benefits.

This is illustrated in *Toscano v. Nimmo* (1983), in which a Title VII violation was found when the granting of sexual favors was a condition for promotion. Similarly, in *King v. Palmer* (1985), a female plaintiff prevailed when another female was promoted after she had sexual relations with a male supervisor.

The EEOC also warns that "widespread favoritism" may constitute hostile environment sexual harassment. Accordingly:

> If favoritism based upon the granting of sexual favors is widespread in a workplace, both male and female colleagues who do not welcome this conduct can establish a hostile work environment in violation of Title VII regardless of whether any objectionable conduct is directed at them and regardless of whether those who were granted favorable treatment willingly bestowed the sexual favors. In these circumstances, a message is implicitly conveyed that the managers view women as "sexual playthings," thereby creating an atmosphere that is demeaning to women. Both men and women who find this offensive can establish a violation if the conduct is "sufficiently severe or pervasive" to alter the conditions of [their] employment and create an abusive working environment.

In short, though certainly not within the mainstream of pro-nepotism policies, employers and supervisors must be aware that coercing employees into paramour status is illegal under both the quid pro quo and hostile environment theories of harassment.

SUMMARY AND CONCLUSIONS

The purpose of this chapter was to present legal issues associated with nepotism in the workplace. Policies relating to both anti-nepotism and pro-nepotism were addressed under constitutional principles, Title VII adverse impact and disparate treatment theory, and state laws.

Under constitutional law, anti-nepotism policies are generally deemed rationally related to legitimate government interests and are difficult to defeat even when there are claims that the policies in question are selectively enforced. The main barrier in constitutional claims is that anti-nepotism policies do not generally interfere with fundamental rights such as the freedom to marry and associate.

On the other hand, plaintiffs have succeeded in challenging anti-nepotism policies via Title VII using both adverse impact and disparate treatment theory. Successful claims in adverse impact theory involve statistical proof that the policy disproportionately affects women, and the employer cannot justify the policy via business necessity. Employers have also lost under disparate treatment theory when it is provable that the policy is selectively enforced and is a pretext for discrimination based on sex. Plaintiffs have also succeeded in defeating anti-nepotism policies in select cases in which there are state laws prohibiting discrimination against marriage, unless the employer can prove that its policy is a legitimate conflict of interest.

Closely related to anti-nepotism policies are policies that address who and under what circumstances employees can enter into sexual relationships. All things being equal, it is legal for state or local agencies to exclude applicants or employees who are engaged in adulterous or presumably illicit relationships as long as the information obtained regarding these relationships is not done in a way that infringes on the constitutional right of privacy.

Pro-nepotism policies are generally legal under constitutional provisions but are illegal under Title VII when they differentially impact or directly discriminate against protected Title VII classes. Most of these cases occurred in homogeneous workplaces with little or no minority representation. These policies have been defeated under adverse impact and disparate theory, both for explicit union policies conditioning membership on familial association with an existing member and for word-of-mouth recruitment. Additionally, though it is not generally illegal to give preferences to spouses or paramours, it is illegal under quid pro quo sexual harassment theory when the paramour status is coerced, and under hostile environment sexual harassment theory where sexual favoritism is widespread.

ENDNOTES

1. See http://nihrecord.od.nih.gov/newsletters/03_19_2002/story04.htm for a complete account of the events surrounding Earl Stadtman's decision to decline the offer from the University of Chicago.

2. For example, in the much-anticipated 1992 ruling (*Planned Parenthood v. Casey*), to which advocates and opponents of abortion rights objected, the Supreme Court upheld abortion as a fundamental right but also ruled that a restriction by the State of Pennsylvania (i.e., parental approval for teens) passed the strict scrutiny test, ruling that the state had a compelling interest in restricting abortions in teens, and that the law itself was narrowly tailored to serve that interest.

3. That said, the rational basis test is not always a slam dunk. For example, in *City of Cleburne v. Cleburne Living Center* (1985), the Supreme Court ruled that a city zoning law that blocked construction of a home for mentally retarded people was "irrational and arbitrary." The same would apply, for example, if a state or municipality wishing to create a speed trap posted a 20 mph speed limit on a major highway that is not under repair.

4. One major exception is Section 1981, a 13th Amendment statute that covers discrimination based on race, color, religion, and national origin, but not sex.

5. Adverse impact theory is also available in the Age Discrimination in Employment Act (ADEA), but the adverse impact rules in the ADEA are dramatically different than in Title VII. It should be noted that adverse impact theory, applied in *EEOC v. Steamship*, was not generally available in Title VII until after *Griggs v. Duke Power* (1971). However, the pattern or practice of discrimination was a statutory violation in original Title VII language.

6. The reasons why adverse impact theory is unavailable in constitutional claims are beyond the scope of this chapter. Readers interested in this topic should read the Supreme Court rulings in *Washington v. Davis* (1976), *Arlington Heights v. Metropolitan Housing Corp.* (1977), and *Personnel Administrator v. Feeney* (1979).

7. Readers interested in learning more about pattern or practice theory should read the Supreme Court's landmark rulings in *International Teamsters v. US* (1977) and *Hazelwood School District v. US* (1977).

8. It should be noted that adverse impact theory, which was applicable to the *Steamboat* case, was not generally available prior to the Supreme Court's landmark ruling in *Griggs v. Duke Power* (1971).

9. Readers interested learning more about retaliation theory should read the Supreme Court's landmark rulings *Robinson v. Shell Oil* (1997) and *Burlington Northern Santa Fe Railway Company v. White* (2006).

10. The 21 states are Alaska, California, Connecticut, Delaware, Florida, Hawaii, Illinois, Maine, Maryland, Michigan, Minnesota, Montana, Nebraska, New Hampshire, New Jersey, New York, North Dakota, Virginia, Washington, and Wisconsin.

11. It should be noted that in *Adamson v. Multi Community Diversified Services* (2008), another frequently cited case, a father, wife, and daughter were terminated based on a broad anti-nepotism policy and sued on ground that the policy adversely impacted families. Additionally, the policy was challenged for disparate treatment based on age (for the father) and disparate treatment based on sex (for the mother and daughter). The 10th Circuit ruled that "familial" adverse impact is an invalid charge, and that there were no grounds for supporting any of the disparate treatment claims.

12. Summary judgment for the defendant is granted if the trial judge assumes that all the plaintiff's statements are true, and the judge concludes that even under these assumptions, a reasonable trier of fact (judge or jury) would be unlikely to rule in favor of the plaintiff.
13. This guidance is available on the EEOC.Gov Web site at http://www.eeoc.gov/eeoc/foia/letters/2006/titlevii_adea_preemployment_inquiries.html. See also http://www.eeoc.gov/eeoc/foia/letters/2004/all_statutes_inquiries.html and http://www.eeoc.gov/policy/docs/race-color.html for related guidance.
14. This guidance is available on the EEOC.Gov Web site at http://www.eeoc.gov/policy/docs/sexualfavor.html.
15. There are generally two types of sexual harassment. In quid pro quo harassment, sexual favors are demanded under threat to terms and conditions of employment, such as demotion, failure to promote, and termination. In hostile environment harassment, the abuses must be sufficiently severe or pervasive so as to interfere with the employee's ability to perform her or his job. However, a connection to specific terms and conditions of employment is not required.

REFERENCES

Gutman, A., Koppes, L., & Vodanovich, S. (2010). *EEO law and personnel practices* (3rd ed.). New York: Routledge.

CASES CITED

Adamson v. Multi Community Diversified Services (CA10 2008) 514 F.3d 1136
Amey v. Delta Airlines (D ND Ga.1980) U.S. Dist. LEXIS 16292
Arlington Heights v. Metropolitan Housing Corp. (1977) 429 US 252
Beecham v. Henderson County (CA5 2005) 422 F.3d 372
Boaden v. Illinois (1996) 664 N.E.2d 61, 171 Ill.2d 230
Bonilla v. Oakland Scavenger Company (CA9 1982) 697 F.2d 1297
Bowers v. Attorney General of Georgia (CA11 1966) 114 F.3d 1097
Burlington Northern Santa Fe Railway Company v. White (2006) 548 US 53
City of Cleburne v. Cleburne Living Center (1985) 105 S. Ct. 3249
DeCinto v. Westchester County Medical Center (CA2 1986) 807 F.2d 304
Domingo v. New England Fish (CA9 1984) 727 F.2d 1429
Dothard v. Rawlinson (1977) 433 US 321
EEOC v. Consolidated Services Systems (CA7 1993) 989 F.2d 233
EEOC v. Rath Packing Company (CA8 1986) 787 F.2d 318
EEOC v. Steamship (CA1 1995) 48 F.3d 594
Ellert v. University of Texas (CA5 1995) 52 F.3d 543
Espinoza v. Thomas (CA8 1978) 580 F.2d 346
Fuller v. Architect of the Capitol (D DC 2002) U.S. Dist. LEXIS 7285

Gibson v. Local 40 (CA9 1976) 543 F.2d 1259
Grant v. Bethlehem Steel (CA2 1980) 635 F.2d 1007
Griggs v. Duke Power Co. (1971) 401 US 424
Harper v. TWA (CA8 1975) 525 F.2d 409
Hazelwood School District v. United States (1977) 433 US 299
Herman v. Western Financial (1994) 696 P.2d 595
Holder v. City of Raleigh (CA4 1989) 49 Fair Empl. Prac. Cas. 47, 49 Empl. Prac.
International Brotherhood of Teamsters v. United States (1977) 431 US 324
Keckeisen v. Independent School District 612 (CA8 1975) 509 F.2d 1062
Kilgo v. Bowman Transportation (D ND GA1983) 570 F. Supp. 1509
King v. Palmer (D DC 1985) 598 F. Supp 65
Kotch v. Board of River Port Pilot Commissioners (1947) 330 US 552
Local 53 v. Vogler (CA5 1969) 407 F.2d 1047
Marcum v. McWhorter (CA6 2002) 308 F.3d 635
McDonnell Douglas Corp. v Green (1973) 411 US 792
McDowell v. Mississippi Power and Light (S SD Miss1986) 641 F. Supp. 424
Mercure v. Van Buren Township (D ED Mich 2000) 81 F. Supp. 2d 814
Montgomery v. Carr (CA6 1996) 101 F.3d 1117
Parks v. Warner Robbins, GA (CA11 1994) 43 F.3d 609
Personnel Administrator v. Feeney (1979) 442 US 256
Planned Parenthood v. Casey (1992) 510 US 1309
Pucci v. Ninth District Court (D ED Mich 2008) 565 F. Supp. 792
Reuter v. Skipper (D Ore1993) 832 F. Supp. 1420
River Bend v. Illinois Human Rights Commission (Ill.App. 1992) 597 N.E. 842
Robinson v. Lorillard (CA4 1971) 444 F.2d 791
Robinson v. Shell Oil (1997) 117 S.Ct. 843
Roche v. Town of Waream (D Mass 1998) 24 F. Supp. 146
Roe v. Wade (1973) 410 US 113
Ross v. Stouffer Hotel (Haw. 1991) 816 P.2d 302
Shuman v. Philadelphia (E.D.Pa. 1979) 470 F. Supp. 449
Siler-Khodr v. University of Texas Health Science Center San Antonio (CA5 2002) 261 F.3d
    542
Sioux City Police Officers Assoc. v. City of Sioux City (Iowa 1993), 496 N.W.2d 687
Sowards v. Loudon County (CA6 2000) 203 F.3d 426
Taken v. Oklahoma (CA10 1997) 125 F.3d 136 6
Taylor v. LSI, Minn. Ct. App., No. A09-1410, 4/27/10
Thomas v. Metroflight (CA10 1987) 814 F.2d 1506
Thomas v Washington County School Board (CA4 1990) 915 F.2d 922
Thorne v. City of El Segundo (CA9 1983) 726 F.2d 459
Toscano v. Nimmo (D Del 1983) 570 F. Supp. 1197
United States v. City of New York (D SD NY 2010) 2010 U.S. Dist. LEXIS 47267
United States v. Virginia (1996) 116 S. Ct. 2264
Vaughn v. Lawrenceburg Power System (CA6 2001) U.S. App. LEXIS 22508
Washington (Mayor, DC) v. Davis (1976) 426 US 229
Waters v. Gaston County, NC (CA4 1995) 57 F.3d 422
Wright v. MetroHealth Medical Center (1995) 58 F.3d 1130
Yancey v. Weyerhaeuser CA8 (2002) 277 F.3d 1026
Yuhas v. Libbey-Owens-Ford Co. (CA7 1977) 562 F.2d 496

3

The Nepotistic Organization: What Is This Place and How Do the People Make It?

Paul M. Muchinsky
University of North Carolina at Greensboro

It would be reasonable to conclude *nepotism* is a dirty word. The paucity of references to it in bodies of literature suggests authors do not like to write about it, or editors do not like to publish anything about it. I found more books with "devil worship" than "nepotism" in the title. The definition of nepotism is "patronage bestowed or favoritism shown on the basis of family relationship, as in business or politics" (www.dictionaryreference.com, 2010). The word first appeared in the 1600s, and its etymological origin is the Italian work for nephew, *nepo*. Its origin is related to the papacy. Newly elected popes appointed relatives, typically brothers and nephews, and provided them with resources to preserve their newly created social and political status. The pope would "surround himself with intimates of unquestionable personal loyalty. Ties of blood were seen as the guarantors against intrigue and factionalism" (Scott, 1991, p. 4). Being celibate, sons were replaced by nephews in the pope's cadre.

The suffix *-ism* is defined as "a distinctive doctrine, theory, system, or practice." Although *nepotism* is the most frequently found form of the word, this chapter will use less frequently found versions of the word: *nepot* and *non-nepot* (Cambreleng, 1969). Eschewing the *-ism* places more emphasis on the actors and the culture of the organization (*nepotistic*) than on the doctrine itself.

The literature on nepotism can be grouped into three categories. There is a body of literature from a legal perspective, mostly derived from case law, as presented in Chapter 2 by Gutman in this volume. Second is an admixture of two primary themes: (a) conceptual statements about nepotism in general (for example, Bellow, 2003; Ewing, 1965; Ford & McLaughlin, 1996; Vinton, 1998); and (b) isolated articles primarily about the hiring of dual-career couples (for example, Padgett & Morris, 2005; Pingree, Butler, Paisley, & Hawkins, 1978; Reed, 1988; Werbel & Hames, 1996).

However, it is the third body of literature upon which most of our knowledge about nepotism is based: the family business. While there is a substantial and growing body of literature on family business, family business researchers rarely cite *nepotism* or any of its linguistic derivatives. Why? Perhaps the simplest answer was provided by Chrisman, Chua, and Sharma (1996): "Nepotism is a given in the family business" (p. 23). Vinton offered a pragmatic statement: "This [nepotism] human resource practice/policy is the one that is most uniquely family business oriented" (p. 297). In short, while nepotism is inevitably linked with family business, as a doctrine it is not frequently cited as an explanatory concept.

It is customary for authors to cite statistical evidence to support the importance of the topic being addressed. In this case the relevant statistic pertains to the percentage of the U.S. economy that is derived from a family business. The criterion problem associated with what constitutes a family business is of significant magnitude. Shanker and Astrachan (1996) and Astrachan and Shanker (2003) addressed this issue in their research based on data from the census and Internal Revenue Service (IRS) tax records. Loosely defined, a *family business* could consist of businesses that are sole proprietorships, partnerships, and businesses that are owned but not operated by families. Using this definition, approximately 59% of the U.S. economy is based upon a family business. However, excluding legal and taxation justifications for potentially including companies as family businesses, the results are considerably different. Using the narrow definition of a family business (and one that conforms to the intent of an analysis of nepotism from a psychological perspective), Astrachan and Shanker reported there are 3 million businesses in the United States, involving 27% of the workforce, representing 36 million people. The narrow definition produces a description of a family business as multigenerational, typically with a grandparent founder, two or three offspring in top management positions, and cousins in entry-level positions.

Research-based books on family business embody several major themes: cross-cultural differences, family business as entrepreneurship, providing consulting services to family businesses, and life cycles of family businesses. These areas of research are also addressed in scientific journals that focus on the study of family businesses (for example, *Family Business Review* and *Families in Business*) as well as journals directed toward family therapy where business-related issues are discussed.

My purpose in writing this chapter is to propose avenues for intellectual and scientific inquiry into the seemingly taboo topic of nepotism. The approach I followed was to take several major interest areas within industrial–organizational (I–O) psychology and demonstrate their potential applicability to the study of nepotism. However, influence can also flow in the opposite direction. The scientific study of nepotism, in all its forms and manifestations, can serve to broaden the domain of I–O psychology, not only conceptually but also methodologically. Those readers interested in an exhaustive literature review of scholarly research published within I–O psychology on nepotism will be disappointed. There is none to review. Likewise, no model will be offered in this chapter nor will the results from a meta-analysis be presented. This chapter is one of potentials and possibilities for our field to pursue. Throughout my career as both an academic and consultant I have had several experiences pertaining to nepotistic organizations and issues. I have also experienced some in my personal life. I have described seven of them and presented them in the form of "Field Notes" interspersed within the text. Their purpose is to animate the conceptual material under consideration. Readers interested in real-life examples may find them illustrative. Critics may dismiss them as $n = 1$ anecdotes.

WHAT DOES *NEPOTISTIC* MEAN?

This question is posed from the perspective of its psychological (construct) meaning, not its legal standing or definition. As is the case with all constructs in psychology, there is no singular standard of meaning. Those who surmise the research literature on family business might provide a strong foothold to the meaning of *nepotistic* will be disappointed (but perhaps not surprised). Chrisman et al. (1996) identified 34 different definitions of a family business in their review of the literature published between 1971 and 1995. As such, the likelihood of a singular definition of nepotistic seems highly unlikely. However, I believe it would be instructive to delineate its attributes.

1. Schneider (1987) famously stated, "The people make the place." His statement provides an initial foundation for meaning. A nepotistic organization is defined by the particular people within the organization at a particular time in the organization's history. It is an interactionistic perspective. An organization may begin with a nepotistic culture based on its members. If those members leave the organization, the nepotistic culture of the organization disappears, although its legacy may endure regarding selected cultural rites and rituals.

2. It is possible for every member of an organization to be nepots, but more often the organization is populated with nepots and non-nepots. The nepotistic organization may be populated by multigenerational members or members from a single generation.

3. There is psychological meaning in terms of attributes and behaviors for both nepots and non-nepots within an organization (i.e., it matters which group you are in). This attribute is similar to Graen's (Graen & Schiemann, 1978) notion of in-group and out-group members. However in Graen's conception, in-group members were consistently regarded and treated with greater favor than out-group members. In the case of a nepotistic organization, the in-group (the nepots) may be the recipients of favorable treatment in some regard, but possibly unfavorable treatment in others, compared with non-nepots.

4. Nepotistic organization cultures can range from weak to very strong in terms of their influence on nepots and non-nepots alike. A weak nepotistic culture would be characterized by little differentiation in attitudes or behavior between nepots and non-nepots, or among the nepots. In a very strong nepotistic culture, there are clear differences between how individuals are regarded within the organization based on their family-member status.

5. Finally, there is nothing inherently positive or negative about a nepotistic organizational culture. Any value (positive or negative) is a function of the particular behavior under consideration and whose interests are being served by the behavior in question. However, nepotism is regarded negatively to the point that laws and organizational policies have been enacted to prevent its occurrence (see Gutman, this volume, Chapter 2).

These attributes are not intended to be exhaustive and are presented to provide a framework for understanding the meaning of nepotistic organizational cultures.

INITIAL TYPOLOGY OF NEPOTISTIC ORGANIZATIONS

Historically, I–O psychology has been more interested in understanding variation in human behavior within organizations (e.g., productive versus counterproductive workplace behavior) than understanding variations in organizational types. Pinder (2008) cited an observation by Lyman Porter regarding the study of organizational behavior (OB) that we seem to know more about "the B than the O." Attempts to understand nepotistic organizations may compel us to develop a typology of organizations in which nepotistic cultures exist. Gutman provided a thorough listing of all types of familial relations that comprise the legal basis of nepotism (see Field Note 1). A basic typology of nepotistic organizational forms would be as follows:

1. *Complete*—In this organization every employee is related by blood or marriage to every other employee. An example would be a family-owned and operated restaurant. Every member would be classified as a nepot. An analysis of this type of organization could focus on differentiations among nepots (perhaps by generation or gender), and interorganizational relations between this organization and vendors (e.g., suppliers) compared to non-nepotistic organizations.

2. *Hierarchical*—This type of organization is the archetype of a nepotistic structure. The formal leaders of the organization (e.g., president, vice presidents, senior managers, and so forth) are nepots, while the rest of the organization is staffed by non-nepots. An analysis of this type of organization might focus on differential organizational expectations between nepots and non-nepots, and interaction between the two groups.

3. *Stratified*—The leaders of this type of organization would not be nepots but at some level(s) beneath the top are nepots. An analysis of this type of organization might focus on the relationships between the nepots and the non-nepots both above and below them in the organizational hierarchy.

4. *Multinepotic*—This type of organization would be populated with multiple sets of nepots, although non-nepots may be represented in top management. An example would be a coal mining company. Coal mining has long attracted multigenerational workers and breadth of members within a generation (brothers, in-laws, cousins)

from multiple families. Organizations of this type have been studied primarily from a sociological perspective.

5. *Isolated*—This type of organization would be populated primarily with non-nepots but in isolated cases the company might employ spouses, siblings, in-laws, and so forth. For the most part, however, the nepots are a small minority of the workforce. An analysis of this type of organization might address the placement of nepots within the organization, perhaps to the detriment of the nepots or organization, for the purpose of negating concerns about alleged favoritism.

FIELD NOTE 1: FUNCTIONAL NEPOTISM

A major university had a regulation forbidding nepotism in any superior–subordinate relationship. A tenured professor within the department was selected by the provost (the senior academic officer of the university) to assume the position of department head. In his second year as department head he entered into a personal relationship with an untenured female professor within the same department. Before too long, the female professor began to cohabitate with her boss, the department head. News of their common living arrangement eventually made its way to the provost. Upon verifying the accuracy of the information brought to his attention, the provost demanded a meeting with department head over the matter. The department head said he was not in violation of the anti-nepotism regulation because he was not married to his female professor colleague. The provost dismissed the legitimacy of the department head's explanation. The provost immediately removed the professor from his role as department head, claiming he was engaging in "functional nepotism" with the female professor. The professor returned to his previous role as a faculty member within the department. No longer in a superior–subordinate relationship, there were no prohibitions against the two professors continuing to live together. However, the former department head had to recuse himself from any evaluation of his junior colleague.

This typology of nepotistic organizations is intended only to be representative of how a nepotistic presence might manifest itself within an organization. My purpose in creating the typology is to underscore that nepotistic influences can be arrayed along a continuum of strength or intensity, pertaining, for example, to power distribution, openness of communication, or trust.

I–O PSYCHOLOGY AND NEPOTISTIC ORGANIZATIONS

It is not difficult to imagine how many traditional content areas of I–O psychology could be enriched by consideration of nepotistic issues. I have selected four major areas for discussion.

Work–Family

It has been convention to partition the 24-hour day into three 8-hour sessions of approximately equal magnitude: 8 hours of sleep, 8 hours of work, and 8 hours of nonwork. The nonwork segment has been variously labeled as family, leisure, or personal time. The importance of time away from work for our psychological health in the form of holidays, vacations, and weekends is well documented. Three major theories (spillover, compensation, segmentation) have been proposed to explain the psychological effect that work and family segments of our lives have on each other. Much attention has been given to how we balance the two in our lives to sustain our mental and emotional well-being. On-site child day-care services and telecommunicating are examples of how we allow the presence of one segment into the space and time traditionally allocated for the other. At the core of work–family theories and organizational interventions is the basic premise of this segmentation of our existence. Although there are times in our lives when we are not confronted with this duality (e.g., childhood and retirement), for the most part it is an omnipresent fact of life.

The nepotistic organization, depending upon its type, can conflate this duality. Rather than conceptualizing life as the relationship between the two domains, nepotistic organizations offer us the opportunity to consider their homogenation. As described in Masuda and Visio's chapter (this volume, Chapter 7), work–family relations for nepots might be regarded as a special or extreme case of the spillover model. Neither a work-centric nor family-centric orientation can fully capture the psychological dynamics of a nepotistic organization, particularly of the complete or hierarchal type for the nepots. Any distinctions between work and family issues may be limited only to the physical location of the nepots at any given moment in time. The concept of "going to work" began to manifest itself in the Industrial Revolution of the 1840s. Prior to that time, work and family life was enacted in the same physical space. Vestiges of that lifestyle continue with the family farm and the shopkeeper who resides in the same building that houses the business. In one sense, nepotistic organizations can be viewed as a social anachronism in contemporary society.

Work–family theories speak to space and time as buffers, protecting us from the (typically adverse) impacts of one against the other. The home is the forum for emotive expressions of love, empathy, and caring, but also the expression of negative emotions as anger, jealousy, and resentment. Workplaces were created as sites where emotive displays of behavior were discouraged or suppressed. Although the workplace is typically guided by formal rules of conduct, replete with policies and procedures designed to control behavior, there is no codification of rules and procedures—the equivalent of the employee handbook—in home life. It can be the absence of formal and enforceable rules of conduct that can facilitate family tension.

Nepots are at the nexus of work and family. They are the members of society who are devoid of the formal boundary between work and family. The degree of the void depends upon the strength of the nepotistic effect (and thus the type of the nepotistic organization). The magnitude of their conjoining influences on each other dictates the degree to which their work and personal lives become homogenated.

Nepots are regarded as beneficiaries of privilege through the accident of birth or, as described by Vinton, members of the "lucky sperm club." A perception of nepots is they enjoy the simultaneous benefits of both work and family. However, research on nepots may yield an alternative depiction of work–family relationships. A potentially valuable line of research would be how nepotistic organizations reward nepots. Privilege of membership is one basis of favoritism. Another basis could be that nepots are disproportionately rewarded within the organization. Some nepots may retain employment only because of their family status. Moreover, some successfully performing nepots may receive perquisites that exceed the value of their contributions (see Field Note 2). Perhaps families regard themselves as placing disproportionate pressures on nepots to legitimate or justify (to the nepots or others) the disproportionate rewards they receive, an interpretation based on equity theory. Especially in hierarchical nepotistic organizations, nepots operate within an informal system of greater control compared to non-nepots. Although nepots can exert greater influence over their work lives, the nepots are also subject to greater organizational control than other employees who are not part of the web of family influence.

FIELD NOTE 2: DYSFUNCTIONAL FAMILY FEUD

A president of a midsize company had his sons staff three of the top four positions in the company. The father referred to the four of them as the "senior management" of the company. The two older brothers as well as the nonfamily member were solid performers for the company, but the youngest son was a chronic underachiever. The youngest son joined the company at the urging of his mother who pressured her husband "to find a place" for him within the company. The president (and father) reluctantly hired his younger son "to keep the peace within the family."

The older two sons were married to women who were very socially competitive, especially with each other. If one got a new car, the other had to have a new car. When the middle son bought a new (and larger) house, the older son soon thereafter followed suite. The youngest son was divorced, but what his two siblings and their wives received from their father became a comparative standard.

The father found himself being asked by his older two sons for the company to subsidize their lifestyles. The father acquiesced on several occasions to pay raises for his two older sons based on their exhortations about needing more money to support their spending habits. In so doing, the sons made far more money than they would have earned by being in comparable positions with other companies. Additionally, the sons successfully induced their father to pay for perquisites including country club memberships, company cars, and additional vacation time.

Because the two older sons made valuable contributions to the company, the father could justify to himself the additional compensation expenses being paid. However, in order to maintain a sense of fairness within the senior management staff, the two other people also benefited from the president's largess. The youngest son also received pay raises and perquisites as provided to his two brothers. Initially such enhancements were not immediately forthcoming to the youngest son. However, upon learning of them he cajoled his father for "equal treatment." When that tactic occasionally failed to produce the desired results, he complained to his mother about it. In turn she pressured her husband to treat the three sons "equally and fairly." The father's explanation to his wife that "fair does not necessarily have to be equal" fell on deaf ears. The father learned that what he provided for one son should be provided for all three.

Meanwhile, the fifth member of the management team, the nonfamily member, was the lucky recipient of the same perquisites extended to the three brothers by the father. However, he did not receive the salary enhancements given to the others. He surmised their existence from off-hand comments occasionally made by the youngest son. As an outsider to the family and its dynamics, he recognized his collateral privileges within the company. He privately referred to his employment as being a contestant on "Dysfunctional Family Feud."

One differentiation between nepots and non-nepots is the strength and magnitude of the buffer between work and family. It would be hypothesized the buffering effect may be negligible for nepots in complete and hierarchical nepotistic organizations. A second distinction pertains to the role of the family. For non-nepots, the research literature indicates the effects of family on work can be negative, neutral, or positive, depending on the particular issues in question (e.g., attentional demands). For nepots, however, the effects may more likely be bimodal, either expressly positive or negative, and perhaps less issue specific. The continuous interplay between work and family roles may compel families to become less variable in their affective responses to work pressures. Nepots offer an opportunity to examine work–family relations from an inverted position from the norm. Instead of understanding the balance between two domains, nepots represent the consequence of their fusion (see Field Note 3).

FIELD NOTE 3: COMMAND PERFORMANCES

A man founded an asphalt paving company. His business quickly grew as he was successful in securing both residential and commercial accounts. He had two sons and a daughter (the youngest of the three children). During high school, his sons worked at the company over the summer. After graduating from high school, both sons entered the business on a full-time basis. Both sons were hard working and dedicated to the business. Within a few years, both sons had become heads of satellite locations of the company. The daughter went on to college, graduated, got married, and her husband also joined the business. The father and two sons (who also married) were very close and all three lived within a few blocks of one another. The daughter and her husband moved back to her hometown and lived about 10 miles from her parents and siblings. The daughter grew up hearing stories of the family business shared over the dinner table, but by the time she was a teenager her brothers had left the family home.

The parents were highly sociable and often held parties, picnics, and barbeques attended by the families. When the families would meet for social occasions, the conversation invariably turned to various aspects of the family business. The constant stream of shoptalk seemed natural for the father and two sons, and the new son-in-law felt obligated to participate.

However, the daughter grew tired of the singular theme to most family gatherings. She privately complained to her mother about it. Her mother said the family was simply talking about family matters and business was part of it. Her two sister-in-laws seemed preoccupied talking to each other about their respective children.

Attempts by the daughter to keep business issues from dominating family discussions were initially met with wry acceptance. When other family members wanted to talk about work-related issues, they would pair off and speak in hushed voices so as not to offend the daughter. Upon seeing this pattern of conversation, the daughter would exclaim, "You're talking about work again!" Eventually the family grew weary of the daughter's attempt at control. Comments began to be made questioning whether she felt socially superior to the others because of her level of education and her living in a different section of town. The daughter was hurt from the rebuke by her own family. She ceased complaining about the business talk and retreated into silence. She developed disdain for family gatherings, especially at holidays, and disparagingly referred to them as "command performances."

Entrance and Ascension

Vocational Choice

The evolutionary process by which individuals develop vocational interests has been the object of scientific inquiry for over 70 years. Our vocational interests appear to crystallize in adolescence and are shaped by life experience and education. The combination of vocational interests tempered by abilities permits us to entertain membership in certain occupations and exclusion from others. Depending upon employment opportunities, ultimately we select a job with the realization that over our lifetime we will change jobs within occupations as well as possibly change occupations. The overall process is typically characterized by undecidedness, ambiguity, and the felt need to ultimately make some choice so as to join the working population.

For families that operate their own business, the possibility of their children joining them in employment is an option unavailable to others. A child can be regarded as a potential nepot from birth. Depending upon the will of the family and the demeanor of the child, offspring can be groomed from an early age to enter the family business (see Field Note 4). As such, there can be a sense of preordination to vocational choice for children from a business family (see Van Hooft and Stout, this volume, Chapter 4).

Nepots can avoid the often unsettling process in adolescence of having to select a career path. However, in adulthood, the comfort and security from having a place within a family business may be offset by the realization of foreclosure of other career options that are afforded to non-nepots. There is little empirical research on the vocational interests and choices of family members who elect to enter into or reject employment within a family business. There is empirical research on enhancing the effective transfer of the family business across generations. For example, Ambrose (1983) reported a successful transfer is more likely if the family children became involved in the business at an early age.

FIELD NOTE 4: "IT'S IN OUR BLOOD"

There is a jewelry store that has been in business for over 100 years. The founder opened the first store in the 1890s. The grandson of the founder, now in his 70s, still comes to work every morning and stays until closing time. He had two sons, now in their 40s, who are also in the business. Their father first took them to New York by train when they were about 10 years old. They would visit the famous diamond district and watch master diamond cutters create facets on uncut diamonds. Their father taught them about the color and clarity of diamonds, and how the shape of a diamond is selected to amplify the stone's strengths and minimize its flaws. I asked one son why he became the fourth generation of the family to be in the jewelry business. His response was, "It's in our blood." His brother had a son who had just graduated from high school. I asked if his nephew had committed to becoming the fifth generation of the family to enter the jewelry business. He deadpanned, "Yes, he just doesn't know it yet."

Recruitment, Selection, and Placement

Recruitment and selection are among the mainstream topics in I–O psychology. They have relevance for family businesses including whether families selectively recruit some members to join the business but not others. Another line of inquiry could be by gender (with preference for one over the other, perhaps as a function of the nature of the family business), and the recruitment potential of late arriving members to the family, such as in-laws, new spouses and step-children (see Field Note 5 for a gender-related nepotistic issue). Why some family members refuse to join the business is unclear, including the consequences for both the individual and the family business. Lansberg (1999) described how some family businesses want the nepot to work outside the business for several years before joining the business (preferably for a company within the same industry). Such a procedure seemingly has no analogue with non-nepots, other than a candidate is rejected for lack of experience. However, the nepot is assured of employment with the family business prior to beginning this work experience with another company. As such, this type of experience represents a hybrid between selection and training. One hundred years of research on recruitment and selection has provided I–O psychology with expertise on these topics. We do not know the degree to which this knowledge generalizes to nepots.

FIELD NOTE 5: CONCERNS ABOUT FAIRNESS

I was a consultant to a large chemical company that had an anti-nepotism regulation as a condition of employment. To allay any possible concerns about issues of favoritism or unfairness in any employment decisions, the company forbade more than one member of a family (spouses, siblings, parent–child) from working at the company. Any attempt at deception about a family relationship within the workforce was grounds for termination. A man and a woman who worked at the company decided to get married to each other. Both knew the consequences of their decision to marry: one of them would no longer continue to work there. The same situation happened several years previously with two other pairs of workers at the company. In each of the three cases the man held a position of higher authority and greater pay than his spouse. In all three cases it was the woman who gave up her employment with the company.

A recently hired vice president of human resources felt uneasy about the pattern of resignations that was unfolding within the company. He decided when the next three pairs of employees decided to get married, it would be the man who would relinquish his employment within the company, not the woman. The vice president cited gender fairness in anti-nepotism as the justification for his decision. Although unrelated to my particular consulting work with the company, he asked me for my opinion of his decision. I asked him if it mattered which gender held a higher position than the other. He acknowledged that could happen in theory, but in reality there were more men than women in upper-level jobs. He was resolute that the next three employees to leave the company due to marriage would be male. He felt the anti-nepotism policy was designed to be "gender blind" but the company's actions indicated otherwise.

Placement is a topic rarely discussed in I–O psychology, and most of what we know is derived primarily from the military. Learning how nepots are assigned to particular jobs within the family business would greatly enhance our knowledge of placement. Furthermore, it seems plausible that some family businesses do not have a position opening that a nepot fills as much as they create one for the nepot. Because the family already has extensive awareness of the nepot's strengths and weaknesses prior to employment, it would be possible for the business to fashion job duties around the attributes of the nepot. As such, family businesses exercise their own version of job design. Complete and hierarchical nepotistic organizations (in particular) would have the capacity to unbundle existing work duties within the family business and reconstitute them in the form of a newly created position for the nepot. Work functions within a nepotistic organization could be conceived as a set of duties that can be synthetically combined and reconstituted in the form of different positions within the business. The primary purpose would be the skill enhancement of the new nepot. Existing nepots within the business may relinquish performing duties as part of their own jobs, secure in the knowledge their continued employment with the business is not in jeopardy. Such a system would serve (in theory) to mitigate the notion of "turf" and the sense of territoriality that is inherent in assigned job titles and commensurate duties. The family business could be structured as an incubator of professional development for the nepots, orchestrated for the primal purpose of enhancing the likelihood the family (business) will survive and prosper. Of particular note might be the capacity and felt need of the nepotistic organization to do so.

Perhaps family businesses have the potential to enhance our understanding of organizational change. The synthetic creation of positional duties built around the need to enhance the professional development of its members (and thus enhance the longevity of the business) is an adaptive organizational response that is deserving of our attention. Such an adaptive response is not convention in non-nepotistic organizations.

Succession

I–O psychology has addressed the topic of succession (usually referenced as "executive succession"), promotion, or advancement, but it has not been examined with the depth or breadth of employee selection. Paradoxically, family research devotes scant research to selection, whereas the topic of succession commands great interest (see Field Note 6). Indeed the topic of succession has been the theme of Shakespearean plays and historically was at the heart of intrigue within both royalty and the papacy. Much of the conflict within family business centers on issues pertaining to differing leadership styles across successive leaders (especially across generations). Research on family business has revealed patterns and styles of leadership as a function of the life cycle of the business. Lansberg differentiated leadership styles of individual family business leaders from the emergence of differing leadership forms used to govern the business. Most family businesses begin with one person who had a vision of a market need that his or her business could meet. The style of the business founder is often heavily autocratic, which Lansberg referred to as the "controlling owner" leadership form. The decision as to who succeeds the founder among multiple sibling candidates has been the basis for conflict, sometimes devastating, within the family business. If there is little or no power struggle regarding the succession, the autocratic style of leadership may suffice for the second generation of the family business. Lansberg referred to perpetuating the leadership style of the founder through the next generation as a "recycle." However, if the conflict among the potential successors is severe, Lansberg proposed a different leadership form for the business, a "sibling partnership." Depending upon the breadth of nepot membership in the organization that becomes the third generation of the business, Lansberg proposed a third leadership form can be used to run the company, a "cousin consortium."

FIELD NOTE 6: "THE NEXT PRESIDENT MUST HAVE AN MBA"

The president and founder of a small meat processing company was in his mid-1970s. His problem was a classic one—succession planning. He had two sons plus a son-in-law who served as his management team. The president did not have a college degree. He was the epitome of the shrewd, streetwise businessman who graduated from the school of hard knocks. His sons had graduated from college, as did his son-in-law. He did not place much value on formal education as a requirement for his successor. He stated the next president must have an MBA—a "mop bucket attitude." His successor should learn the business the same way he learned it, by mopping the floor in the abattoir at the end of the day and have a demeanor reflective of such humble actions.

He questioned whether either of his sons was sufficiently committed to head the company. He held his son-in-law in higher regard but conceded if he passed over his two sons it would cause irreparable damage to his family. The possibility of a triumvirate running the company was deemed by him as unworkable. Selecting an outsider to be his successor was regarded as being offensive to everyone. His succession problem seemed intractable. He avoided the decision by delaying his own retirement, a course of action that was becoming increasingly unacceptable due to his own declining health.

The need for these differing leadership forms for family businesses is due to the high potential for destructive conflict among the nepots. Conflict may be inevitable in organizational successions, but its potency is particularly acute in the family business. The issue of "rightful succession" in a family business is further compounded by belief in the ancient principle of *primogeniture*, that family power and authority flows from the father to the firstborn son. As a succession guiding principle, contemporary family businesses may find the concept of primogeniture to be anachronistic. However, its merit emerges indirectly in that the firstborn son probably has more years of experience in the business and most likely was directly mentored by the founder. Both of these factors can provide a basis of legitimacy for ascension into the top leadership position of the company.

The issue of succession within nepotistic organizations, unlike traditional leadership issues examined in non-nepotistic organizations, has a very strong interactionistic property to it. The interaction is between the individual and the state of the organization in its life cycle. Traditional leadership research in I–O psychology tends to view the leadership needs of an organization in terms of its stated goals or desired directions at a given point in time. Perhaps it is because non-nepotistic organizations are less fragile than nepotistic organizations. The relative lack of potentially destructive conflict allows the non-nepotistic organization to focus on the qualities of the individual candidates, on the presumption there is no need to consider alternative leadership forms (the analogues of the sibling partnership and cousin consortium) found in nepotistic organizations. However, it is possible that rapidly changing business conditions confronted by contemporary organizations may compel them to consider alternate forms of leadership, especially given the emergence of mergers and acquisitions involving global organizations. Counterintuitive as it may seem, global organizations may find value in the various leadership forms that evolve from the need to govern successive generations of small family businesses.

Conflict

De Dreu and Gelfand (2008) edited a book on conflict as part of the Society for Industrial and Organizational Psychology (SIOP) Frontiers series. A total of 17 chapters were presented on organizational conflict in various contexts (e.g., union management, work teams, and so forth). No chapter was devoted to conflict in work families. Conflict is often at the core of family business, it is of deep concern of leaders of family business, and the capacity of a family business to manage its internal conflict often dictates its ultimate fate. To illustrate the potency of conflict within family business organizations (see Field Note 7), the following are titles of books and journal articles written on the topic over the past 30 years:

- "Conflicts That Plague Family Businesses" (Levinson, 1971)
- "How to Keep Kids From Suing Each Other" (Cantor, 1982)
- "Family Firms Can Leave the Feuds Behind" (Topolnicki, 1983)
- *Steinberg: The Breakup of a Family Empire* (Gibbon & Hadekel, 1990)
- "Dynasty Undone: U-Haul's Patriarch Now Battles Offspring in Bitterest of Feuds" (Tomsho, 1990)
- "Penetrating the Cycle of Sustained Conflict" (Kaye, 1991)
- *Blood & Wine: The Unauthorized Story of the Gallo Wine Empire* (Hawkes, 1993)
- *The House of Gucci: A Sensational Story of Murder, Madness, Glamour, and Greed* (Forden, 2000)
- *The Bronfmans: The Rise and Fall of the House of Seagrams* (Faith, 2006)

FIELD NOTE 7: BIRTHRIGHT

A man founded a small company in the 1920s that provided coal for home heating. The company held its place in the market and the founder ultimately passed his business down to his son. By the late 1940s, coal had been replaced by oil, gas, and electricity as the primary means of heating homes. The son transformed the business to being a provider of home heating oil, and also became a wholesale provider of branded gasoline for local gas stations. By the late 1960s, the son of the founder wanted to have his two sons enter the family business. The younger son took an active interest in the company, but the older son showed only a passive interest in doing so. The father provided both sons with opportunities to learn the business under his tutelage. The younger son quickly emerged as the heir apparent based upon his business sense and interest in commerce. The older son found his father's business to be intellectually unappealing. Furthermore, he performed awkwardly in a business role, especially in his dealings with other employees. After 18 months on the job, by mutual agreement the older son left the company to pursue a PhD in history.

The father kept most of his financial assets within the company. He lived modestly but comfortably and made few visible displays of the wealth he had accumulated in his company. Within 2 years of his older son leaving the company, the father died suddenly. He left his personal estate to his wife. However, the bulk of the father's financial assets were with the company, which now was controlled by the younger son. Soon after the death of his father, the older son demanded his brother pay him a multimillion dollar sum out of the company. It was the older brother's position that the company assets should flow equally to the two sons following the death of their father, and it was immaterial whether one worked for the company and one did not. The younger son (and now president of the company) refused to honor his brother's demand for money. In turn, the older brother filed multiple civil lawsuits against his brother alleging (among other things) undue influence by the younger brother to have the father oust the older brother, and thereby cut him out of the family business money. The older brother stated he was entitled to that money as a "birthright." News of the lawsuits eventually made its way back to the company. Some employees feared for their jobs and wondered whether they would be asked to testify in a trial for one side or the other. The lawsuits and various appeals dragged on for years and both sides incurred large legal fees. Ultimately, the younger brother prevailed. The relationship between the two brothers was irreparably harmed. They never saw or spoke to each other again after the trial, and the bitterness between the two continued until the death of the older brother (by suicide).

Gordon and Nicholson (2008), in their book *Family Wars*, described the polarizing forces that simultaneously pull nepots together and can also pit them against each other. Both forces are grounded in the most primal emotions, and the behavioral manifestations of these emotions are the sum and substance of the paradox of family business relationships. On the positive side, family members have intimate knowledge of one another, and their relationships can be characterized by emotional strength not found in any other social institution. However, family life also provides inevitable occasions for jealousy and anger to develop. If the family has no mechanisms to dissipate the emotional pain from temporal conflict, the negativity festers and grows disproportionately to the initial reasons for its occurrence. When carried outside of the immediate family unit, relationships among nepots have a new forum in which to express themselves.

Gordon and Nicholson (2008) posited threats to personal identity as the basis for the intensity of conflict within family business. Families provide the initial foundation of self-esteem and personal attachment in our lives. Therefore, perceived attacks on our self-esteem from the original source that first provided it are among the most painful. Hodson (1995) proposed the concept of personal dignity that is violated through conflict. Research suggests conflict in family business is more intense than typically found in nonfamily business. The conflict can be so virulent that perhaps existing research on organizations will not help us to further understand it. Rather it is the research on families, and the psychodynamics of the internal relations among constituent members, that may offer the greater likelihood of its comprehension. Thus, I–O psychologists interested in studying nepotistic conflict may find the research literature on families to be more insightful than research written from a traditional organizational perspective.

Family businesses are not only characterized by conflict but also the open expression of it. Non-nepotistic organizations are perhaps no less conflicted, but because of lower thresholds for job loss, disputants must find ways to resolve the conflict or develop more subtle mechanisms for its dissipation. With less fear of job loss, nepots are less constrained in seeking oblique forms of this expression. Researchers interested in the confluence of emotions in the workplace and organizational conflict may find the family business as a rich source of data.

Organizational Justice

Anti-nepotism laws and policies were enacted to prevent some candidates being advantaged in the selection process, by birth or marriage, relative to other candidates. This section examines underlying psychological issues associated with nepots in their relationship to the organization, especially in relationships to non-nepots.

One of the precepts of organizational justice is that employees will be treated fairly, with the equality rule being operative. It is acceptable to treat employees unequally if the differential treatment is based on merit. That is, high performers are more likely rewarded with promotions and larger pay raises than low performers, and low performers are more likely to be sanctioned than high performers. Although there is ample room for bias in judgments of performance and their concomitant effects on personnel decisions within the organization, the merit-based system itself is deemed a reasonable and defensible way to govern an organization.

However, in a nepotistic organization, there can be the perception that distribution rules differ between nepots and non-nepots. Neither of the two distribution rules (merit and equality) within organizations can provide a legitimate explanation of the differential allocations. Nepots do not necessarily exhibit better performance in their work roles compared with non-nepots. Assertions of equality between nepots and non-nepots would have to be carefully considered on the basis of the specific outcomes or behaviors in question. Nepots and non-nepots may be equal in terms of adherence to a dress code, for example. However, with regard to such distributed outcomes as rates of advancement and office location, for example, there might be no illusions regarding equality.

The assumption that nepots are the consistent recipients of more favorable treatment than non-nepots may be unfounded. Nepots may be held to higher standards than non-nepots (e.g., longer work weeks) and be the recipients of harsher rebukes for perceived shortcomings. Nepots may be subjected to higher expectations because they are contributing not only to the welfare of the organization but also of the family. What is regarded as discretionary behavior for non-nepots may be required for nepots. Rules that guide behavior of non-nepots may be deemed inapplicable (or of lesser applicability) to nepots. The status associated with being a family member in a nepotistic organization may be a double-edged sword. Greater benefits may indeed be bestowed on nepots, but nepots could be held to different standards and have different expectations imposed on them compared to non-nepots. Nepotistic organizations may operate under two sets of rules (and thus two standards of fairness): one for nepots and one for non-nepots. In all likelihood, the two sets of rules may overlap with regard to selected outcomes or processes. Where they diverge is part of the construct meaning of a nepotistic organization. While the general perception may be that nepots are recipients of better visible outcomes than non-nepots, there may be latent costs associated with being members of a privileged subset. Nepots have traditionally been described as being "entitled" to receive preferential treatment and status within the organization. Their entitlement may include sanctions that are not as openly recognized as the more manifest rewards.

EXTENDED CONSIDERATIONS OF NEPOTISTIC ORGANIZATIONS

Quasi-Nepotistic Organizations

Nepotistic organizations make selection decisions based on family membership. Anti-nepotism regulations and laws were enacted to prevent favoritism on the basis of family relationships. However, it is possible for organizations to exhibit favoritism in selection decisions based on other considerations besides family relations. As such, these decisions would not be classified as nepotism, but would still reflect preferences based on group membership. Organizations that engage in this type of practice might be classified as *quasi-nepotistic* (*quasi*, meaning "resembling or seeming").

This type of preference is reflected in the actions of cliques and clans, resulting in cronyism. Examples might include a preference for individuals who attended certain schools or served in particular branches of the military. Decisions based on these groups are not covered by anti-discrimination employment laws, but their effect is clearly discriminatory, just not "unfairly" so in a legal sense. The awarding of contracts and grants could be made on the basis of idiosyncratic preferences that, while not illegal, result in unequal chances of selection. More important, the basis for these preferences may be unrelated to merit or performance. Organizations that engage in these practices may create the illusion of open competition and equal opportunity, but in the parlance of cronyism, the organization runs a "closed shop" and the decisions are "wired." Nepotistic organizations exhibit preferences based of family relationships. Quasi-nepotistic organizations exhibit preferences in making decisions that do not violate the letter of any law, but the spirit of the principle that every candidate being judged solely on merit is violated. These decision variables might co-vary with protected group membership but not necessarily so. For example, it is illegal to deny applications for insurance on the basis of race, but a surrogate for race, geographic location, can achieve a comparable outcome. This practice is called *redlining* (Squires & Espenshade, 1997). Other variables might be used to make selection decisions that produce less conspicuous outcomes and are thus more likely to elude scrutiny. Nepotism and cronyism are both manifestations of favoritism. Laws and organizational policies have been enacted to prevent the former, while the latter's *sub-rosa* status permits it to more efficiently operate within the penumbra of an organization's span of influence.

DISCIPLINARY TYPE II ERROR

The study of nepotism compels I–O psychology to examine, in large part, work families. The vast majority of research on work families is case based. These case narratives about families—sometimes named families (as reported in the section on conflict)—produce most of what we know about nepotism. The research method of choice is qualitative in nature. Although it is possible to use quantification with qualitative research (Flick, 2009), for the most part each method has its respective advocates and each has produced its own body of research findings.

I–O psychology seems to have no fondness for qualitative research methods. A casual reading of the premier empirical journals in I–O psychology would support that conclusion. The paucity of research on nepotism was the justification for commissioning the writing of this book. It was previously mentioned that the Frontiers book on conflict did not contain any material on conflict in nepotistic organizations. I do not believe this is attributable to a lack of interest in nepotistic organizations. More likely it is the product of a topic (family business) not registering on our disciplinary radar screen because the topic is traditionally studied with research methods unpopular in I–O psychology.

Nepotistic organizations, and all that they embody, are out there to be studied. By failing to recognize their existence, the discipline of I–O psychology has committed its own type II error—we missed what is there to be found. If I–O psychology continues to avoid or ignore topics that are typically researched in ways we don't value or respect, it is our loss. By the most conservative of standards, nepotistic organizations comprise a meaningful portion of our economy. Furthermore, they are replete with psychological meaning and substance. We know little about them. I hope this volume serves as a catalyst for their study in I–O psychology.

REFERENCES

Ambrose, D. M. (1983). Transfer of family-owned business. *Journal of Small Business, 21,* 49–56.

Astrachan, J. H., & Shanker, M. C. (2003). Family businesses' contribution to the U.S. economy: A closer look. *Family Business Review, 16,* 211–219.

Bellow, A. (2003). *In praise of nepotism: A natural history.* New York: Doubleday.

Cambreleng, R. W. (1969). The case of the nettlesome nepot. *Harvard Business Review, 47*(2), 14.

Cantor, G. M. (1982). How to keep kids from suing each other. *Inc.,* February 1.

Chrisman, J. J., Chua, J., & Sharma, P. (1996). *A review and annotated bibliography of family business studies.* Boston: Kluwer.

De Dreu, C. K., & Gelfand, M. J. (Eds.). (2008). *The psychology of conflict and conflict management in organizations.* New York: Lawrence Erlbaum.

Ewing, D. W. (1965). Is nepotism so bad? *Harvard Business Review, 43*(1), 22.

Faith, N. (2006). *The Bronfmans: The rise and fall of the House of Seagrams.* New York: St. Martin's Press.

Flick, U. (2009). *Introduction to qualitative research* (4th ed.). London: Sage.

Ford, R., & McLaughlin, F. (1986, November). Nepotism: Boon or bane? *Personnel Administrator, 31,* 79–89.

Forden, S. G. (2000). *The House of Gucci: A sensational story of murder, madness, glamour, and greed.* New York: Perennial.

Gibbon, A., & Hadekel, P. (1990). *Steinberg: The breakup of a family empire.* Toronto: Macmillan of Canada.

Gordon, G., & Nicholson, N. (2008). *Family wars.* London: Kogan Pane.

Graen, G., & Schiemann, W. (1978). Leader member agreement: A vertical dyad leader approach. *Journal of Applied Psychology, 63,* 206–212.

Hawkes, E. (1993). *Blood & wine: The unauthorized story of the Gallo wine empire.* New York: Simon & Schuster.

Hodson, R. (1995). Worker resistance: An underdeveloped concept in the sociology of work. *Economic and Industrial Democracy, 16,* 79–110.

Kaye, K. (1991). Penetrating the cycle of sustained conflict. *Family Business Review, 4,* 21–44.

Lansberg, I. (1999). *Successive generations.* Boston: Harvard University Press.

Levinson, H. (1971). Conflicts that plague family businesses. *Harvard Business Review, 49,* 90–98.

Padgett, M. Y., & Morris, K. A. (2005). Keeping it "all in the family": Does nepotism in the hiring process really benefit the beneficiary? *Journal of Leadership & Organizational Studies, 11,* 34–45.

Pinder, C. C. (2008). *Work motivation in organizational behavior* (2nd ed.). New York: Psychology Press.

Pingree, S., Butler, M., Paisley, W., & Hawkins, R. (1978). Anti-nepotism's ghost: Attitudes of administrators toward hiring professional couples. *Psychology of Women Quarterly, 3,* 22–29.

Reed, C. M. (1988). Anti-nepotism rules and dual career couples: Policy questions for public personnel administrators. *Public Personnel Management, 17,* 79–89.

Schneider, B. (1987). The people make the place. *Personnel Psychology, 40,* 437–454.

Scott, J. B. (1991). *Images of nepotism: The painted ceilings of Palazzo Barberini.* Princeton, NJ: Princeton University Press.

Shanker, M. C., & Astrachan, J. H. (1996). Myths and realities: Family businesses' contributions to the U.S. economy—A framework for assessing family business statistics. *Family Business Review, 9,* 107–119.

Squires, G. D., & Espenshade, T. J. (Eds.). (1997). *Insurance redlining: Disinvestment, reinvestment, and the evolving role of financial institutions.* Baltimore: Urban Institute Press.

Tomsho, R. (1990, July 16). Dynasty undone: U-Haul's patriarch now battles offspring in the bitterest of feuds. *The Wall Street Journal*, p. A1.

Topolnicki, D. M. (1983). Family firms can leave the feuds behind. *Money, 12*, 83–89.

Vinton, K. L. (1998). Nepotism: An interdisciplinary model. *Family Business Review, 11*, 297–303.

Werbel, J. D., & Hames, D. S. (1996). Anti-nepotism reconsidered: The case of husband and wife employment. *Group & Organization Management, 21*, 365–379.

4

Nepotism and Career Choice, Job Search, and Job Choice

Edwin A. J. van Hooft
University of Amsterdam

Tracy Stout
Missouri State University

Psychologists have long been interested in questions related to how people choose an occupation or a career, how they search for suitable job opportunities, and how they evaluate and decide between available job alternatives. This is not surprising, since choosing well-fitting careers and jobs positively predicts outcomes related to performance, well-being, and health (for example, Kristof-Brown, Zimmerman, & Johnson, 2005; Tsabari, Tziner, & Meir, 2005). Furthermore, in modern dynamic labor markets, both career decision making and job seeking are no longer limited to graduating students and unemployed people, but form an integral aspect of people's working lives.

Career decision making can be described as the psychological process of organizing relevant career information, deliberating among career alternatives, and making a commitment to a course of action (cf. Harren, 1979). The process of career decision making consists of several stages, with many models distinguishing between stages of exploration and search, and stages of evaluation and choice (for example, Mihal, Sorce, & Comte, 1984; Soelberg, 1967). Career exploration, for example, encompasses activities directed toward enhancing knowledge of oneself and of the external environment in order to foster progress in developing one's career (Blustein, 1992). Job search can be defined as referring to a goal-directed motivational process that includes identifying possible job opportunities, acquiring information about the identified opportunities, and actively pursuing these job opportunities (Barber, Daly, Giannantonio, & Phillips, 1994;

Kanfer, Wanberg, & Kantrowitz, 2001). Active job search and job pursuit behavior may lead to one or more job offers. The subsequent evaluation of these job offers and the decision-making process for accepting an offer is usually referred to as job choice (Chapman, Uggerslev, Carroll, Piasentin, & Jones, 2005).

It is interesting that both the career and the job search and choice literatures highlight the importance of social factors in influencing people's decision-making processes and career and job choices. For example, Fouad (2007) notes that, in vocational psychology "one of the major areas of emphasis in that past decade has been on examining the role of relationships in facilitating or hindering career development" (p. 551). In the job search literature, using social networks is character- ized as an important method to gather information about employment opportunities (for example, Van Hoye, Van Hooft, & Lievens, 2009; Wanberg, Kanfer, & Banas, 2000), and people's social context has been shown to affect their job search intensity, decision making in the pur- suit process, and job attainment (Kanfer et al., 2001; Jaidi, Van Hooft, & Arends, 2011).

The present chapter will discuss the role of social context in career decision making, job search, and choice from the lens of nepotism and cronyism. As described in the first chapter of this book, nepotism gener- ally refers to "a set of psychological and social processes associated with observed phenomena with respect to family membership (broadly defined) in and around organizations" (Jones, this volume, Chapter 1). More spe- cifically, nepotism can be defined as "the bestowal of patronage by reason of relationship regardless of merit" (Simon, Clark, & Tifft, 1966, p. 344). This includes favoritism based on kinship, but may also refer to favoritism based on other relationships than simple consanguinity (Bellow, 2003), such as (long-standing) friendship (also known as cronyism). Nepotism is traditionally viewed from the perspective of the organization, referring to the use of nepotism as a basis for organizational decisions, such as hiring employees (Jones et al., 2008). Bellow (2003) supplements this traditional perspective by suggesting a modern version of nepotism, highlighting the perspective of the job seeker. Based on Bellow (2003), this so-called new nepotism refers to the notion that people may choose the same profession or job as their parents or close friends, or may be willing to take advantage of opportunities provided by family and close friends.

The present chapter focuses on nepotism from the perspective of the career decision maker or job seeker rather than from the perspective of the selecting organization. As such, we define nepotism in career decision making and job search as career and job choices and job search methods that are instigated by, or make use of opportunities provided by relatives or friends. In the following, we first discuss the role of nepotism in career choice, addressing questions related to why people make nepotistic career choices, and how nepotistic choices relate to employment outcomes such as career satisfaction and advancement. Second, we discuss nepotism in the context of job search and job choice. Specifically, we focus on nepotistic job search methods and their effects on employment outcomes such as job attainment and employment quality. Third, we will summarize and provide an agenda for future research on nepotism in career decision making.

NEPOTISM AND CAREER CHOICE

Theory and Research on Career Choice

A widely accepted notion in the career decision making literature is the idea that, in choosing a career, people need to understand themselves, the career alternatives that are out there, and the relationship between the two (Fouad, 2007). One of the most widely used theories addressing the importance of this person–environment (P–E) fit notion in career decision making is Holland's (1997) theory. P–E fit generally refers to the alignment of the characteristics of both people and their environment, which is assumed to lead to positive outcomes. Holland (1997) extended this idea to vocational choice, theorizing that, when people's personality patterns resemble their occupational environment, people experience congruence and find their environments satisfying. This means that individuals will search for vocations in an environment they perceive to have opportunities related to their interests. The positive outcomes associated with a high level of P–E fit are achievement, satisfaction, and vocational stability; whereas negative outcomes such as dissatisfaction and leaving the job are associated with low levels of P–E fit (Kristof-Brown et al., 2005; Sekiguchi, 2004; Tsabari et al., 2005).

Holland's P–E fit theory, although one of the most popular, is also relatively static. Other theories have been developed to try to create a more dynamic P–E fit. An example of this is the theory of work adjustment (TWA). Instead of placing the focus on fit, the TWA focuses on something similar labeled as "correspondence." Correspondence occurs when there is a "reciprocal relationship in which the work personality and work environment are mutually responsive, with the individual fulfilling the requirements of work environment and the work environment fulfilling the requirements of the individual" (Rounds, Dawis, & Lofquist, 1987, p. 298). Where the emphasis is on an individual's characteristics in P–E fit, the main focus of the TWA is on a process. Specifically, the process through which individuals attempt to obtain and maintain correspondence with their environments is referred to as work adjustment. It is theorized that, within their jobs, individuals will attempt to either change themselves or the environment around them in order to have fit. Many job environments are not static and may change, which leads to changes in fit/correspondence, and also leads to changes in work adjustment outcomes. Based on research by Rounds et al. (1987), work adjustment outcomes are directly related to correspondence and, according to TWA, "satisfaction is a function of the correspondence between the reinforcer pattern of the work environment and the individual's needs" (p. 298).

Another theory that focuses on a process between individuals and organizations is Schneider's (1987) attraction–selection–attrition (ASA) model (see Dickson, Nieminen, & Biermeier-Hanson, this volume, Chapter 5). The P–E fit theories suggest that, in order for positive outcomes to occur and for individuals to be effective in their job, individuals must fit the environment. According to Sekiguchi (2004), this indicates that the individual's behavior becomes "a function of the person and the environment" (p. 181). In contrast to this, the ASA model claims that it is the individuals that make the environment. Fit between people and environments is derived through a process of attraction, selection, and attrition (Schneider, 1987). Specifically, attraction refers to the idea that individuals are attracted to organizations that match their personal characteristics (which is similar to Holland's theory). Selection (i.e., the organization's formal and informal selection procedures) entails the recruitment and hiring of those individuals that the organization feels fitting. Attrition refers to the idea that individuals leave the organization when they no longer perceive a fit with the organization. Thus, fit perceptions may not only explain initial career choice and attraction to organizations, but also why people leave organizations and change careers.

In addition to the desire for fit, self-efficacy is a central concept in the career decision-making literature (Fouad, 2007). According to social cognitive career theory (Lent, Brown, & Hackett, 1994), self-efficacy influences the career decision-making process by predicting people's career interests, the career goals they set, and the effort they invest in pursuing these goals. Betz and Hackett (1981), for example, demonstrated that self-efficacy expectations for a specific occupation strongly predicted students' interest in that occupation. Also, Bandura, Barbaranelli, Caprara, and Pastorelli (2001) found that academic self-efficacy plays an important role in the development of children's occupational self-efficacy beliefs, which in turn predict their occupational choices. These results confirm previous research conducted in this area as reviewed by Lent and Hackett (1987), who concluded that self-efficacy expectations can affect a whole range of career-related behaviors (e.g., choice of career options, occupational searching behavior—both initiating searching and depth or effort of searching—and ultimately deciding on a career).

Because self-efficacy beliefs are highly significant to career-related behaviors, it is important to understand how these efficacy expectations are developed. Bandura (1986) hypothesized that efficacy expectations are acquired through four major methods: enactive attainment (or performance accomplishments), vicarious experience (including observational learning through modeling), verbal persuasion, and one's physiological state. Bandura states that these four methods for acquiring efficacy expectations influence an individual's actions by affecting judgments of their own performance. In 1977, Bandura also asserted that contextual variables could influence self-efficacies and that these included family experiences.

Another factor in career decision making that has received a lot of research attention is the role of the family, more specifically the parents. In their review of the literature, Whiston and Keller (2004) concluded that both family structure variables, such as the parent's occupations, and family process variables, such as support and attachment, affect career development. For example, Kniveton (2004) states that "the family can provide information and guidance, either directly, or indirectly, to influence a young person's choice of career" (p. 48). Keller and Whiston's (2008) study pointed to the correlation between parents' behaviors (specifically career-related and supportive) and their adolescent children's self-efficacy. They concluded that "young adolescents value their parents' opinions about career issues and hence, may believe in their own career decision-making abilities only to the degree to which they think their parents believe in them" (p. 210). They also alluded to the notion that the strong influence of family is due to the fact that individuals begin to think about occupations during their middle-school years, which is also the time during which self-efficacy expectations begin to form (Keller & Whiston, 2008).

Research conducted by Small and McClean (2002) described the very significant influence parents can have simply by being an example for their children. Another way they found that parents have strong influences on their children was by offering support for particular occupational choices, which they discovered tended to follow their own occupations. There is an incredibly long history related to this concept of children being influenced into the same occupations as their parents. The idea of the eldest son following in his father's footsteps has been around for centuries. It may be that the family is even more influential than studies can demonstrate, as this influence may be deeply ingrained.

Nepotistic Career Choice

As mentioned in the introduction of this chapter, nepotistic career choices refer to career choices that are instigated by or make use of opportunities provided by relatives or close friends. Based on the theory and research discussed earlier, we can speculate about reasons why people would make a nepotistic career choice. First, extending fit perspectives (i.e., Holland's theory, theory of work adjustment, ASA model) to nepotism in career decision making, people may engage in nepotistic career choices for reasons of fit. For example, children may choose the same occupation as their parents because they perceive high fit between their own personality and values and their parent's occupation. That is, based on Holland's (1997) theory and the ASA model, it can be assumed that parents have occupations that are congruent with their personalities. Further, because personality has a substantial biological basis (for example, Jang, McCrae, Angleitner, Riemann, & Livesley, 1998), children's personalities are likely to resemble their parents' personality. Combining these notions, children can be expected to choose similar occupations as their parents based on perceptions of increased fit for those occupations.

Second, nepotistic career choices can be explained from a social cognitive perspective (cf. Bandura, 1986; Lent et al., 1994). Specifically, occupational choice is theorized and found to be predicted by occupational self-efficacy. Further, self-efficacy beliefs may develop based on observational learning and modeling. Therefore, it can be expected that parental occupational modeling positively affects children's occupational self-efficacy, which in turn may lead to nepotistic career choices. Related to this self-efficacy explanation for nepotistic career choice is the human capital explanation raised by Lentz and Laband (1989). As a by-product of growing up in close proximity to one's parent's job, children may acquire career-specific human capital. Such human capital transfer may result in higher self-efficacy, motivation, and knowledge of the parent's occupations relative to alternative occupations. According to Whiston and Keller (2004), parents do share a considerable amount of career-relevant knowledge with their children. Some offspring may choose the same occupation as their parents due to occupational lending of relevant knowledge and skills from parent to child (Laband & Lentz, 1992). For example, lawyers transfer their knowledge of the law to their children, and this transferred knowledge is a significant factor in the child's decision to follow in the lawyer parent's footsteps. One study found that only 5% of sons from nonlawyer parents had an interest in law, compared to 35% of lawyers' sons (Laband & Lentz, 1992). This finding suggests that the decision to choose the same occupation as one's parent could be based on transfer of occupation-specific knowledge and skills from one generation to the next.

The fit explanation, the self-efficacy explanation, and the human capital transfer explanation for nepotistic career choice all assume that individuals freely choose their career. However, not all people may see the choice of a career as being completely under one's own control (Kniveton, 2004). Some individuals may be influenced toward occupations that they may not necessarily believe to be a good fit or feel efficacious about. For example, a study by Paolillo and Estes (1982) demonstrated that parental influence affected the selection of a profession among accountants, attorneys, engineers, and physicians. Furthermore, for centuries, birth order played a huge role in determining one's occupation. As noted by Spraggs (2001), the oldest son would inherit the estate, the second son would join the church, and the third son would join the military. A study by Wall (1996) confirms that, for the eldest son, this custom still occurs to this day within certain occupations. This is especially true for family-owned companies.

Kets de Vries (1993) claims that 80% of all businesses are family controlled and one-third of the Fortune 500 companies are family controlled in the United States. Thus, in the case of family business, for example, offspring may feel pressured to join the family business.

A fourth explanation for nepotistic career choice relates to perceived opportunities and favoritism. Parents, for example, can use their positions within an organization to obtain opportunities for their children. Offspring who have been provided these opportunities can choose to accept or pass on these opportunities. There are various reasons why children would accept such opportunities. For example, some may choose the opportunity simply because it was presented to them by a parent and it seems to be an easy career path to follow compared to trying to find a job on their own. Alternatively, children may choose the same career as their parent(s) simply for the opportunity of financial gain, as illustrated by a study where men were found to earn 5% to 8% more if they chose the same occupation as their father compared to other individuals in the same occupation (Worklife, 2002). Taking advantage of possible favoritism and provided opportunities may also increase chances for success. Lentz and Laband (1989), for example, found that doctors' children were admitted into medical school nearly 14% more often than those who were comparable to them except for the fact that neither parent was a doctor.

Summarizing the aforementioned literature, we can identify four hypotheses for why people may engage in nepotistic career choices: (a) the fit explanation (people perceive higher fit for such occupations), (b) the self-efficacy and human capital explanation (people feel an increased self-efficacy and are better skilled for such occupations), (c) the pressure explanation (people are or feel pressured or coerced to choose such occupations), and (d) the opportunities explanation (because of favoritism, people have or perceive increased opportunities in such occupations).

These four explanations for nepotistic career choice can be distinguished in the extent to which they reflect autonomous or controlled motivation as described in Deci and Ryan's (2000) self-determination theory (SDT). SDT is a motivational theory distinguishing between several forms of motivation based on the concept of autonomy or self-determination (Deci, Koestner, & Ryan, 1999). Self-determination involves autonomous regulation in which there is a feeling of choice and full volition. When a decision is made autonomously, behavior will have more perceived importance and will be more compatible with the decision maker's values. A non-self-determined or controlled decision involves (perceived) pressure or coercion. A decision based on control instead of self-determination is made due to such factors as feelings of threat, demand, reward, or guilt.

In a study of career choice among lawyers, Stout and Jones (2006) distinguished between self-determined nepotism and coercive nepotism based on SDT. Self-determined nepotism occurs when an individual accepts a job offer by a family member because they strongly believe that the job offered is in their desired and chosen career path. Coercive nepotism is non-self-determined and occurs when an individual accepts a job offer from a family member because they feel they are coerced into the decision. This coercion could be based on pressure from family members to be in the same occupation, thus continuing a sort of family tradition. A third type of proposed nepotism is opportunistic nepotism, in which an individual accepts a job offer from a family member without feelings of family pressure or coercion, or without freely choosing the position. This type of nepotism is based more on accepting what is being offered due to feelings of ease in finding a good job, not really choosing a certain career path.

Stout and Jones (2006) examined the validity of the distinction between these three types of nepotism (self-determined, coercive, and opportunistic) in a sample of 275 lawyers. Lawyers were chosen for this study due to the findings of prevalence of nepotism within this occupation. Stout and Jones developed the Occupational Nepotism Scale (ONS) to assess the three types of nepotistic career choices. Sample items include "because I felt this occupation was suited for me" for self-determined nepotism, "because I felt pressure from my family to obtain this job" for coercive nepotism, and "because my parents or family member(s) could help me get a job if I chose this occupation" for opportunistic nepotism. Their findings illustrated that the three types of nepotistic career choice were empirically distinguishable, and differentially related to general self-determination and to the extent to which they were employed in a nepotistic environment. Specifically, when general self-determination levels were higher, coercive nepotism levels were lower. This finding supports the premise that if individuals are highly self-determined, they are less likely to be forced by family members to choose a career that they do not wish to pursue. Furthermore, both coercive nepotism and opportunistic nepotism were positively related to the actual presence of family members at their workplace. This finding indicates that nepotistic environments increase the likelihood for career choices based on pressure or opportunities, supporting the pressure explanation and the opportunities explanation for nepotistic career choice. Last, general self-determination was positively related to self-determined nepotism, meaning that participants who were highly self-determined tended to choose their occupation independently of family pressures. This occurred regardless of whether people were employed in a nepotistic environment. This finding relates to the original idea of new nepotism in which family members take a personal interest in a previous generation's occupation, possibly experience a transfer of occupation-specific knowledge, and then base their career decision on this knowledge, rather than on the basis of coercion.

In addition to general levels of self-determination, nepotistic career choice is also likely dependent on people's career decision-making styles. Career decision-making style is a cognitive construct referring to a habitual pattern that individuals use in making career choices (Harren, 1979). An important typology of decision-making styles is that of Harren (1979), which distinguishes between rational, intuitive, and dependent decision making. A rational style is characterized by making decisions deliberately and logically ("I am very systematic when I go about making an important decision"). An intuitive style is characterized by making decisions based on feelings and emotional satisfaction ("When I make a decision I just trust my inner feelings and reactions"). A dependent style is characterized by making decisions based on the expectations and opinions of others ("When I make a decision it is important to me what my friends think about it"). According to Harren's model, a rational style is most likely to result in effective decision making and self-actualization. A dependent style, in contrast, likely leads to perceiving limited options resulting in a lack of fulfillment and personal satisfaction. Research generally supported these assumptions, for example, showing that a rational style positively and a dependent style negatively relates to gathering occupational information, planning, and problem solving (Mau, 2000). Extending this model to nepotistic career choice, it is likely that people with a dependent style are more inclined to engage in nepotistic choice, because nepotistic choices are instigated by or make use of relatives or close friends. This would especially hold true for coercive and opportunistic nepotism and less so for the more self-determined nepotistic career choices.

Similarly, consistent with a dependent style, a nepotistic choice is likely to be based on restricted information or options. For example, in the cases of coercive nepotism and opportunistic nepotism, the individual likely chooses a specific occupation not because of rational arguments based on a consideration of a wide array of alternatives, but rather because of pressure or seemingly attractive chances for this one specific alternative. A nepotistic career choice is therefore likely related to low levels of career exploration. Career exploration entails an active process of gathering information about oneself and the environment (Stumpf, Colarelli, & Hartman, 1983). Whereas self-exploration refers to the examination of one's goals, values, skills, needs, and interests, environmental exploration refers to gathering information about the occupational environment, such as different jobs, work demands, and organizational cultures. As noted by Werbel (2000), both self-exploration and environmental exploration are important in order to make accurate assessments of P–E fit with different employment opportunities (Werbel, 2000). Thus, nepotistic career choices based on pressure or expected favoritism (opportunistic) are likely to be characterized by low levels of career exploration. For nepotistic career choices based on the fit explanation (e.g., self-determined nepotism) this is less likely to be the case.

Consequences of Nepotistic Career Choices

This section discusses the sources of opinions relating to nepotism and also of the consequences, whether positive or negative, associated with nepotism. The feelings and attitudes toward nepotism seem to be varied, but many people still view nepotism negatively and classify it as undesirable. Because of the negativity that sometimes surrounds nepotism, some organizations have even established anti-nepotism policies. Slack (2001) suggests that negative attitudes towards nepotism occur because many believe it goes against the American values of self-reliance and egalitarianism. Nepotism can be viewed as unfair by some since "those who benefit from nepotism are seen as advancing their careers by relying on family connections rather than individual merit" (Padgett & Morris, 2005, p. 34).

From an organizational perspective, nepotism can have several negative consequences. First, nepotism may result in reduced fairness perceptions. Pelletier and Bligh (2008), for example, discussed the results of a 1990 International Public Management Association survey in which questions were posed about dual-career couples in the workplace. They discovered that 40% thought spouses in the same organization produced ethical dilemmas. Further, results showed that employees believed nepotism was less fair than hiring based on merit and did not positively view those who had been hired based on family ties instead of based on ability. Also, Padgett and Morris (2005) asked students to review scenarios about merit-based versus nepotistic hiring, and showed that nepotism was perceived to be unfair and unethical. A few other investigations into nepotism focus more on favoritism, where a person in a higher position has the authority to offer an occupational opportunity to an individual based solely on their relationship (e.g., a relative) rather than on the individual's work qualifications. For example, Mutlu (2000) discussed the problems within a police organization in which the police force was comprised of individuals who had been appointed based on favoritism and nepotism. In this specific situation, the environment created by favoritism was so negatively viewed that it was thought to disturb the basic morality of the police force and would carry immorality to the societal level. This study portrayed an extensive case of nepotism and how it was viewed. Second, a study by Arasli and Tumer (2008) showed that perceived nepotism and cronyism may lead to increased job stress among organizational employees, for example, as a consequence of conflicts when dealing with underqualified employees that are hired because of nepotism. Third, nepotism is associated with lowered organizational satisfaction and commitment (see Becker, this volume, Chapter 6). Padgett and Morris (2005), for example, reported that people had lower organizational commitment when their supervisor was hired based on nepotism. Arasli and Tumer (2008) found that nepotism and cronyism were related to lower job satisfaction and increased turnover intentions among organizational employees. In addition to increased stress and lower employee attitudes and morale, Hernandez and Page (2006) and Khatri and Tsang (2003) suggest that nepotism is associated with a variety of other organizational dysfunctions, including the hiring and promotion of underqualified candidates, lower organizational performance, conflicts of interest, gossip and rumors about the unfair practices, legal complications (e.g., discrimination), reduced organizational diversity (which may lead to reduced flow of new ideas and perspectives), and lower organizational ability to learn and adapt to changes.

From the perspective of the individual who "benefits" from nepotism, a number of negative consequences may be present, although much less research has addressed this issue. First, insofar as nepotistic career choice is characterized by lower levels of self-exploration and environmental exploration and by a less rational and more dependent decision-making style, it likely results in less information about possible career alternatives and probably leads to lower quality jobs. This may especially be true for the less self-determined types of nepotistic career choice. In support of this argument, Stout and Jones (2006) found that nepotistic career choices based on coercion related to lower job satisfaction. Second, individuals hired through nepotistic practices may face the negative reactions of fellow workers, leading to reduced well-being. For example, Padgett and Morris (2005) found that people judged their supervisor as less capable when he or she was hired based on nepotistic practices.

Even though it may appear so, not all views of nepotism are negative. For example, Bellow (2003) advocates for certain types of nepotism, as indicated by the title of his book: *In Praise of Nepotism*. Hernandez and Page (2006) can also see a positive side to nepotism and claim that favoritism does not have to be dysfunctional, depending on how an organization chooses to use it. Their view is that an organization can potentially hire someone with family ties and end up with a person who already has a certain degree of skills and aptitudes, consistent with the fit and human capital explanations. Hernandez and Page (2006) argue that hiring a family member "can be a source of distinctive competence—the transmission of property, knowledge, and authority from one generation to the next" (p. 8). When qualified employees are selected through nepotism, they offer the following advantages: (a) consistent with the human capital explanation noted earlier, people's training may be more extensive as they grew up around a business or vocation and its value system; (b) people may have stronger networks in the specific field; (c) the selection process is less costly; and (d) because family ties are lasting, loyalty and commitment will be high.

The key word in the previous passage is *qualified*. Hiring a qualified family member or friend may greatly change the organizational and employee outcomes when compared to hiring an individual simply based on nepotism. Bellow (2003) claims that, when hiring relatives, there is a "chain of generosity and gratitude," meaning that most family members will be appreciative of their position and be a good employee in return. The study by Hernandez and Page (2006) demonstrated that individuals recruited by family members have higher levels of commitment than individuals recruited by other means (e.g., newspaper advertisement). They hypothesized that this higher level of organizational commitment and possibly job performance may be due to the individuals trying harder to uphold the reputation of the family member who referred them.

NEPOTISM AND JOB SEARCH, PURSUIT, AND CHOICE

Theory and Research on Job Search and Choice

In their influential review of job seeking theory and research, Schwab, Rynes, and Aldag (1987) stated that finding employment and the quality of employment depend on the sources that job seekers use to acquire information about job opportunities and the intensity of their job search. Based on this notion, job search is usually conceptualized as the number of sources that people use to acquire information about possible job opportunities (i.e., *job search sources*), and the general amount of time and effort that people spend on looking for and pursuing job opportunities (i.e., *job search intensity*) (Barber et al., 1994; Kanfer et al., 2001). Regarding job search sources, the gathering of information about potential job leads can be done by using formal channels or by using informal channels (Barber et al., 1994; Blau, 1994). Whereas formal channels refer to intermediaries such as recruitment advertisements, search firms, and employment agencies, informal channels relate to networking with personal contacts such as relatives and family, friends, acquaintances, current or former colleagues, or other business or professional contacts.

In addition to job search sources and job search intensity, it has been theorized that people may adopt different *job search strategies*, varying from systematic and focused to random or haphazard (Stevens & Beach, 1996; Stumpf et al., 1983). Based on this theorizing, Crossley and Highhouse (2005) conceptually and empirically distinguished between three job search strategies: a focused strategy (i.e., concentrating search efforts on a small number of carefully screened potential employers), an exploratory strategy (i.e., examining several potential employment options and actively gathering information), and a haphazard strategy (i.e., passively gathering information both inside and outside one's area of expertise using a trial and error approach). An alternative classification of job search strategies builds upon Simon's (1956) distinction between two choice-making strategies: maximizing and satisficing. Whereas a maximizing job search strategy entails seeking the best possible job, which requires an exhaustive search of all possibilities, a satisficing job search strategy refers to engaging in job seeking until a job option is encountered that is good enough (cf. Iyengar, Wells, & Schwarz, 2006).

Nepotistic Job Search

Combining the literature about job search sources, intensity, and strategies with the definition of nepotism in career decision making as stated at the beginning of this chapter, we can develop a description of what a nepotistic job search may look like. That is, a nepotistic job search can be defined as a job search relying exclusively on selective informal channels such as networking with relatives and friends. As such, a nepotistic job search may be characterized as using a relatively narrow range of available job search sources, resulting in a relatively less effortful job search. A nepotistic job search is further likely to be a focused strategy, as it is restricted to finding a job through one's network of relatives and friends, rather than casting a wider network of acquaintances and professional contacts or using a broader array of more formal job search sources. Last, a nepotistic job search likely is more a satisficing than a maximizing strategy, because it relies on a selective and narrow rather than an exhaustive search of all possible job opportunities.

Antecedents and Consequences of a Nepotistic Job Search

Based on this description, we can speculate about possible antecedents and consequences of a nepotistic job search. Regarding *consequences*, the recruitment and job search literatures provide some ideas for possible outcomes of a nepotistic job search. Several studies examined the effects of using informal sources, such as word of mouth (i.e., "interpersonal communication, independent of the organization's [formal] recruitment activities, about an organization as an employer or about specific jobs"; Van Hoye & Lievens, 2005, p. 180), as a job search method. Word of mouth is perceived to be a more credible source than recruitment advertising (Van Hoye & Lievens, 2005), and affects people's organizational attractiveness perceptions, job pursuit, and actual job choices (Collins & Stevens, 2002; Jaidi et al., 2011). Furthermore, job seeking research found that the intensity with which people use networking in their job search positively predicts the number of job offers that people receive (Van Hoye et al., 2009), and increases people's chances to find employment (Wanberg et al., 2000). Last, a consistent finding in the recruitment source literature is that employees hired via informal sources (e.g., employee referrals) stay longer, perform better, and are more satisfied than employees hired via formal sources, possibly because informal hires get a more realistic job preview (Barber, 1998; Zottoli & Wanous, 2000).

Thus, in general, both the recruitment and job seeking literatures would suggest that a nepotistic job search has positive effects for the job seekers on outcomes such as the job opportunity pool they can choose from, their chances to find a job, and the quality of that job. However, a few comments should be made concerning this conclusion. First, all the studies cited earlier use concepts that are somewhat broader than what we define as a nepotistic job search. That is, informal recruitment sources, employee referrals, word of mouth, and networking all refer to personal contacts in general. This includes not only relatives and close friends, but also acquaintances, colleagues, business contacts, and other professional contacts. As such it is not clear whether the positive effects would also hold true for a nepotistic job search, which is limited to using relatives and close friends.

In fact, social network theory would suggest the contrary, based on the concept of tie strength (i.e., the closeness of the social relationship between the individual and other people in the network) (Granovetter, 1973). Relatives and close friends are strong ties, whereas acquaintances and former colleagues are examples of weak ties. In his strength-of-weak-ties hypothesis, Granovetter (1973) stated that people to whom we are weakly tied are more likely to move in circles different from ours and thus have access to information different from that which we already receive. The strength-of-weak-ties hypothesis would suggest that a nepotistic job search (i.e., networking with strong ties) indeed is harmful because it leads to more redundant and less unique information about job opportunities (Brown & Konrad, 2001; Granovetter, 1973; Van Hoye et al., 2009). In support of this idea, Van Hoye and colleagues (2009) found that networking intensity was more negatively related to person–organization fit in the newfound job for job seekers with more strong ties in their network. Thus, based on this reasoning, we propose that a nepotistic job search (i.e., networking with strong ties) will result in lower quality jobs as opposed to a non-nepotistic job search (i.e., networking with weak ties).

Second, the studies on the positive effects of formal recruitment sources, employee referrals, word of mouth, and networking did not take the network quality into consideration. Network quality refers to the characteristics of the other people in an individual's social network, and reflects the quality of the information that they can provide (Adler & Kwon, 2002). For example, unemployed individuals or individuals low in the organizational hierarchy are less likely to have useful information on job opportunities and are less likely to have influence on hiring decisions than employed people or individuals high in the organizational hierarchy. Operationalizing network quality in terms of the educational, occupational, and general status of people's ties, Van Hoye et al. (2009) found that network quality moderates the effect of networking intensity on employment status, such that networking increases the probability to find a job only when network quality is high. Similarly, research on gender differences in job seeking has demonstrated that women using informal sources are more likely to end up in low paid and female-dominated jobs than women using formal sources (Drentea, 1998; Huffman & Torres, 2001). Based on her findings, Drentea (1998) concluded that "networks may not help women as much as men because women may have inferior access to influential people" (p. 323), possibly because women's networks are less diverse and more family and friend based than men's networks. Extending these findings suggests that a nepotistic job search is only beneficial when one's relatives and friends are of high status in terms of having a job, having access to information about job opportunities, or having influence on hiring decisions. If not, then a nepotistic job search likely results in lower quality jobs.

A special situation may be the case of minority groups that are discriminated against at the labor market. For example, Bertrand and Mullainathan (2004) demonstrated that resumes with African-American names received 50% less interview invitations as compared to resumes with White-sounding names. Similarly, Derous, Nguyen, and Ryan (2009) showed that resumes with Arab names and affiliations were rated lower on job suitability than resumes with White names and affiliations. For ethnic minorities who are discriminated against at the labor market, a nepotistic job search may be more beneficial. That is, cases where so-called *ethnic economies* and ethnic labor markets exist, a nepotistic job search may increase chances to find employment in the ethnic labor market because hiring discrimination is not an issue then.

As defined earlier, a nepotistic job search relies exclusively on selective, informal channels, such as networking with relatives and friends. As such, a nepotistic job search is likely characterized by low job search intensity, a focused job search strategy, and a satisficing strategy. Using the job search literature, these characterizations would predict a mixed pattern of outcomes of a nepotistic job search. First, job search intensity is fairly consistently found to relate positively to the number of job interviews, the number of job offers, and the probability to find a job (Kanfer et al., 2001; Saks, 2005). Thus, to the extent that a nepotistic job search would mean low job search intensity, this would likely limit the number of job choices and employment probabilities. Second, Crossley and Highhouse's (2005) findings on the effects of different job search strategies indicate that a focused strategy does not predict the number of job offers (whereas an exploratory strategy does) but is positively related to people's job satisfaction in the newfound job. Iyengar et al.'s (2006) findings on the effects of maximizing versus satisficing in job search indicate that a maximizing strategy leads to higher paying jobs but to more negative affect and less satisfaction with the newfound job as compared to a satisficing strategy. Thus, to the extent that a nepotistic job search entails a focused and satisficing strategy, this likely results not so much in more job offers or a greater chance to find a job, but in more satisfaction with the newfound job.

In describing job seeking in China, Song and Werbel (2007) introduced the term *guanxi search*, which refers to using personal networks of strong ties to find employment, and as such highly resembles our definition of nepotistic job search. In their theorizing about guanxi search, Song and Werbel (2007) raise another drawback of nepotistic job search. That is, using personal networks to find jobs may restrict one's freedom to search for and accept jobs outside these networks. Because of the mutual relationship with a personal contact, people tend to be obligated to accept a job that is offered through a nepotistic or guanxi search in order not to endanger the relationship (Song & Werbel, 2007). Not accepting such an offer may be insulting and lead to losing face, shame, or feelings of guilt. Although this may be especially salient in more collectivistic cultures, guanxi and nepotistic job searches thus likely lead to prioritization of maintaining a good relationship over pursuing individual work goals. Thus, as theorized by Song and Werbel (2007), a nepotistic job search or guanxi search may result in "compromises in career decision making which reflect interdependent rather than independent career choice" (p. 54).

Regarding the *antecedents*, it would be of interest to study possible individual differences and situational circumstances that may cause people to engage in a nepotistic job search. Regarding individual differences, based on Stout and Jones (2006), we can expect that people with low levels of self-determination are more likely to engage in a nepotistic job search, especially the coerced and opportunistic types. Further, extending Simon's (1956) choice-making strategies to the dispositional level, individuals with satisficing personalities will likely be more inclined to engage in a nepotistic job search than individuals with maximizing personalities, who are more likely to cast a wide net, use multiple sources, and examine a broad range of opportunities. Similarly, to the extent that a nepotistic job search is less effortful, those individuals with lower achievement motivation, ambition, and conscientiousness are more likely to engage in a nepotistic job search as it may offer an "easy" alternative. In addition, people who are higher on conformity or motivation to comply are likely to be more sensitive to social pressure in their job search (cf. Van Hooft & De Jong, 2009), and therefore more likely to engage in a nepotistic job search, especially the coerced type.

In addition to personal factors, we can also identify several situational factors that may instigate a nepotistic job search. First, there should be some opportunity for nepotism. For example, a nepotistic job search is more likely when a family business is present or when one has relatives or friends at positions in organizations with the possibility to affect hiring decisions. Consistent with this notion, Stout and Jones (2006) found a positive relationship between the presence of family members at one's job and people's ratings of coercive and opportunistic nepotistic career choices. Second, a nepotistic job search is probably more likely when there is a lack of other ways to find a job. For example, when one is living in a rural area or small community, or when unemployment rates are high, there may be a lack of non-nepotistic alternatives. Similarly, when the chances to find employment on the general labor market are reduced because of discrimination, it may be more likely for ethnic groups to engage in a nepotistic job search at the ethnic labor market. Third, there may be cultural differences and differences between nations in the extent to which people engage in a nepotistic job search and in the extent to which it is beneficial. Werbel, Song, and Yan (2008), for example, theorized that domestic labor markets differ in the extent to which external recruitment (i.e., recruitment using formal sources) are being used. They demonstrated that the United States, as compared to China, can be characterized by a higher proportion of large companies, and therefore a greater reliance on formal recruitment. A nepotistic job search is therefore likely to be less common and less effective in labor markets that heavily rely on formal recruitment methods.

CONCLUSION

The present chapter discussed nepotism from the perspective of the career decision maker or job seeker rather than from the perspective of the hiring organization. Nepotistic career choice and nepotistic job search were defined as career choice and job search methods that are instigated by or make use of opportunities provided by relatives or (close or long-standing) friends. In reviewing the literature on career decision making, we proposed that nepotistic career choices may be understood from the perspective of increased perceptions of fit, higher occupational self-efficacy, human capital transfer, (perceived) pressure, and increased (perceived) opportunities. Stout and Jones (2006) went a step further by distinguishing between different types of nepotistic career choices (i.e., self-determined, opportunistic, and coercive), drawing on self-determination theory. Nepotistic career choice and job search methods were proposed to be characterized by low levels of career exploration, both about oneself and the environment, relying on a relatively narrow range of sources, resulting in a relatively low effortful job search that is characterized by a focused and satisficing strategy.

Extending the career decision making and job search literatures, we derived several expectations about possible antecedents and consequences of nepotistic job searches and career choices. Regarding the antecedents, we distinguished between personal and situational factors. Nepotistic job search and career choice may be expected to be more likely among individuals with low levels of self-determination; dependent decision-making styles; satisficing personalities, low levels of achievement motivation, ambition, and conscientiousness; and high levels of conformity and motivation to comply. Aside from personal factors, several situational contingencies may make nepotistic job searches and career choices more likely, including the presence of opportunities (e.g., family business, strong ties at influential positions), a lack of non-nepotistic alternatives (e.g., due to a secluded location, high unemployment, discrimination), and cultural factors (e.g., collectivism–individualism, reliance on external recruitment).

Regarding the consequences, we shortly reviewed the literature outlining organizational consequences of nepotism. This literature generally shows a host of negative consequences of nepotistic hiring on the other employees (e.g., lower fairness and ethical climate perceptions, lower job satisfaction and organizational commitment) and the organization in general (e.g., increased job stress, conflicts, gossip, and reduced performance and adaptation to change). Although a nepotistic job search and career choice may be an easy option, we theorized that it may also have negative consequences for the individual. Because a nepotistic search relies on strong rather than weak ties, a nepotistic job search is likely to result in fewer job opportunities and in lower quality jobs. Furthermore, especially in collectivistic cultures, it may result in obligations to accept unwanted jobs offered by personal contacts. However, the severity of the negative organizational and individual consequences likely depends on two factors: (a) the skills and abilities of the individual in relation to the job, and (b) the level of self-determination in the nepotistic search and choice. That is, when the individual is highly qualified for the job (thus was hired not only based on nepotism but also based on merit), negative organizational consequences are likely to be less pronounced. Further, when the nepotistic search and choice is highly autonomous (rather than coerced), it may not restrict people's options and actually result in higher quality jobs.

It should be noted that the characteristics, antecedents, and consequences of nepotistic job searches and career choices are derived from a very limited research base. As such, these expectations are speculative and future research should test these proposed antecedents and consequences as well as the underlying assumptions. Specifically, future research should examine: (a) what individual and situational factors predict whether people engage in nepotistic career decision making, (b) what factors predict what type of nepotism people engage in (i.e., self-determined, fit, self-efficacy, opportunistic, coercive), and (c) what factors (i.e., individual, situational, and type of nepotism) predict whether a nepotistic job search and career choice have negative or positive consequences. Last, future research should consider different relational levels in nepotism. There is nepotism based on the hiring of blood relatives, the hiring of spouses, and the hiring of friends. These are usually labeled as nepotism, favoritism, or cronyism.

It is of great interest to investigate whether these levels of nepotism have different effects on chances to find employment and the quality of the found jobs.

REFERENCES

Adler, P. S., & Kwon, S.-W. (2002). Social capital: Prospects for a new concept. *Academy of Management Review, 27,* 17–40.

Arasli, H., & Tumer, M. (2008). Nepotism, favoritism and cronyism: A study of their effects on job stress and job satisfaction in the banking industry of North Cyprus. *Social Behavior and Personality, 36,* 1237–1250.

Bandura, A. (1977). *Social learning theory.* Englewood Cliffs, NJ: Prentice-Hall.

Bandura, A. (1986). *Social foundations of thought and actions: A social cognitive theory.* Englewood Cliffs, NJ: Prentice-Hall.

Bandura, A., Barbaranelli, C., Caprara, G. V., & Pastorelli, C. (2001). Self-efficacy beliefs as shapers of children's aspirations and career trajectories. *Child Development, 72,* 187–206.

Barber, A. E. (1998). *Recruiting employees: Individual and organizational perspectives.* Thousand Oaks, CA: Sage.

Barber, A. E., Daly, C. L., Giannantonio, C. M., & Phillips, J. M. (1994). Job search activities: An examination of changes over time. *Personnel Psychology, 47,* 739–766.

Bellow, A. (2003). *In praise of nepotism: A natural history.* New York: Doubleday.

Bertrand, M., & Mullainathan, S. (2004). Are Emily and Greg more employable than Lakisha and Jamal? A field experiment on labor market discrimination. *The American Economic Review, 94,* 991–1013.

Betz, N. E., & Hackett, G. (1981). The relationship of career-related self-efficacy expectations to perceived career options in college women and men. *Journal of Counseling Psychology, 28,* 399–410.

Blau, G. (1994). Testing a two-dimensional measure of job-search behavior. *Organizational Behavior and Human Decision Processes, 59,* 288–312.

Blustein, D. L. (1992). Applying current theory and research in career exploration to practice. *Career Development Quarterly, 41,* 174–185.

Brown, D. W., & Konrad, A. M. (2001). Granovetter was right: The importance of weak ties to a contemporary job search. *Group & Organization Management, 26,* 434–462.

Chapman, D. S., Uggerslev, K. L., Carroll, S. A., Piasentin, K. A., & Jones, D. A. (2005). Applicant attraction to organizations and job choice: A meta-analytic review of the correlates of recruiting outcomes. *Journal of Applied Psychology, 90,* 928–944.

Collins, C. J., & Stevens, C. K. (2002). The relationship between early recruitment-related activities and the application decisions of new labor-market entrants: A brand equity approach to recruitment. *Journal of Applied Psychology, 87,* 1121–1133.

Crossley, C. D., & Highhouse, S. (2005). Relation of job search and choice process with subsequent satisfaction. *Journal of Economic Psychology, 26,* 255–268.

Deci, E. L., Koestner, R., & Ryan, R. M. (1999). A meta-analytic review of experiments examining the effects of extrinsic rewards on intrinsic motivation. *Psychological Bulletin, 125,* 627–668.

Deci, E. L., & Ryan, R. M. (2000). The "what" and "why" of goal pursuits: Human needs and the self-determination of behavior. *Psychological Inquiry, 11*, 227–268.

Derous, E., Nguyen, H.-H., & Ryan, A. M. (2009). Hiring discrimination against Arab minorities: Interactions between prejudice and job characteristics. *Human Performance, 22*, 297–320.

Drentea, P. (1998). Consequences of women's formal and informal job search methods for employment in female-dominated jobs. *Gender & Society, 12*, 321–338.

Fouad, N. A. (2007). Work and vocational psychology: Theory, research, and applications. *Annual Review of Psychology, 58*, 543–564.

Granovetter, M. S. (1973). The strength of weak ties. *American Journal of Sociology, 78*, 1360–1380.

Harren, V. A. (1979). A model of career decision making for college students. *Journal of Vocational Behavior, 14*, 119–133.

Hernandez, E. H., & Page, R. A. (2006). Nepotism in the employment recruitment process: How nepotism builds organizational commitment. *Journal of Business Management and Change, 1*, 3–13.

Holland, J. L. (1997). *Making vocation choices: A theory of vocational personalities and work environments* (3rd ed.). Odessa, FL: Psychological Assessment Resources.

Huffman, M. L., & Torres, L. (2001). Job search methods: Consequences for gender-based earnings inequality. *Journal of Vocational Behavior, 58*, 127–141.

Iyengar, S. S., Wells, R. E., & Schwartz, B. (2006). Doing better but feeling worse: Looking for the "best" job undermines satisfaction. *Psychological Science, 17*, 143–150.

Jaidi, Y., Van Hooft, E. A. J., & Arends, L. R. (2010). *Recruiting the top-talents: A study on the relationship between recruitment information sources, the theory of planned behavior, and actual job pursuit*. Manuscript submitted for publication.

Jaidi, Y., Van Hooft, E. A. J., & Arends, L. R. (2011). Recruiting highly educated graduates: A study on the relationship between recruitment information sources, the theory of planned behavior, and actual job pursuit. *Human Performance, 24*, 135–157.

Jang, K. L., McCrae, R. R., Angleitner, A., Riemann, R., & Livesley, W. J. (1998). Heritability of facet-level traits in a cross-cultural twin sample: Support for a hierarchical model of personality. *Journal of Personality and Social Psychology, 74*, 1556–1565.

Jones, R. G., Stout, T., Harder, B., Levine, E., Levine, J., & Sanchez, J. I. (2008). Personnel psychology and nepotism: Should we support anti-nepotism policies? *The Industrial/Organizational Psychologist, 45*(3), 17–20.

Kanfer, R., Wanberg, C. R., & Kantrowitz, T. M. (2001). Job search and employment: A personality-motivational analysis and meta-analytic review. *Journal of Applied Psychology, 86*, 837–855.

Keller, B. K., & Whiston, S. C. (2008). The role of parental influences on young adolescents' career development. *Journal of Career Assessment, 16*, 198–217.

Kets de Vries, M. F. R. (1993). The dynamics of family controlled firms: The good and the bad news. *Organizational Dynamics, 21*(3), 59–71.

Khatri, N., & Tsang, E. W. K. (2003). Antecedents and consequences of cronyism in organizations. *Journal of Business Ethics, 43*, 289–303.

Kniveton, B. (2004). The influences and motivations on which students base their choice of career. *Research in Education, 72*, 47–57.

Kristof-Brown, A. L., Zimmerman, R. D., & Johnson, E. C. (2005). Consequences of individuals' fit at work: A meta-analysis of person–job, person–organization, person–group, and person–supervisor fit. *Personnel Psychology, 58*, 281–342.

Laband, D. N., & Lentz, B. F. (1992). Self-recruitment in the legal profession. *Journal of Labor Economics, 10*, 182–201.

Lent, R. W., & Hackett, G. (1987). Career self-efficacy: Empirical status and future directions. *Journal of Vocational Behavior, 30*, 347–382.

Lent, R. W., Brown, S. D., & Hackett, G. (1994). Toward a unifying social cognitive theory of career and academic interest, choice, and performance. *Journal of Vocational Behavior, 45*, 79–122.

Lentz, B. F., & Laband, D. N. (1989). Why so many children of doctors become doctors: Nepotism vs. human capital transfers. *Journal of Human Resources, 24*, 396–413.

Mau, W.-C. (2000). Cultural differences in career decision-making styles and self-efficacy. *Journal of Vocational Behavior, 57*, 365–378.

Mihal, W. L., Sorce, P. A., & Comte, T. E. (1984). A process model of individual career decision making. *Academy of Management Review, 9*, 95–103.

Mutlu, K. (2000). Problems of nepotism and favouritism in the police organization in Turkey. *Policing: An International Journal of Police Strategies & Management, 23*, 381–389.

Padgett, M. Y., & Morris, K. A. (2005). Keeping it "all in the family": Does nepotism in the hiring process really benefit the beneficiary? *Journal of Leadership and Organizational Studies, 11*, 34–45.

Paolillo, J. G. P., & Estes, R. W. (1982). An empirical analysis of career choice factors among accountants, attorneys, engineers, and physicians. *The Accounting Review, 57*, 785–793.

Pelletier, K. L., & Bligh, M. C. (2008). The aftermath of organizational corruption: Employee attributions and emotional reactions. *Journal of Business Ethics, 80*, 823–844.

Rounds, J. B., Dawis, R. V., & Lofquist, L. H. (1987). Measurement of person–environment fit and prediction of satisfaction in the theory of work adjustment. *Journal of Vocational Behavior, 31*, 297–318.

Saks, A. M. (2005). Job search success: A review and integration of the predictors, behaviors, and outcomes. In S. D. Brown & R. W. Lent (Eds.), *Career development and counseling: Putting theory and research to work* (pp. 155–179). Hoboken, NJ: Wiley.

Schneider, B. (1987). The people make the place. *Personnel Psychology, 40*, 437–454.

Schwab, D. P., Rynes, S. L., & Aldag, R. J. (1987). Theories and research on job search and choice. In K. M. Rowland & G. R. Ferris (Eds.), *Research in personnel and human resources management* (Vol. 5, pp. 129–166). Greenwich, CT: JAI Press Inc.

Sekiguchi, T. (2004). Toward a dynamic perspective of person-environment fit. *Osaka Keidai Ronshu, 55*, 177–190.

Simon, H. A. (1956). Rational choice and the structure of the environment. *Psychological Review, 63*, 129–138.

Simon, R. J., Clark, S. M., & Tifft, L. L. (1966). Of nepotism, marriage, and the pursuit of an academic career. *Sociology of Education, 39*, 344–358.

Slack, C. (2001, September). Breeding success. *MBA Jungle*, pp. 82–88.

Small, J. & McClean, M. (2002) Factors impacting on the choice of entrepreneurship as a career by Barbadian youth: A preliminary assessment. *Journal of Eastern Caribbean Studies, 27*, 30–54.

Soelberg, P. O. (1967). Unprogrammed decision making. *Industrial Management Review, 8*, 19–29.

Song, L. J., & Werbel, J. D. (2007). Guanxi as impetus? Career exploration in China and the United States. *Career Development International, 12*, 51–67.

Spraggs, G. (2001). *Outlaws and highwaymen: The cult of the robber in England from the Middle Ages to the nineteenth century.* London: Pimlico.

Stevens, C. K., & Beach, L. R. (1996). Job search and job selection. In L. R. Beach (Ed.), *Decision making in the workplace: A unified perspective* (pp. 33–49). Mahwah, NJ: Lawrence Erlbaum Associates.

Stout, T., & Jones, R. G. (2006). *Career choice and nepotism: Opportunism, coercion, and self-determination.* Unpublished manuscript.

Stumpf, S. A., Colarelli, S. M., & Hartman, K. (1983). Development of the career exploration survey (CES). *Journal of Vocational Behavior, 22,* 191–226.

Tsabari, O., Tziner, A., & Meir, E. I. (2005). Update meta-analysis on the relationship between congruence and satisfaction. *Journal of Career Assessment, 13,* 216–232.

Van Hoye, G., & Lievens, F. (2005). Recruitment-related information sources and organizational attractiveness: Can something be done about negative publicity? *International Journal of Selection and Assessment, 13,* 179–187.

Van Hoye, G., Van Hooft, E. A. J., & Lievens, F. (2009). Networking as a job search behaviour: A social network perspective. *Journal of Occupational and Organizational Psychology, 82,* 661–682.

Van Hooft, E. A. J., & De Jong, M. (2009). Predicting job seeking for temporary employment using the theory of planned behaviour: The moderating role of individualism and collectivism. *Journal of Occupational and Organizational Psychology, 82,* 295–316.

Wall, R. (1996). Marriage, residence, and occupational choices of senior and junior siblings in the English past. *The History of the Family, 1,* 259–271.

Wanberg, C. R., Kanfer, R., & Banas, J. T. (2000). Predictors and outcomes of networking intensity among unemployed job seekers. *Journal of Applied Psychology, 85,* 491–503.

Werbel, J. D. (2000). Relationships among career exploration, job search intensity, and job search effectiveness in graduating college students. *Journal of Vocational Behavior, 57,* 379–394.

Werbel, J. D., Song, L. J., & Yan, S. (2008). The influence of external recruitment practices on job search practices across domestic labor markets: A comparison of the United States and China. *International Journal of Selection and Assessment, 16,* 93–101.

Whiston, S. C., & Keller, B. K. (2004). The influences of the family of origin on career development: A review and analysis. *The Counseling Psychologist, 32,* 493–568.

Worklife. (2002). In their fathers' footsteps. *Worklife Report, 14,* 12.

Zottoli, M. A., & Wanous, J. P. (2000). Recruitment source research: Current status and future directions. *Human Resource Management Review, 10,* 353–382.

5

Nepotism and Organizational Homogeneity: How the Attraction–Selection–Attrition (ASA) Process Is Accelerated by Nonmerit-Based Decision Making

Marcus W. Dickson
Wayne State University

Levi R. G. Nieminen
Denison Consulting

Benjamin J. Biermeier-Hanson
Wayne State University

It is a rare week that goes by without some allegation of nepotism reaching the front pages of the national news media. Recently, for example, Senator Max Baucus of Montana came under fire when it was revealed that he had nominated his romantic partner (who at the time was his employee) to a position as U.S. district attorney in his home state, without having revealed their relationship in the nominations process (Hulse & O'Connor, 2009). We, writing here in the city of Detroit, Michigan, have seen a parade of news stories unfolding in the past few years suggesting that the former mayor of Detroit, Kwame Kilpatrick, made a practice of appointing family members and friends to government positions, often positions for which they did little work (McGraw, 2008). When people read of these types of nepotism—especially the hidden types of nepotism, such as those cited— they are often dismayed, or (having seen it all before) they respond with resignation to a seemingly unending drumbeat of nepotism.

It is not only in politics, of course, where nepotism occurs. Virtually every person with whom we discussed this chapter as we were writing it was able to provide at least one example of a coworker hired or promoted based on (what at least appeared to be) their relationships rather than on their capabilities. Companies have anti-nepotism policies to oppose this process, generally with strong support. Over 40 years ago, *Harvard Business Review* (Ewing, 1965) found that 85% of surveyed managers generally opposed the use of nonmerit factors in hiring and other personnel decisions, and there is no evidence that this proportion is growing smaller.

Despite these well-publicized examples of nepotism, which led to public outcry against the practice, many organizations find that relying solely on merit-based considerations in hiring is itself problematic. Colleges and universities often give preferential treatment in admissions to the children of alumni, arguing that "legacy preferences help build cross-generational relationships with institutions and cement relationships with alumni donors" (Jaschik, 2008). The increase in dual-earner couples seeking to manage the demands of work and family have led some companies to either weaken, make exceptions to, or eliminate their anti-nepotism rules (Werbel & Hames, 1996). And the 85% of managers surveyed in 1965 who said that they opposed the use of nepotism in hiring? They also said that they sometimes used it in specific circumstances, despite their general opposition to the practice.

Other chapters in this book have focused in depth on the processes and the pros and cons of nepotism as an organizational practice. In this chapter, we focus on one particular process that occurs in organizations and how that process is affected by nepotistic practices. Specifically, our focus is on organizational culture, including the attraction–selection–attrition (ASA) cycle, and the natural tendency in organizations toward homogeneity of personality and values among organization members.[1]

Clearly, the presence of nepotism within an organizational system can affect that organization's culture, although the direction of that effect is not necessarily clear. Ram (2001) presented a qualitative analysis of a small consulting firm in which the spouse of the CEO was hired as a consultant and expected to be integrated into projects, despite her seeming lack of qualifications or skills for the job. The organization's culture of hard work and merit-based recognition—in place prior to the active participation of the spouse—suffered significantly, as other consultants felt the need to include the spouse, but then to redo almost any work that she had completed. Denison, Lief, and Ward (2004), on the other hand, found that family-run firms (in which hiring and promotion was at least somewhat based on family membership rather than strict merit) had more positive (i.e., more productive) organizational cultures in general than did businesses without any sort of family affiliation, and that this more positive culture was the result of both "who they are" (i.e., the types of people who make up the firm) and "what they do" (i.e., the strategic decisions the firms make). Additionally, kinship or friendship ties can serve to threaten the culture when relationship conflicts external to the organization are introduced or strengthen it when kinship ties allow for "holding each other accountable" (Gordon & Nicholson, 2008).[2]

To begin this chapter, then, we need to lay some groundwork. First, it is important to recognize the difference between cases in which hiring and promotion decisions are based solely on family or friendship ties,[3] and those in which merit and relationship are both part of the personnel decision process. Here, we draw a parallel to a distinction offered by Bellow (2003) between "old" and "new" forms of nepotism. In contrast to the traditional or old view of nepotism, which focused on nepotism as a coercive action by the benefactor and as oppressive from the beneficiary's perspective, a new view of nepotism recognizes that nephews (and sons, daughters, etc.) willingly join family enterprises to capitalize on several unique advantages that would not be available elsewhere. Taking a perspective more closely aligned with the newer conceptualization, it should not be assumed that beneficiaries of nepotism are not also highly qualified for the positions they inherit through family relationships. In fact, nepotism likely advances the qualifications of motivated family employees who seek to learn the family business from a young age.

We also need to differentiate nepotism from cronyism, in which the appointed or hired friend or relative recognizes their lack of qualifications and is expected to support their long-standing benefactor. Barnett (2005) notes that Alexander Hamilton's Federalist Paper No. 76 is often cited in reference to cronyism, in that it describes why the consent of the Senate is required for presidential appointments:

> He would be both ashamed and afraid to bring forward, for the most distinguished or lucrative stations, candidates who had no other merit than that of coming from the same State to which he particularly belonged, *or of being in some way or other personally allied to him, or of possessing the necessary insignificance and pliancy to render them the obsequious instruments of his pleasure.* [Emphasis added]

Further, we need to differentiate nepotism, as an unsupported organizational practice, from family hiring within a family firm, in which the intention to hire family members for key positions is well known to all within the firm.

We also need to recognize that there are many topics that we could pursue within this chapter. But, to clarify the starting point for our work in this chapter, we have assumed that nepotism is an intentional or conscious process originating with an organizational leader (often with the founder), that the decisions that are made and the apparent reasons for them are seen by other employees, and that their subsequent behaviors and perceptions are shaped by the actions of the leader. We also recognize that individual difference variables (e.g., personality, equity sensitivity) are likely to affect one's reactions to and interpretations of organizational events, but were unable to explore these issues within the space limitations of the present chapter.

We will address the nepotism–culture linkage by first defining and describing organizational culture, with a focus on issues of culture and climate strength as they relate to homogeneity of personality, values, and perceptions. We will then describe the ASA model developed by Benjamin Schneider (Schneider, 1987; Schneider, Goldstein, & Smith, 1995), and others (Dickson, Resick, & Goldstein, 2008). We will consider the acceleration of the ASA process in nepotistic settings, addressing each of the three components of the ASA model, as well as organizational socialization. We will address several important contingency factors, including organizational size, life-cycle stage, and external environment. Finally, we will draw conclusions and present avenues for future research. As with many of the chapters in this volume, the definitive literature on this topic is lacking, and so we will at times speculate, though we will support our speculations wherever possible.

ORGANIZATIONAL CULTURE AND CLIMATE

Though organizational culture has been defined in many different ways (Ashkanasy, Wilderom, & Peterson, 2000), for ease of discussion we rely on the model of culture presented by Schein (1993), which is both concise and well known. In Schein's model, there are three primary levels at which culture can be considered. The first level, referred to as "artifacts," is the most visible level, and refers to aspects of organizational functioning that are able to be seen (e.g., the structure of the work space) or which leave behind detritus (e.g., memos, policies, and so forth). This level, while easy to gather data from, provides the least definitive and most ambiguous information about the culture of the organization. The second level, referred to as "espoused values," is made up of the cognitively available explanations that people hold for the ways in which their organization functions. The final level, and the level at which Schein believes culture actually resides, he refers to as "basic assumptions." At this level of culture are the fundamental, taken-for-granted, often preconscious assumptions about the nature of work and of humanity that come to be shared within the organization. As the organization wrestles with challenges and finds strategies and explanations that work, basic assumptions are passed on to other members as the right ways to think and perceive.

In our exploration of nepotism, we will focus primarily at the levels of basic assumptions and (to some extent) espoused values, as these are the values and cognitively available explanations that serve to drive nepotism as an organizational practice. Further, we believe that hiring nepotistically would serve to strengthen the sharedness of basic assumptions and espoused values in a unit or organization.

We have already noted the work by Denison et al. (2004), in which family firms had more positive (i.e., productive) cultures than did nonfamily firms. Similarly, Vallejo (2008) found statistically significant differences between family and nonfamily firms on 9 of 12 organizational culture dimensions: involvement, identification, loyalty, working atmosphere, trust, participation, reinvestment, leadership, and cohesion. Vallejo goes on to conclude that family firms' cultures differ from those of nonfamily firms on several key points, including:

1. The employees of family firms show higher levels of loyalty, involvement, and identification, which translate into a stronger commitment to their firm.
2. There is a better working atmosphere in family firms, and higher levels of participation and trust between individuals, which translates into a greater organizational harmony.

3. These firms reinvest their profits more, making their management more oriented toward long-term outcomes.
4. The leadership exercised in family firms is more transformational, which in turn leads to a higher degree of cohesion among the members of this type of organization compared to those of nonfamily firms. (p. 273)

Each of these processes is likely to lead to increased levels of agreement among organization members on key values. For example, those people who are highly committed to an organization and those who work in positive and trusting atmospheres are likely to share values among themselves, as are those led by a transformational leader who emphasizes values (House, 1977). The level of agreement on perceptions of organizational cultures and on the values that comprise the culture is often referred to as "culture strength" (for example, O'Reilly, 1989), and firms with strong cultures have been found in earlier research to outperform firms with weak cultures (for example, Burt et al., 1994; Gordon & DiTomaso, 1992; Kotter & Heskett, 1992).

We now have two related concepts to consider: (a) culture strength, which is based on the levels of agreement among culture members around cultural elements; and (b) organizational homogeneity, which is the condition of having organization members who share similar characteristics, including personality (for example, Schneider, Smith, Taylor, & Fleenor, 1998) and values (for example, Giberson, Resick, & Dickson, 2005). To better assess the relationship between these constructs and the likelihood that nepotistic practices will affect them, we turn to the ASA model, which describes an oft-supported process by which organizations come to comprise individuals with higher levels of homogeneity than one might expect.

INTRODUCTION OF THE ASA MODEL

As the ASA model is one of the primary focuses of this chapter, it is useful to introduce it conceptually before exploring how it can be used as a lens through which to examine the effect of nepotism in organizational cultures. This model was proposed by Schneider in 1983, clarified in

1987, and updated in 1995 (Schneider, 1983, 1987; Schneider et al., 1995). Its central premise is that people are not randomly assigned to organizations. Instead, people are attracted to, are selected into, and may leave organizations due to their fit (or lack thereof) with the organization's values, goals, strategies, and processes. The primary implication of this model is that, over time, the people within an organization become more homogeneous in their goals, values, and behaviors. As Schneider noted, "The people make the place." Thus, this homogeneity in people leads to a similarly homogeneous organizational culture. We believe nepotism may accelerate the ASA process, thus leading to cultural outcomes that may potentially be unique to nepotistic organizations.

The ASA model consists of three primary components: attraction, selection, and attrition. Socialization into the organizational culture is also an important component of this model, though it is not explicitly included (Schneider, 1983, 1987). Although these parts were each originally conceptualized as separate decision points, recent advances in ASA have posited that the process cannot be delineated quite this clearly (Dickson et al., 2008). Instead, this process is both continuous and, at times, simultaneous. This is particularly evident in the potential overlap during both attraction and selection. For example, an organization could be attracted to a potential job applicant, leading to recruitment. Concurrently, a job applicant could become attracted to an organization. Throughout the selection process, the organization and applicant may continue to be attracted to each other, up until potential entry into the organization. Once in the organization, the new employee will become further socialized into the values of the organizational culture. If, at any point, the employee is no longer attracted to the organization, he or she may choose to leave the organization in search of a better fit.

Attraction

Although the various points of the ASA model are continuous and overlapping (Dickson et al., 2008), it is necessary to define its parts at each individual decision point for the ease of explication later. Attraction is based on the premise that people do not generally take any job that comes along. Instead, they are attracted to organizations that they perceive will fit their skills, values, and personalities. Considerable research has been conducted on Chatman's (1991) person–organization fit (P–O

fit) theory that supports the assertion that people are attracted to organizations with values that are perceived to be congruent with their own
(for example, Cable & Edwards, 2004; Cable & Judge, 1997). Additionally,
research into personality and organizations has shown that there are
moderate relationships between the personality of the job applicant and
the nature of the organization (Kristof, 1996). Both approaches have
demonstrated that the perceived fit between a potential applicant and an
organization determines whether an individual is attracted to a particular organization.

Selection

As noted before, selection is the potentially concurrent process that could
be considered attraction from the organization's perspective. Instead of
an applicant assessing potential fit in an organization, the organization
assesses the potential fit of an employee in both the organizational culture
and in the skills and abilities the employee may provide to the organization. Although not always explicit, recruiters often rely on implicit P–O
fit judgments to distinguish between job applicants (Westerman & Cyr,
2004). Additionally, attraction and selection may be interactive as well as
concurrent (Dickson et al., 2008). That is, an individual (or organization)
may be attracted to the organization (or individual) and, through use of
impression management tactics throughout the selection process, attempt
to increase their own attractiveness to the other party. If the attraction
is mutual throughout the entire selection process, then the individual is
likely to be formally selected into the organization.

Attrition

The attrition portion of ASA suggests that an employees' perception of
poor perceived fit with an organization is one of the primary reasons an
employee may ultimately choose to leave in order to seek a better fit elsewhere (for example, Schneider, 1987; Schneider et al., 1995). Although
there has been a good amount of research done on the attraction and
selection components, primarily through the P–O fit research (for
example, Chatman, 1991), there has been considerably less investigation
into attrition. This is primarily due to the difficulty in collecting reliable
data from employees who have turned over. Lauver and Kristof-Brown

(2001) did find support for attrition due to fit, however, when examining person–job and person–organization fit and their relationship to intent to turnover. They found that both types of fit impact intent to turnover, with P–O fit accounting for more variance. Although there is little literature supporting attrition due to lack of fit, there is evidence that attrition can occur due to perceived lack of fit from either the individual or organizational perspective.

Socialization

Although socialization is not, as noted before, a specific component of ASA, it deserves mention due to its importance in the overall process and its potentially differential manifestation in nepotistic organizations. Socialization has the potential to increase perceived fit following selection (Thomas & Anderson, 1999). Conversely, it is possible that socialization can illustrate poor fit that was not apparent during attraction and selection (Dickson et al., 2008). Socialization thus has implications for organizational homogeneity, as it either leads to better fit or recognition of poor fit and eventual attrition.

ASA and Nepotism

Although it has not been explicitly studied, we believe nepotism has a variety of interesting implications for the ASA process. Specifically, we believe nepotistic practice may accelerate the ASA process. While homogeneity is a natural outcome of ASA, we believe it may be even stronger in nepotistic organizations. In the next section, we will discuss potential effects nepotism may have on each component of the ASA model and the subsequent effects these practices may have on organizational culture.

CONSEQUENCES OF NEPOTISM THROUGH THE ASA FRAMEWORK

Schneider and colleagues (1995), in their update of the ASA framework, note that the goals and values of an organization's founder lead to many of the policies and strategies for that organization, including selection strategies. Nepotistic policies are frequently one of these strategies, particularly in young organizations (Ford & McLaughlin, 1985). Often, the original employees of an organization are hired to carry out the founder's goals and vision, and share the same assumptions as the founder (Schein, 1993). If nepotism is a fundamental practice at the beginning of an organization, it is reasonable to conclude that nepotism is likely to persist in some manner throughout the organization's lifespan, particularly given that the majority of organizations in the United States are family owned (Dyer, 1986). Although some studies have found no significant performance differences between founder-managed and professionally managed companies (Willard, Krueger, & Feeser, 1992), potential implications for organizational culture remain, particularly given the strong relationship between the founder's values and strategy, and the culture of the organization as a whole (Ogbonna & Whipp, 1999).

Now that we have introduced ASA and discussed the link between an organization's original practices and culture, we can elaborate on how we believe nepotism can accelerate the ASA process at each stage and the resulting consequences for organizational homogeneity and culture. Although we discuss nepotism at each decision point, we believe that it affects the ASA process in the same temporally continuous and overlapping manner as the ASA model itself operates (Dickson et al., 2008). That is, while we discuss the effect of nepotism on the ASA model at attraction, selection, attrition, and socialization, respectively, we believe that this process can occur at multiple decision points simultaneously. Additionally, as we have discussed before, the effects of nepotism are likely contingent upon many factors, such as organizational size or age. When appropriate, we will discuss these contingencies at each point in the ASA model.

ATTRACTION

Attraction to a nepotistic organization almost certainly differs depending on whether one is a member of the family (or friend of the family) or an unrelated family member. Attraction is likely to be considerably different if one is part of the family. It is not necessarily accelerated in the traditional sense because attraction may be a gradual process throughout an individual's childhood and teenage years. Nonetheless, we consider this process accelerated when compared to nonfamily members.

Family Members

In both old and new nepotism (Bellow, 2003), family members are likely to have a very clear sense of the organization's values, goals, structures, and processes. Some evidence exists that individuals often share work-related attitudes that are acquired from their parents through social learning (for example, O'Shea & Kirrane, 2008). These shared attitudes coupled with an intimate knowledge of the organization make it reasonable to conclude that family members are likely attracted to the family business and will fit within it. Even if family members do not share similar values, the attraction process is likely to be considerably accelerated. That is, family members will know with greater certainty than nonfamily members whether they fit into the organization. They will not have to engage in the same information-seeking procedures that lead to attraction of nonfamily members. This would seem to be a distinct advantage for family members.

There are several other potentially attractive features of a family-run organization for a family member that may affect the attraction component of the ASA model. A guarantee of employment would most likely make an organization quite attractive to a potential familial employee. Additionally, new nepotism suggests that familial employees often undergo considerable training, whether on the job or in school, to prepare them for a position in the family business. Furthermore, the positive and negative information about the family business that is likely gained during a lifelong grooming process provides what could be considered a realistic job preview (Premack & Wanous, 1985; Wanous, 1976). Other factors, such as close family support at work, also could be considered advantages that would accelerate attraction.

It should be noted that there are potential disadvantages that may deter people from employment in the family business. Some family members may feel coerced into going into the family business, either because that is the familial norm or because of factors within the family. Family employees also may experience uncertainty about their value to the organization. For example, a family employee may be unsure whether a promotion was due to merit or due to kinship. While these are potential disadvantages, the effect on attraction remains the same. Attraction can be a moot point for individuals who perceive disadvantages in joining their family's organizations, but are forced to join anyway. If an individual is coerced into the business, the attraction process is circumvented. On the other hand, individuals who actively divorce themselves from an organization because of perceived coercion or who opt not to join due to other perceived disadvantages still have their attraction decision accelerated, even though it results in unemployment.

The long-term cultural consequences of attraction for the family firm likely depend on whether nepotism at the attraction stage resembles the old or new type. Family employees who were attracted to the family business and voluntarily joined it (i.e., new nepotism) will likely share the same values as the rest of the family in the organization. This will serve to perpetuate the organizational values and goals and thus create a force toward the culture's stability over time. This will likely hold even if family members begin at entry-level positions. Over time, given the family-based culture, family members will likely rise to management and thus perpetuate the existing culture. It is possible, however, that existing cultures may not be sustained if there are family members in the organization who were coerced into it (i.e., old nepotism). Over time, if these individuals also rise in the ranks, their values (which we assume are different from the family values due to the lack of attraction) have the potential to change the existing organizational culture. Further research into the effect that disenfranchised family members have on a familial organization's culture would be a particularly fascinating direction in which to take research on nepotism.

Nonfamily Members

Attraction to nepotistic organizations is clearly very different if a job applicant is a nonfamily member rather than a family member. Attraction, for a nonfamily member, is not a lifelong process leading up to employment. Instead, nonfamily members will likely have to engage in information-seeking behavior to determine whether the organization appears to be a good fit. Dailey and Reuschling (1980), using a self-response survey methodology, found that nonfamily members may be attracted to familial organizations for a variety of reasons. Desirability of working in a warm family atmosphere, improved communications, consistency of policy, smoothness of executive transitions, and acceptance of a family-led organization within a community were all cited as potentially attractive features of a family-based organization. Unattractive features included negative impact on morale and family affairs affecting business decisions. Another potentially unattractive feature, found by Arasli and Tumer (2008), is that nepotism has a high impact on job stress for nonfamilial employees.

The decision to pursue a familial organization may be considerably more difficult for nonfamily members. Assumptions of job stability, consistency, and emphasis on family time, along with the advantages cited earlier, may provide a very attractive fit for certain individuals. Conversely, individuals may perceive a distinct lack of fit due to the reasons cited along with a potential inability to advance within the organization. Perceptions of fit may be more difficult to discern in family businesses, as the nature of the family role in the organization may not be clear.

The cultural implications regarding nonfamily employees are less clear than for family employees, though we can make some educated conjectures. The attraction process may be accelerated for nonfamily members as well, as people may perceive a nepotistic organization as immediately unattractive or attractive. That is, due to its nepotistic nature, people may make assumptions about the organization that may either deter them completely or serve as the primary attractive features. There also may be employees for whom the nepotistic nature of an organization may not accelerate attraction. This is possibly contingent upon both organizational age and size. Nonfamily members may be more attracted to younger, less established organizations where nepotism is merely convenient and not embedded in the culture. Nonfamily members may also be more attracted to large organizations due to perceived opportunities (i.e., family members may run the company, but there are many management opportunities available). Conversely, nonfamily members may be put off if nepotism is embedded and opportunities limited.

Thus, the cultural implications for nonfamily members in nepotistic organizations are various. Nonfamily members attracted to young organizations may have the ability to change the culture if nepotism is not considered a core value. Nonfamily members attracted to older organizations likely will have less effect on the organizational culture, particularly if the responsibility for guiding the organizational goals and values rests with the family. Similarly, nonfamily members attracted to the family-based nature of the organization itself are likely to have congruent values with the organization and will be further socialized as their tenure with the organization continues.

Thus, attraction operates very differently for family members and nonfamily members. Attraction is likely accelerated for family members, resulting in a continuation of the organizational culture and greater homogeneity. Attraction for nonfamily members, however, may or may not be accelerated. Attraction is likely accelerated for nonfamily members who are attracted to the family-based nature of the organization. This, too, would further perpetuate the existing culture and contribute to organizational homogeneity. Attraction may operate normally for nonfamily members attracted to established, older, and larger organizations. These nonfamily employees may still have only a minimal effect on the culture. Nonfamily members attracted to a young organization and family members coerced into working in the family business seem to have the greatest chance at reducing organizational homogeneity and changing the organizational culture, as their values likely differ from those of the founder and other family.

SELECTION

Like attraction, selection of an employee by a nepotistic organization likely differs considerably depending on whether the employee is a family member. Also, like attraction, we believe that selection is accelerated concurrently with attraction for family members but likely remains normal for nonfamily members. Additionally, selection into the organization is potentially contingent upon the level of hire, organizational size, and organizational age.

Family Members

As noted in the attraction section for family members, selection is likely more or less automatic. That is, an individual may have been groomed for years to take a position in the company, thus greatly accelerating selection. Even if the family member in question has not been trained and socialized all their life (i.e., old nepotism or a family member coerced into the organization), selection is likely automatic. There are several attractive aspects inherent to nepotistic selection. Given that non-nepotistic organizations devote considerable time, resources, and energy into assessing value congruence (Cable & Judge, 1997), selection of a family member offers a considerable advantage in cost. The likelihood of turnover, which is also expensive, is lower when hiring family members due to their life-long socialization into the company and shared values. This is, of course, contingent on whether the family employee is willing. Nepotistic policies thus offer a cheap method of attracting and retaining a dedicated, loyal, and committed workforce (Donnelley, 1964; Lansberg, 1983).

Additional resources are saved if one assumes that succession plans are likely in place in family-based firms. Boeker and Goodstein (1993) found support for this assumption, discovering that firm ownership affects successor choice, such that firms owned by insiders are less likely to replace the CEO with an outsider. A family-based organization stands to save considerable money on executive searches if there is a family member primed to step in when a family leader retires. This may have differing consequences for the organization and its culture. One consequence is that the culture remains static and the transition is smooth. Conversely, it is possible that selection of family members at the upper level of an organization will lead to either family or nonfamily infighting, and will result in the formation of subcultures that differ from the broader organizational culture.

The selection process for entry- or middle-level family employees is also likely automatic for several reasons. First, the obvious family connection may make entry-level employment, in particular, automatic. Second, under new nepotism, the family members applying for positions have likely been well trained to join the company and thus are already qualified. Finally, as noted before, organizations are getting a known quantity, thus saving costs.

We posit that, under most circumstances, the selection process is greatly accelerated for family members. The cultural implications when selected family members are at the entry level are likely the same as when family members are promoted to upper management, as it seems probable that these entry-level family members are still being trained to eventually assume higher leadership positions. Thus, selection of family members into an organization will result in greater homogeneity within the organization and a continuation of the core values. The exceptions to this would be unwilling family members in the organizations with different values as well as the differences in values that result from infighting during leadership succession.

There are a few circumstances where the culture may change. These exceptions could lead to greater organizational heterogeneity and an eventual change in organizational culture. It is also possible that family-based organizations may be forced to change their selection procedures as a way of changing their culture. That is, the homogeneity resulting from the ASA process may lead to stagnation, forcing the family to bring in new perspectives to survive. Alternatively, selection procedures may be legally imposed if the current selection procedures are found to discriminate against protected groups (see Gutman, this volume, Chapter 2).

Nonfamily Members

It is difficult to discuss selection of nonfamily members due to the various contingencies mentioned. Selection may actually be decelerated for nonfamily members compared to family members. Selection of nonfamily members may also vary depending on the age and the size of the organization. Smaller, younger organizations may strictly hire family members until they are established enough to take on nonfamily employees, who may require more compensation. However, older organizations that remain small in size may also strictly hire family or friends a means to either "keep it in the family" or to keep selection costs at a minimum. If smaller organizations hire employees that are not friends or family, more effort may be put into ensuring that the employee will fit well, thus actually drawing out the selection process. Large organizations, both young and old, are more likely to select employees in a manner more consistent with non-nepotistic firms, particularly at the lower levels of the organization. If a family-based organization chooses to hire externally for upper-management positions, more care may be taken in the selection process to ensure the new hire fits in with the existing family structure. Additionally, in ensuring fit of non-family members, homogeneity remains a consequence of the ASA model, unless the family deliberately hires someone who fits less well for survival or legal reasons. Thus, with these exceptions, selection of nonfamily members likely only contributes further to the existing homogeneous culture.

SOCIALIZATION

Family Members

Perhaps even more than the previous stages, the process of socialization is likely to differ for family and nonfamily employees. For family employees, socialization into the family-owned business may begin well in advance of organizational entry (or reentry) as an adult. Longenecker and Schoen (1978) described how the process of grooming a family successor begins with the inculcation of the family organization's values as early as childhood. Similarly, Griffeth, Allen, and Barrett (2006) integrated Feldman's (1981) concept of anticipatory socialization (i.e., socialization that occurs prior to full-time employment) into their longitudinal model of succession in family-owned businesses. According to their model, the outcomes of early socialization experiences, such as when a young family member works part time for the family business, will be an important factor in the later decision to seek employment with the family business (i.e., as an adult seeking full-time employment) or elsewhere. Specifically, positive relationship building during this early phase is expected to enhance the individual's satisfaction and commitment, and thereby increase the likelihood of retention later. Conversely, a negative experience during anticipatory socialization is likely to decrease perceptions of fit and lead to withdrawal from the family-owned business.

From this perspective, socialization after organizational entry (or reentry as an adult full-time employee) may be unnecessary to the extent that individual's values are already closely aligned with the owning-family's values. In other words, there may be fewer "rough edges of fit" to be smoothed (Dickson et al., 2008, p. 7) due to anticipatory socialization. Moreover, the social support aspects of socialization (e.g., mentoring, relationship building), which appear to be most strongly related to enhanced perceptions of P–O fit (Cooper-Thomas, Van Vianen, & Anderson, 2004), may be redundant with many of the benefits afforded to family employees simply as a function of having access to familial relationships within the organization. At the same time, effortful socialization may have increased importance for P–O fit outcomes when family employees are only distally related to the owning family or have had little previous exposure to the organization. Nonetheless, in comparison to nonfamily employees, distal relatives are likely to enter the organization with a higher potential for building their social networks. This is because an immediate, albeit perhaps tenuous, connection to members of the owning family can provide a head start toward relationship building and lead to increased visibility within the organization. As a result, assimilation into the existing culture should be similarly accelerated.

Nonfamily Members

Whereas formal socialization mechanisms for family employees may be largely superfluous from a P–O fit perspective, such mechanisms may be very important for the successful assimilation of nonfamily employees and the maintenance of a cohesive organizational culture. In many ways, the process and outcomes of socialization for these nonfamily employees can be expected to mirror those of the more general organizational context in which socialization has been described (see Schneider, 1987; Schneider et al., 1995). However, we can also envision how certain features of socialization may be unique to the scenario involving matriculation of nonfamily employees in nepotistic organizations. An emergent theme from case studies of family-owned organizations is the inclusiveness of the family concept that is engrained in the description of these organizations' cultures. For example, to the extent that family metaphors are used when describing the values of an organization, they are usually intended as evidence of the blurring of divisions between family and nonfamily employees within the larger organizational family (Ainsworth & Cox, 2003). Socialization may be indirectly related to whether such a vision is achieved in practice, as mediated by nonfamily employee perceptions. Along these lines, outcomes of socialization may be directly related to whether nonfamily members perceive themselves as part of the "organizational family" or as a second-class citizens.

An important question for future research to address involves how best to socialize nonfamily employees and promote their inclusion within the dominant family culture. Taking a procedural justice perspective suggests that, at minimum, nonfamily employees should be provided the same benefits of socialization as family employees (e.g., access to mentoring relationships, and so on). However, attention to equality at the level of formal practices alone is unlikely to result in the perception of a level playing field, as when family employees are perceived as benefitting from face time away from the office. For this reason, the development of unique strategies tailored specifically to the evolving needs of nonfamily employees may be necessary. Regardless of the ultimate solution to this complex problem, the consequences of socialization are likely to be reflected in the favorability of employees' reaction to subsequent instances of nepotism by the organization. From a longitudinal perspective, organizational culture may play an important sense-making role in shaping such reactions.

ATTRITION

Family Members

Unlike the previous stages of the ASA model, nepotism may work to slow the process of attrition, particularly for family employees, who may remain due to extraordinary commitment to the organization's mission or a sense of obligation to their family (see Becker, this volume, Chapter 6). Younger generation employees may be motivated by the prospect of one day running the company, or such an arrangement may be implied when a major reason behind starting the business was to provide employment opportunities for the family. Alternatively, some research suggests that the beneficiaries of nepotism may harbor self-doubts (e.g., regarding their competence), particularly young family managers, whose ascension is attributed primarily to their status as a family member and not to merit (Padgett & Morris, 2005). For these persons, employment opportunities elsewhere may be perceived as unattainable or as being associated with a reduction in status, pay, and so on.

From a different perspective, it can be difficult to fire or demote under-performing family employees (Abdalla, Maghrabi, & Raggad, 1998; Ewing, 1965). Managers may be attentive to certain organizational norms involving how family employees are to be handled (e.g., there may be an obligation to give a family employee a second chance, whereas a similar courtesy may not be extended to nonfamily) or may actively seek to avoid the fall out precipitated by removing a family member from his or her post. The difficulty associated with intervening may be particularly dependent on the target employee's status within the family, as well as the family's own beliefs regarding the appropriateness of such actions. Furthermore, those individuals comprising the owning family's innermost circle may be virtually untouchable. For example, Hillier and McColgan (2009) reported that family CEOs were much less likely to leave or be removed following poor performance than nonfamily CEOs.

These factors likely operate together to promote family employees staying with the business, and provide a myriad of disincentives for their departure. The organizational culture of family firms is similarly expected to reinforce values that are aligned with the strategic objective of retaining key personnel (e.g., loyalty, commitment, and identification with the organization as a sort of family) (Vallejo, 2008). This may be especially critical for the circumstances frequently ascribed to small businesses—they operate in very uncertain environments with high failure rates (Esteve-Pérez & Mañez-Castillejo, 2008). A case study presented by Ainsworth and Cox (2003) illustrates the high costs associated with a son's departure from the family business, further underscoring the vested interest these firms should have in maintaining solidarity. After setting up his own firm in direct competition with the family business and poaching many valuable employees, the son's relationship with his parents was subsequently estranged, and his mother died from a heart attack soon thereafter. Power dynamics among family members (e.g., concerning the timing and nature of managerial succession or distribution of control) and other familial divisions (i.e., generational divisions, gender divisions) were a potent source of interpersonal conflict, providing the impetus for the son's departure and the psychological withdrawal of other family employees. Herein, organizational culture may be indirectly related to attrition by influencing the nature of interpersonal relationships and providing organizational members with norms regarding the appropriate ways to resolve conflict. Disagreement among members about these norms (i.e., weak culture) is likely to lead to further conflict and eventual attrition.

Nonfamily Members

Attrition processes are likely to differ for nonfamily employees. For one, nonfamily employees probably do not experience the same pressures to remain with the organization, and may be less protected in the event of downsizing. For those employees who remain in the organization and those employees who choose to leave, fairness perceptions related to nepotism are likely to be an important intervening variable. Specifically, justice violations due to nepotism may lead to employee withdrawal from work and eventually turnover, or alternatively, to disenfranchisement and the formation of subcultures (see later). Although justice perceptions have not been assessed directly by previous studies from this domain, a number of authors have alluded to fairness as a central determinant of employee reactions to nepotism (for example, Arasli & Tumer, 2008; Khatri & Tsang, 2003; Padgett & Morris, 2005; Pelletier & Bligh, 2008).

As noted elsewhere in this volume, a lack of fairness is often implicit in definitions of nepotism. When an organizational event is viewed as unfair, emotional reactions may include paranoia, cynicism, and generalized stress and anxiety (Pelletier & Bligh, 2008). Arasli and Tumer's (2008) study with bank employees in Cyprus found that nepotism was a strong predictor of employee stress levels, which in turn predicted lower job satisfaction and increased turnover intentions.

In addition to being important for individual-level outcomes (e.g., turnover), employees' justice perceptions are likely to be consequential for organizational culture and, by extension, organization-level outcomes, such as performance and long-term viability (Eberlin & Tatum, 2008). Intuitively, a relationship might be anticipated, whereby violated justice perceptions among employees contribute negatively to organizational culture. Networking and contagion models provide a possible vehicle for studying how individual attitudes become represented at the organization level (for example, Monge & Contractor, 2001). Research attempting to link individual attitudes and perceptions to organizational level constructs, such as climate and culture, is limited to date, perhaps due to statistical and methodological issues associated with cross-level studies (see Glisson & James, 2002). However, a recent study by Schepers and Van den Berg (2007) provides one such example. Their study demonstrated that knowledge sharing among employees mediated the effect of procedural justice on perceived workplace creativity, a particular facet of organizational culture. Along similar lines, one might anticipate an indirect effect of violated justice perceptions (due to nepotism) on culture via counterproductive work behaviors (e.g., withholding information, withdrawal).

Subculture Formation

One consequence of nepotism might be the accelerated development of subcultures as a function of increased group salience. Khatri and Tsang (2003) described how cronyism reinforces the existence of a clear in-group and out-group. Management's differential treatment of employees comprising these groups subsequently increases the likelihood of intergroup hostility and the fragmentation of the organization's overall culture. In comparison to members of the in-group, those employees not favored by management may be likely to experience limited support (e.g., less access to mentorship), lower financial reward (e.g., lower pay, slower promotion rates), and reduced job satisfaction. Over an extended time, such demotivational states would be expected to lead to a decrease in job performance and an increase in counterproductive work behaviors (e.g., withdrawal from work). To the extent that these factors do not eventually lead to turnover, members of the out-group may collectively form a subculture, with features that reflect their resentment of being derogated by the in-group. In other words, disenfranchised nonfamily employees who remain with the organization may come to resemble a counterculture, with values that are distinct from those of the broader organization.

There is reason to suspect that disenfranchised nonfamily employees might remain with an organization and form a subculture, as opposed to leaving, which would be predicted by the ASA model. Specifically, the external economic climate may reduce attrition. During a recession, employees typically have fewer job opportunities available, which would reduce the chances of finding a better fit elsewhere. Organizations experiencing a hiring freeze may be similarly reluctant to let these employees go, whereas under other circumstances, to do so could be considered *healthy attrition*. From either perspective, an economic downturn is likely to reduce the mobility of employees as prescribed by ASA processes (Dickson et al., 2008).

Along similar lines, organizational downsizing may represent a unique opportunity for the manifestation of nepotism and is likely to have important cultural consequences for the organization moving forward. In their recent review of the downsizing literature, Datta, Guthrie, Basuil, and Pandey (2010) suggested that justice perceptions are an important intervening variable in the individual-level outcomes associated with downsizing, both for victims and survivors. Though outcomes are generally negative, as reflected in the term *survivor syndrome* (e.g., reduced organizational commitment, increased turnover intent, etc.), an important finding suggests a buffering effect of high procedural justice, such as when employees view the downsizing process as having been conducted in a just and fair manner (Brockner et al., 1994). Because procedural justice encompasses fairness in decision processes, such as freedom from biased decision criteria and adherence to ethical standards, organizations may find it difficult to be both nepotistic and procedurally fair during downsizing. Remaining nonfamily employees may be particularly susceptible to a strong survivor syndrome, with negative effects potentially cascading to the organization level (e.g., a fragmentation of the overall culture). More generally, the idea of downsizing may be difficult to reconcile with the family values that are thought to be fundamental to the cultures of nepotistic family firms (Stavrou, Kassinis, & Filotheou, 2007).

In addition to the formation of family and nonfamily subcultures, the family itself can include a number of divisions, any of which might similarly fragment the overall culture of the organization. These can include gender divisions (e.g., sons versus daughters), generational divisions (e.g., older versus younger generations), and divisions based on closeness of relation to the founding family (e.g., core versus extended family) (Ainsworth & Cox, 2003). It is further interesting to note that some researchers have described a positive relationship between strength of cultural values and the appearance of subcultures (for example, Boisnier & Chatman, 2003). From this perspective, organizations that continually reinforce the importance of family values may inadvertently fuel intergroup rivalries and the development of a counterculture.

IMPORTANT CONTEXTUAL CONSIDERATIONS

Thus far, our discussion has focused primarily on identifying and describing key conceptual themes that are likely to be relevant across a range of organizational contexts. In part, a largely "undifferentiated" discussion of nepotism and organizational culture was necessary in order to remain within the scope of the present chapter. At the same time, we feel that many of the constructs described (e.g., group dynamics, fairness perceptions, and organizational homogeneity) will have generalizable importance for understanding the relationship between nepotism and organizational culture. However, we simultaneously recognize that the cultural issues associated with nepotism will be complex and partly dependent on the specific organizations, families, managers, and employees involved. In the following sections we describe the role of three potentially important contextual variables: *organizational size*, *organizational life cycle*, and *societal culture*. Although by no means an exhaustive list, these variables provide an interesting point of departure from the extant literature on nepotism and culture.

Organizational Size

It is perhaps unsurprising that, historically, academic (and popular) perspectives on nepotism as a business practice have been qualified by the size of the business in question. For the small or family-owned business, nepotism was viewed as essential for the enterprise's survival, providing practical benefits that would otherwise be financially unattainable (e.g., access to dedicated employees) (Dailey & Reuschling, 1980; Ford & McLaughlin, 1986). Indeed, it is difficult to imagine a small family firm divorced from the concept of nepotism, and early attempts to define what does and does not constitute a "family business" reflect the inextricable linkages between the two (for example, Donnelley, 1964). In contrast, nepotism need not be considered part of the essential fabric of larger organizations, even though it may be reflected in the legacy of many of these institutions (Bellow, 2003). More commonly, nepotism has been viewed as a threat to the supposed professionalism and meritocracy of the large corporation, as a form of organizational politics (Pelletier & Bligh, 2008), or worse yet, as an example of corruption and white-collar crime. Survey research dating from the mid-1980s and earlier generally supports this position, finding that nepotism was more frequently practiced in small organizations and less likely to be prohibited either by formal or informal anti-nepotism policies (Ford & McLaughlin, 1986; Wexler, 1982). Similarly, an earlier survey by Ewing (1965) found that managers held substantially less condemnatory attitudes toward nepotism when practiced in small companies. More recently, public scrutiny of nepotism has continued to focus exclusively on large corporations (e.g., Enron).

At the same time that stakeholder perceptions have been more favorable toward nepotism by small organizations, certain disadvantages have been ascribed to these contexts as well (Abdelsamad & Kindling, 1978; Donnelley, 1964; Ford & McLaughlin, 1986). It is first interesting to note how the practice of nepotism is likely to be more visible, if not an obvious reality, to employees of small organizations. Particularly when members of an organization work and live in close proximity to one another, the hiring or promotion of family over nonfamily employees is likely to be a very salient issue with strong cultural consequences (and antecedents). In particular, interpersonal conflict is an emergent theme in several case studies of small family firms. Two specific sources of conflict include spillover of family conflict into the work domain, such as when an argument between spouses affects one or both parties' work performance or reduces the morale of surrounding employees (Pingree, Butler, Paisely, & Hawkins, 1978; Werbel & Hames, 1996), and when family employees are perceived as incompetent by nonfamily employees (Ram, 2001). The smallness of an organization is likely to amplify the presence of these conflicts and make them a central cultural feature. Ram's (2001) aforementioned case study of a very small family consultancy illustrates how these issues became defining features of the organization's culture. This is perhaps unsurprising given that legitimacy and professionalism are cornerstones of consulting enterprises. Nonetheless, the positive aspects of the firm's culture (e.g., warmth, support for work–life balance) were also ascribed to family values. In sum, it seems plausible that the degree to which the consequences (both positive and negative) associated with familial relationships are salient features of an organization's culture will be inversely related to the organization's size, and therefore, most amplified for very small organizations.

In comparison, nepotism is more easily concealed in larger and more structurally complex organizations, where, for example, the spouse of an employee could be hired and placed in a geographically and functionally distinct unit in order to mitigate the negative perceptions of other employees (Ford & McLaughlin, 1985). Werbel and Hames's (1996) survey of employees from small and large organizations provides some support for this position. These authors found that employees from larger organizations had more favorable attitudes toward the possibility of their organization employing married partners. Moreover, attitudes were more favorable toward same-organization spousal hires than same-department spousal hires. In contrast to the traditional perspective, this study provides some support for the idea that nepotism would be less impactful of day-to-day operations within larger organizations.

At the surface, it seems counterintuitive then that nepotism is generally perceived as less acceptable in those contexts where it is most easily hidden and least likely to impact day-to-day functioning (i.e., larger organizations). Organizational culture may provide insight into this seeming contradiction. Given the salience of nepotism in the small business context, it is highly likely that strong cultural mechanisms will be in place for justifying nepotism, from the organization's perspective, and for understanding it, from the employees' perspective. For example, strong family values may provide the impetus for placing family above work matters (Dailey & Reuschling, 1980). From an ASA perspective, nonfamily employees may be attracted to small family firms for this very reason—because they perceive cultural support for balancing work and nonwork aspects of life. Thus, nonfamily employees may tolerate their disadvantaged status in the organization in exchange for these benefits. Alternatively, the culture may be so strong surrounding these values that nonfamily employees come to be viewed as a sort of extended kin over time.

Lenius (2007) provides an interesting description of an organization that has sought to maintain nepotism throughout its 160 years of growth into a mature organization. As evidence of their family culture, Lenius recounts a scenario in which one employee was diagnosed with cancer and the other employees offered to shave their heads in a show of support. In addition, organizational symbols, myths, and stories may serve as a constant reminder of the sacrifices that were made by the founding family. According to Ford and McLaughlin (1985), nonfamily employees may rationalize the occurrence of favoritism by focusing on the personal and financial burden that was endured by the founding family. On the other hand, in large companies, employees are more likely to expect merit-based policies and do not afford the leader (who does not bear the associated risks of ownership) the right to enact nepotistic practices. Taken together, aspects of the culture of the family firm may serve to reinforce management's right to maintain nepotistic practices. By extension, justice violations and related consequences (e.g., withdrawal, counterproductive work behaviors, and so on) may be the result of inadequate cultural support for nepotism in some small organizations, rather than a direct effect of nepotism in and of itself.

Organizational Life Cycle

Taking a temporal view of an organization's growth suggests a number of ways in which the relationship between nepotism and organizational culture may differ over time. Here, we draw certain parallels to Schein's (1993) process model relating leadership to organizational culture over time. Schein's model suggests that the ability of the leader to influence the organization is gradually constrained by the maturing organization's coalescing culture. Similarly, the influence of the family, including its ability to behave nepotistically, has been described as becoming constrained over time, in this case as a function of the maturing organization's movement toward a culture of professionalism. Elstrodt (2003) described how the growth process for successful family-owned organizations entailed limiting the family's governance in certain domains. Most notably, among the firms that were studied, those that successfully grew their enterprise over multiple generations of family ownership enacted a variety of anti-nepotism policies, such as mandating that a percentage of the executive board be occupied by nonfamily and requiring that family members seek outside experience prior to applying for a position with the company. Clearly, these companies viewed nepotism as a danger to long-term sustainability. Moreover, organizational growth typically necessitates increased specialization of roles (Mintzberg, 1979), such that hiring practices become increasingly focused on the skills and abilities of job candidates out of necessity. Failure of the owning family to reconsider its culture, specifically as it pertains to those values associated with nepotism, can present a barrier to growth, or worse yet, can precipitate the decline of the organization (Holland & Boulton, 1984).

Thus, as implied by Schein's model, the organization faces the difficult task of adapting new cultural values that are in alignment with its changing strategic needs. Culture change initiatives in underperforming organizations often start with the task of rooting out sources of cronyism and nepotism. For example, Collins (2001) describes a case in which a turnaround effort began with the removal of certain members of the executive team to send a clear message throughout the organization that family ties were no longer valued. Alternatively, new methods of expressing old values may be necessary, such as family-friendly work policies, company-wide profit sharing, or contributing toward employee education.

Societal Culture

Much has been written regarding the influence of societal culture on organizational culture (for recent overviews, see Dickson, BeShears, & Gupta, 2004; Kwantes & Dickson, 2010). A broad range of theories can be drawn upon to explain the predominant view that organizational cultures generally reflect the cultures of the societies in which they are embedded (Dickson et al., 2004). From this vantage, one might anticipate, as we do, that there are cross-cultural differences in organizational norms concerning nepotism. For example, Arasli and Tumer (2008) suggested that the related practice of cronyism in organizations will be particularly difficult to curb in cultures with strong values surrounding interpersonal relationships. The limited research that is available provides a mixed but mainly incomplete picture. However, a recurrent theme is that organizations in less developed countries will hold more nepotistic values as a result of less anti-nepotistic views at the societal culture level. This is consistent with the historical account offered by Bellow (2003), in that advanced societies have adopted more punitive attitudes toward nepotism over time, or at least the old, more coercive forms of nepotism. The new nepotism that is characteristic of progressive societies is a redefined concept that incorporates merit and free will to a greater degree.

One study by Abdalla et al. (1998) identified several reasons that organizations in developing countries should be more tolerant of nepotism than organizations in developed countries, including: (a) family constitutes a larger portion of one's social network, (b) intense competition for white-collar jobs makes it likely that such positions will be coveted and passed within families, (c) widespread lack of the educational opportunities prevents job seekers from competing on the basis of skills and credentials, and (d) governments are less likely to reject nepotism. However, the results of their survey with human resources managers across a variety of organizations from the United States and Jordan (developing country) failed to uncover significant differences; respondents from both countries viewed nepotism as having mainly negative consequences for organizations. Moreover, a number of survey items targeted perceptions about the implications of nepotism for organizational culture specifically (e.g., "Nepotism is helpful due to having relatives work together and share common goals and values").

A number of other examples from developing countries have documented organizations' struggles to overcome sociocultural acceptance of nepotism. For example, Robinson (2008) provides an example of a rapidly expanding Indian-based firm that attributes its success largely to the organization's ability to instill a culture of professionalism by adhering to strict anti-nepotism policies. Robinson's report suggests that the company prides itself on representing a sort of counterculture in India, where family is a dominant cultural theme both in work and nonwork life. Agnaia (1997) describes the difficulties of training Libyan managers to use professional management practices, given that Arabic culture has traditionally valued seniority and family ties over merit and fairness. Robertson-Snape (1999) pointed to traditional Javanese (the historically dominant ethnic group in Indonesia) customs regarding gift exchange and the centrality of family to professional life as an explanation for the nepotism pervasive in Indonesian politics. As a final example, Arasli and Tumer (2008) describe nepotism as an obstacle to organizational professionalism in Arabic cultures: "Establishing professionalism and institutionalization are quite difficult in these workplaces in small states since employees tend either to be related or to know each other personally" (p. 1238).

To date, the limited research that is available on this topic has focused broadly on the comparison of developed and developing countries and societies. To further understand how societal cultures shape the occurrence and consequences of nepotism within organizations, future research should incorporate existing sociocultural dimensions. Using Hofstede's framework (1983, 1984), two dimensions that may be particularly relevant to nepotism and organization-level culture are collectivism–individualism and power distance. In collectivist cultures, an individual's self-concept is tightly integrated with the identity of the groups or *collectives* to which one belongs (e.g., families, organizations, and so forth). As a result, virtues relevant for the success of the group are among the most highly valued in these cultures, including loyalty, commitment, and relationship building (Hofstede, 1984). As previously suggested, certain cultural outcomes at the organization level associated with nepotism may depend, in part, on the degree to which nonfamily employees can be successfully integrated into the dominant family in-group. Collectivism as a societal culture value may facilitate relationship building at the organization level, such as when an organization adopts explicit goals involving increased group unity or expends a great deal of effort socializing new employees. In the long term, this may decrease some of the cultural strains associated with nepotism and group dynamics among family and nonfamily employees.

Power distance involves the extent to which members of a society are comfortable with autocratic processes and inequality. For example, individuals in high power-distance cultures may be unlikely to expect leader consultation regarding decisions that affect them personally, or equality among leaders and followers (Hofstede, 1984). Thus employees in high power-distance cultures may view nepotistic practices as a legitimate extension of a leader's power. To the extent that leaders' decision making is generally accepted without question in high power-distance societies, the importance of fairness perceptions as a mediating process for the cultural (organization-level) consequences of nepotism is seemingly reduced. Instead, the more important variable might be the leader's ability to maintain legitimate authority over followers, and by extension, the continued privilege to do what he or she sees fit. In this case, nepotism may not be a source of cultural conflict but simply an accepted reality.

CONCLUSIONS

Though we have covered a lot of ground in this chapter, there are many topics that we have not been able to address, including several additional micro- and macrolevel contextual variables. For example, the consequences of nepotism for individuals, which we have described as likely having secondary effects on organizational culture, may depend on how psychologically invested they are in the organization. For this reason, reactions to nepotism likely differ for part-time and full-time employees as well as for those who see their employment as a job as opposed to a career. At the same time, the individuals and organizations affected by nepotism are nested within larger contexts, which also ought to be considered. For example, industry norms likely influence perceptions of the negative and positive effects of nepotism on organizational longevity and performance. All of these are potential moderators of effects we have described in this chapter.

Nonetheless, our review of the literature on this topic leads us to some clear propositions.

Proposition 1: ASA processes are stronger in nepotistic organizations, leading to greater homogeneity of personality and especially of values in nepotistic organizations than in non-nepotistic organizations.

Proposition 2: Attraction processes of the ASA model are accelerated in nepotistic organizations for family members who have easy and long-standing access to important organizational information, but decelerated for nonfamily members, who may have greater difficulty accessing relevant information and determining their level of interest in the organization.

Proposition 3: The effects of nepotism—both positive and negative—are stronger when nepotism is a core value of the organization (e.g., in a family-run business with founders in place, and an active intention to pass the business leadership/ownership on to succeeding generations).

Proposition 4: Perceptions of unfairness or justice violations are significantly lower in organizations characterized by new nepotism than those characterized by old nepotism.

Proposition 5: Old nepotism at the attraction stage creates a force toward eventual culture change in the family business, whereas new nepotism creates a force toward culture stability over time.

Proposition 6: Entry-level selection processes of the ASA model are accelerated for family members in nepotistic organizations (relative to other organizations), but are equivalent to that in other organizations or slightly decelerated for nonfamily members.

Proposition 7: Selection processes relative to promotion within the organization will generate less internal conflict in organizations characterized by new nepotism than those characterized by old nepotism.

Proposition 8: Anticipatory socialization will reduce the effects of formal organizational socialization and integration programs for family members in nepotistic organizations. This differential effect will lead to negative perceptions on the part of nonfamily members unless they are provided with some form of the benefits of socialization provided to family members (e.g., access to mentoring relationships).

Proposition 9: Attrition processes of the ASA model are decelerated for family members in nepotistic organizations (even when they feel poor fit) but may be accelerated for non-family members, especially if expectations (e.g., about opportunities for promotion) are not made clear to nonfamily members during selection and socialization stages.

Proposition 10: The presence of nepotistic selection and promotion practices leads to the acceleration of formation of subcultures within an organization, largely along family and nonfamily lines.

Proposition 11: Economic challenges (e.g., recession leading to demands for downsizing) present greater challenges for new nepotistic organizations than for old nepotistic organizations, as the new nepotistic organizations attempt to balance perceptions of procedural justice in their cost-cutting decisions while at the same time maintaining family ties.

Proposition 12: The negative consequences associated with nepotism (e.g., violated justice among nonfamily employees) will be least evident in small organizations with cultural mechanisms that support nepotism (e.g., strong family values) and most evident in large organizations that lack such cultural mechanisms.

Proposition 13: Nepotism as an organization-wide core value of the organizational culture becomes harder to maintain and more harmful to the organization as the organization grows, as it becomes more complex, and as it moves through multiple generations of family members.

Proposition 14: The individualism–collectivism and power-distance dimensions of societal culture provide boundary conditions for the viability of the propositions presented here.

The current economic challenges and recovery worldwide, the increasing prevalence of cross-national boundary organizational growth, and the increasing understanding of new versus old forms of nepotism all provide opportunities for study of the homogeneity hypothesis of the ASA model in new and exciting ways, and we look forward to seeing those investigations in the years to come.

ENDNOTES

1. Our focus is primarily on the United States and other Western cultures. We fully recognize the large cultural differences in the perceived acceptability and desirability of the practice of hiring friends and relatives.
2. The senior author of this chapter encountered this latter phenomenon on a consulting project for a local government when he found that all 14 of the employees in a particular unit were related to each other, and that hiring had been done within the family for many years. When questioned, the senior employees explained that "if one of my cousins gets out of line here at work, I can take care of it back home, and they all know that."
3. Throughout this chapter, we have used the term *family members* to refer to all of those people who are relationally connected to organizational owners and decision makers, whether they are actually members of the same family, or are connected through friendship, romantic, or other relational ties.

REFERENCES

Abdalla, H. F., Maghrabi, A. S., & Raggad, B. G. (1995). Assessing perceptions of human resource managers toward nepotism: A cross-cultural study. *International Journal of Manpower, 19*, 554–570.

Abdelsamad, M. H., & Kindling, A. T. (1978). Why small businesses fail. *Society for Advanced Management Journal, 43*(2), 24–32.

Agnaia, A. A. (1997). Management training and development within its environment: The case of Libyan industrial companies. *Journal of European Industrial Training, 21*, 2–3.

Ainsworth, S., & Cox, J. W. (2003). Families divided: Culture and control in small family businesses. *Organization Studies, 24*, 1463–1485.

Arasli, H., & Tumer, M. (2008). Nepotism, favoritism and cronyism: A study of their effects on job stress and job satisfaction in the banking industry of north Cyprus. *Social Behavior and Personality, 36*, 1237–1250.

Ashkanasy, N., Wilderom, C. P. M., & Peterson, M. F. (Eds.). (2000). *Handbook of organizational culture and climate*. Thousand Oaks, CA: Sage.

Barnett, R. E. (2005, October 4). Cronyism. Retrieved April 4, 2010, from The Cato Institute Web site: http://www.cato.org/pub_display.php?pub_id=5109.

Bellow, A. (2003). *In praise of nepotism: A natural history*. New York: Doubleday.

Boeker, W., & Goodstein, J. (1993). Performance and successor choice: The moderating effects of governance and ownership. *Academy of Management Journal, 32*, 489–515.

Boisnier, A., & Chatman, J. A. (2003). The role of subcultures in agile organizations. In R. S. Peterson & E. A. Mannix (Eds.), *Leading and managing people in the dynamic organization* (pp. 87–114). Mahwah, NJ: Lawrence Erlbaum.

Brockner, J., Konovsky, M., Cooper-Schneider, R., Folger, R., Martin, C., & Bies, J. (1994). Interactive effects of procedural justice and outcome negativity on victims and survivors of job loss. *Academy of Management Journal, 37*(2), 397–409.

Burt, R. S., Gabbay, S. M., Holt, G., & Moran, P. (1994). Contingent organization as a network theory: The performance culture contingency. *Acta Sociologica, 37*(4), 345–370.

Cable, D., & Judge, T. (1997). Interviewers' perceptions of person–organization fit and organizational entry. *Journal of Applied Psychology, 824*, 294–311.

Cable, D. M., & Edwards, J. R. (2004). Complementary and supplementary fit: A theoretical and empirical integration. *Journal of Applied Psychology, 89*, 822–834.

Chatman, J. A. (1991). Matching people and organizations: Selection and socialization in public accounting firms. *Administrative Science Quarterly, 36*, 459–484.

Collins, J. (2001). Level 5 leadership. *Harvard Business Review, 79*, 66–76.

Cooper-Thomas, H. D., Van Vianen, A., & Anderson, N. (2004). Changes in person-organization fit: The impact of socialization tactics on perceived and actual P–O fit. *European Journal of Work and Organizational Psychology, 13*, 52–78.

Datta, D. K., Guthrie, J. P., Basuil, D., & Pandey, A. (2010). Causes and effects of employee downsizing. *Journal of Management, 36*, 281–348.

Dailey, R. C., & Reuschling, T. L. (1980). Human resource management in the family owned company. *Journal of General Management, 5*(3), 49–56.

Denison, D., Lief, C., & Ward, J. L. (2004). Culture in family-owned enterprises: Recognizing and leveraging unique strengths. *Family Business Review, 17*(1), 61–70.

Dickson, M. W., BeShears, R. S., & Gupta, V. (2004). The impact of societal culture and industry on organizational culture: Theoretical explanations. In R. J. House, P. J. Hanges, M. Javidan, P. W. Dorfman, & V. Gupta (Eds.), *Culture, leadership, and organizations: The GLOBE study of 62 societies* (pp. 74–90). Beverly Hills, CA: Sage.

Dickson, M. W., Resick, C. J., & Goldstein, H. W. (2008). Seeking explanations in people, not in the results of their behavior: Twenty-plus years of the attraction-selection-attrition model. In D. B. Smith (Ed.), *The people make the place: Exploring dynamic linkages between individuals and organizations* (pp. 5–36). Mahwah, NJ: Lawrence Erlbaum.

Donnelley, R. (1964). The family business. *Harvard Business Review, 61*, 47–56.

Dyer, W. G. (1986). *Culture change in family firms: Anticipating and managing business and family transactions*. San Francisco, CA: Jossey-Bass.

Eberlin, R. J., & Tatum, B. C. (2008). Making just decisions: Organizational justice, decision making, and leadership. *Management Decision, 46*, 310–329.

Elstrodt, H. P. (2003). Keeping the family in business. *McKinsey Quarterly, 4*, 94–103.

Esteve-Pérez, S., & Mañez-Castillejo, J. A. (2008). The resource-based theory of the firm and firm survival. *Small Business Economics, 30*, 231.

Ewing, D. (1965). Is nepotism so bad? *Harvard Business Review, 43*, 22–40.

Feldman, D. C. (1981). The multiple socialization of organizational members. *Academy of Management Journal, 2*, 309–318.

Ford, R., & McLaughlin, F. (1985). Nepotism. *Personnel Journal, 64*(9), 57–60.

Ford, R., & McLaughlin, F. (1986). Nepotism: Boon or bane. *Personnel Administrator, 31*, 78–89.

Giberson, T., Resick, C. J., & Dickson, M. W. (2005). Embedding leader characteristics: An examination of homogeneity of personality and values in organizations. *Journal of Applied Psychology, 90*, 1002–1010.

Glisson, C., & James, L. R. (2002). The cross-level effects of culture and climate in human service teams. *Journal of Organizational Behavior, 23*, 767–794.

Gordon, G. G., & N. DiTomaso (1992). Predicting corporate performance from organizational culture. *Journal of Management Studies, 29*, 783–799.

Gordon, G., & Nicholson, N. (2008). *Family wars: Classic conflicts in family business and how to deal with them.* London: Kogan Page.

Griffeth, R. W., Allen, D. G., & Barrett, R. (2006). Integration of family-owned business succession with turnover and life cycle models: Development of a successor retention process model. *Human Resource Management Review, 16*, 490–507.

Hillier, D., & McColgan, P. (2009). Firm performance and managerial succession in family managed firms. *Journal of Business Finance & Accounting, 36*(3/4), 461–484.

Hofstede, G. (1983). Dimensions of national cultures in fifty countries and three regions. In J. B. Deregowski, S. Dziurawiec, & R. C. Annis (Eds.), *Explications in cross-cultural psychology* (pp. 335–355). Lisse, Netherlands: Swets and Zeitlinger.

Hofstede, G. (1984). The cultural relativity of the quality of life concept. *Academy of Management Review, 9*, 389–398.

Holland, P. G., & Boulton, W. R. (1984). Balancing the "family" and the "business" in family business. *Business Horizons*, March/April, 16–21.

House, R. J. (1977). A 1976 theory of charismatic leadership. In J. G. Hunt & L. L. Larsen (Eds.), *Leadership: The cutting edge* (pp. 189–207). Carbondale, IL: Southern Illinois University Press.

Hulse, C., & O'Connor, A. (2009, December 6). Baucus acknowledges recommending girlfriend. *The New York Times*, p. A41.

Jaschik, S. (2008, November 20). Looking to the past to ban legacy admissions. *Inside Higher Ed.* http://www.insidehighered.com/news/2008/11/20/legacy.

Khatri, N., & Tsang, E. W. K. (2003). Antecedents and consequences of cronyism in organizations. *Journal of Business Ethics, 43*, 289–303.

Kotter, J. R., & Heskett, J. L. (1992). *Corporate culture and performance.* New York: Free Press.

Kristof, A. L. (1996). Person-organization fit: An integrative review of its conceptualizations, measurement, and implications. *Personnel Psychology, 49*, 1–49.

Kwantes, C., & Dickson, M. W. (2010). Organizational culture in a societal context: Lessons from GLOBE and beyond. In N. Ashkanasy, C. Wilderom, & M. Petersen (Eds.), *Handbook of organizational culture and climate* (2nd ed., pp. 494–514). Thousand Oaks, CA: Sage.

Lansberg, I. S. (1983). Managing human resources in family firms: The problem of institutional overlap. *Organizational Dynamics, 12*, 39–46.

Lauver, K. J., & Kristof-Brown, A. (2001). Distinguishing between employees' perceptions of person–job and person–organization fit. *Journal of Vocational Behavior, 59*, 454–470.

Lenius, P. (2007). A family affair. *Supply House Times, 50*, 40–44.

Longenecker, J., & Schoen, J. (1978). Management succession in the family business. *Journal of Small Business Management, 16*, 1–6.

McGraw, B. (2008, September 5). The rise and fall of Kwame Kilpatrick: Detroit's mayor an example of the best—and worst—of city. *Detroit Free Press*, p. 6S.

Mintzberg, H. (1979). *The structuring of organizations*. Englewood Cliffs, NJ: Prentice-Hall.

Monge, P. R., & Contractor, N. S. (2001). Emergence of communication networks. In F. M. Jablin & L. L. Putnam, (Eds.), *The new handbook of organizational communication: Advances in theory, research, and methods* (pp. 440–502). Thousand Oaks, CA: Sage.

O'Reilly, C. A., III. (1989). Corporations, culture and commitment: Motivation and social control in organizations. *California Management Review, 31*, 9–25.

Ogbonna, E., & Whipp, R. (1999). Strategy, culture, and HRM: Evidence from the UK food retailing sector. *Human Resources Management Journal, 9*(4), 75–90.

O'Shea, D., & Kirrane, M. (2008). The transmission of work-related attitudes: A social learning analysis. *Journal of Managerial Psychology, 23*, 524–557.

Padgett, M. Y., & Morris, K. A. (2005). Keeping it "all in the family": Does nepotism in the hiring process really benefit the beneficiary? *Journal of Leadership and Organizational Studies, 11*, 34–45.

Pelletier, K. L., & Bligh, M. C. (2008). The aftermath of organizational corruption: Employee attributions and emotional reactions. *Journal of Business Ethics, 80*, 823–844.

Pingree, S., Butler, M., Paisley, W., & Hawkins, R. (1978). Anti-nepotism's ghost: Attitudes of administrators toward hiring professional couples. *Psychology of Women Quarterly, 3*(1), 22–29.

Premack, S. L., & Wanous, J. P. (1985). A meta-analysis of realistic job preview experiments. *Journal of Applied Psychology, 70*, 706–719.

Ram, M. (2001). Family dynamics in a small consulting firm: A case study. *Human Relations, 54*, 395–418.

Robertson-Snape, F. (1999). Corruption, collusion and nepotism in Indonesia. *Third World Quarterly, 20*, 589–602.

Robinson, S. (2008, January 7). The newest model. *Time International* (South Pacific Edition), 51/52, 110.

Schein, E. H. (1993). *Organizational culture and leadership*. San Francisco, CA: Jossey-Bass.

Schepers, P., & Van den Berg, P. T. (2007). Social factors of work–environment creativity. *Journal of Business & Psychology, 21*, 407–428.

Schneider, B. (1983). Interactional psychology and organizational behavior. *Research in Organizational Behavior, 5*, 1–31.

Schneider, B. (1987). The people make the place. *Personnel Psychology, 40*, 437–453.

Schneider, B., Goldstein, H. W., & Smith, D. B. (1995). The ASA framework: An update. *Personnel Psychology, 48*, 747–773.

Schneider, B., Smith, D. B., Taylor, S., & Fleenor, J. (1998). Personality and organizations: A test of the homogeneity of personality hypothesis. *Journal of Applied Psychology, 83*, 462–470.

Stavrou, E., Kassinis, G., & Filotheou, A. (2007). Downsizing and stakeholder orientation among the Fortune 500: Does family ownership matter? *Journal of Business Ethics, 72*(2), 149–162.

Thomas, H. D. C., & Anderson, N. R. (1999). Changes in newcomer psychological contracts during organizational socialization: A study of recruits into the British Army. *Journal of Organizational Behavior, 19*, 745–767.

Vallejo, M. (2008). Is the culture of family firms really different? A value-based model for its survival through generations. *Journal of Business Ethics, 81*, 261–279.

Wanous, J. P. (1976). Organizational entry: From naïve expectations to realistic beliefs. *Journal of Applied Psychology*, 61, 22–29.

Werbel, J. D., & Hames, D. S. (1996). Anti-nepotism reconsidered: The case of husband and wife employment. *Group & Organization Management, 21*, 365–379.

Westerman, J. W., & Cyr, L. A. (2004). An integrative analysis of person-organization fit theories. *International Journal of Selection and Assessment, 12*, 253–261.

Wexler, J. G. (1982). Husband and wives: The uneasy case for anti-nepotism rules. *Boston University Law Review, 52*, 75–142.

Willard, G. E., Krueger, A., & Feeser, H. R. (1992). In order to grow, must the founder go: A comparison of performance between founder and non-founder managed high-growth manufacturing firms. *Journal of Business Venturing, 7*, 181–194.

6

Nepotism and the Commitment of Relevant Parties

Thomas E. Becker
University of Delaware

Nepotism is favoritism to a relative on the basis of a personal relationship ("Nepotism," 2001b). It is often seen as a person with power favoring relatives or friends, especially by giving them jobs. According to the *New Oxford American Dictionary* ("Nepotism," 2001a), the origin of the word dates from the 17th century and derives from the French *népotisme*, meaning nephew. This etymology refers to privileges bestowed on the "nephews" of popes who were in many cases their illegitimate sons. Thus, from the beginning, the concept of nepotism has carried with it a rather seedy connotation involving the misuse of power and having something to hide.

Although under certain conditions nepotism may have benign effects (Bellow, 2003; Jones et al., 2008), a major thesis of this chapter is that nepotism can also generate dysfunctional conflict through the multiple commitments held by relevant parties. However, I will maintain that the links among nepotism, commitment, and conflict are complex and that simple statements about direct relationships are likely misguided. Prior to further discussion, let me be clear about what I mean by conflict and commitment. Dysfunctional conflict means confrontation that interferes with progress toward desired goals (Amason, 1996). Such conflict is typically negative, personalized, emotionally driven, and competitive (Lumsden & Lumsden, 2000; Pace, 1990).

Commitment is a psychological bond with one or more organizational, interpersonal, or behavioral targets (foci) (Becker, 1992; Klein, Becker, & Meyer, 2009; Reichers, 1985). Commitment also has a number of possible bases or motives, including positive affect or emotion, perceived obligation, and a lack of available alternatives (Allen & Meyer, 1990; Meyer, Stanley, Herscovitch, & Topolnytsky, 2002). In the next section, I discuss

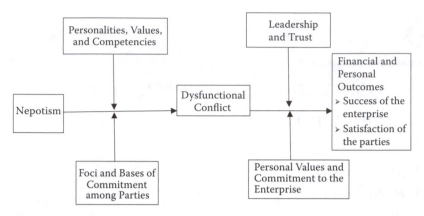

FIGURE 6.1
Model of nepotism, commitment, and conflict.

specific ways in which multiple foci and bases of commitment may generate conflicts among parties, including founders, potential successors, family members, and employees. Next, I address potential solutions to these conflicts, including an analysis of the role of rational self-interest. I conclude with a discussion of research directions and practical implications.

Figure 6.1 presents a model of nepotism, commitment, and conflict that I will use to organize the chapter. The model contains two fundamental propositions. First, the effects of nepotism on dysfunctional conflict depend upon the characteristics of the parties involved and on the mix and patterns of commitments exhibited by the parties. Second, the effects of conflict on financial and personal outcomes depend upon certain aspects of the parties' individual attributes (personal values and commitment to the enterprise) and interpersonal relationships (leadership and trust). The implications of these propositions are the focus of much of what follows. In addition, I will use the model and related discussion to provide sample propositions, that is, a limited set of predictions that may not be fully developed but serve the purpose of illustrating implications of the model and suggesting potential research directions.

NEPOTISM AND DYSFUNCTIONAL CONFLICT

Parties' Personalities and Values

There are many reasons why nepotism may or may not lead to conflict. Among these are the personalities and values of the relevant parties. With respect to personality, for instance, given the same circumstances a conscientious family member who is appointed company president by a parent is probably less likely to provoke employees' resentment than is a less dependable, hardworking relative. As another example, compared to a mistrusting, neurotic relative, one high in agreeableness and emotional stability may feel less alienated and upset with the founder's decision to elevate someone besides him- or herself.

With respect to values, Jones et al. (2008) suggest that shared values among family members may sometimes lead to benefits such as greater interpersonal support and human capital advantages from early interest in the enterprise. This is a plausible argument, but its truth likely depends upon the particular values held by relevant parties. The literatures on procedural and distributive justice suggest that some employees are more sensitive to issues of fairness than are others (Van Offen & De Cremer, 2007; Vermunt, Van Knippenberg, Van Knippenberg, & Blaauw, 2001). Those who particularly value justice may be more likely to become angered when they perceive that employee advancement is based more on shared genes than on merit. In addition, those who highly value honesty can be expected to be most dissatisfied with dishonesty (Locke & Woiceshyn, 1995), including a founder's disingenuous explanations for nepotism. More broadly, relevant parties with high integrity will react most negatively to apparently underhanded tactics in others (Becker, 1998, 2005).

In addition to effects related to the particular values held by one or more parties, dysfunctional conflict is a probable outcome of nepotism if parties have incongruous values. For instance, many successful founders have a profound appreciation of ability in others, including in their employees (Locke, 2000). If a spouse of such a founder believes that an eldest son of dubious competence is entitled to be the company heir, then a heated and perhaps irresolvable clash between the founder and his or her spouse may be unavoidable. Similarly, if employees are loyal to a talented and benevolent manager, they may become indignant if the founder decides to allow a relative to run the firm.

In both of these cases there is a potential clash between the value of merit on one hand and kinship on the other. It is important to note, however, that an interaction between merit and nepotism is likely. When merit of the beneficiary is low, nepotism (versus no nepotism) may lead to increased negative reactions due to the kinds of concerns with competence and fairness raised earlier. However, when merit is high, reactions may be unaffected because concerns with competence and fairness are reduced. Depending on whose reactions are being measured, the high-merit, high-nepotism condition could even lead to favorable reactions (e.g., both parents are happy, the mean satisfaction of employees with the succession is higher).

Proposition 1: Nepotism is more likely to lead to dysfunctional conflict when the relative in question is low in agreeableness, conscientiousness, emotional stability, or some combination of the three.

Proposition 2: The more that nonbeneficiary parties value fairness and integrity, the more likely that nepotism will to lead to dysfunctional conflict involving these parties.

Proposition 3: The lower the competence of the beneficiary, the greater the dysfunctional conflict among nonbeneficiaries, especially when the beneficiary has the traits identified in Proposition 1, the nonbeneficiaries have the values specified in Proposition 2, or both.

In sum, I suggest that, in terms of relative parties' reactions to nepotism, there is interplay among personalities, values, and competencies. Dysfunctional conflict can and does occur, but different kinds of people respond differently to nepotistic practices. This is a complex process and is about to become more complicated by the consideration of commitment.

Foci and Bases of Commitment

There is ample evidence that people become attached to others due to value congruence or shared values (Becker, 1992; O'Reilly & Chatman, 1986; Vandenberghe, 2009). As illustrated earlier, it would not be surprising to find that value incongruence associated with divergent commitments generates conflict. There are other likely sources of commitment-related conflict as well. As Allen and Meyer (1990) first demonstrated, there are at least three mindsets that accompany commitment. The first, commonly referred to as affective commitment, involves a positive emotional attachment to a specified individual, group, or organization. Individuals high in affective commitment maintain a relationship with the target because they want to. With normative commitment, people feel obligated to maintain the relationship because they believe they ought to. Continuance commitment involves an awareness of the costs associated with leaving the target and, possibly, an inopportunity to dissolve the relationship. People high in continuance commitment maintain a relationship with a target out of perceived necessity.

The implications of the different mindsets are illustrated in Figure 6.2. These illustrations are for exposition purposes only and are not meant to serve as formal hypotheses or a complete set of commitment-conflict types. The figure addresses one general kind of conflict, that between a founder and a relative who will become the successor. The cells in the figure are predicated on the conditions under which the founder has offered succession and which the relative has accepted or intends to accept. One might normally think that this would be a conflict-free situation, but this is not

Relevant Party/Basis of Commitment	Founder/AC	Founder/NC	Founder/CC
Successor/AC	1 No conflict	2 Founder resentment	3 Founder enmeshment
Successor/NC	4 Successor resentment	5 Mutual resentment	6 Founder enmeshment, Successor resentment
Successor/CC	7 Successor incompetence	8 Founder resentment, Successor incompetence	9 Founder enmeshment, Successor incompetence

FIGURE 6.2
Examples of conflicting interpersonal commitments: founder and relative.

necessarily the case. True, where the founder makes the offer out of a positive emotional attachment to the relative and the relative has responded in kind (Cell 1), commitment between these parties is likely to be high and conflict low. However, the other cells identify potential types of conflict linked to different patterns of commitment within the dyad, as follows.

In Cell 2, the founder is normatively committed to the relative and the relative is affectively committed to the founder. In this instance, the founder gives the relative the job out of obligation, as in the cases of ethnic traditions or familial habits; for example, "My father gave me my first start and I should do the same for my child." Normative commitment can be positive and, indeed, when the target is "the organization," it usually leads to desirable outcomes (Meyer et al., 2002). In the interpersonal realm, however, obligation can breed resentment when it involves feeling pressured to do something one does not want to do or making a decision that one does not think best (Berg, Janoff-Bulman, & Cotter, 2001; Berkowitz & Connor, 1966). Thus, even though the relative earnestly accepts the position, resentment on the part of the founder may be expected. The situation may be worse in Cell 5, where both founder and relative feel obligated to each other and make their decision to offer and accept the position on this basis. Again, obligation in and of itself need not create friction, but when it involves doing what one does not want to do it normally will. Worse still is the situation in Cell 8. As before, the founder offers the job out of felt obligation to the relative. In this case, though, the relative accepts not out of desire or obligation but, rather, because the relative has no other options. Why might a relative of working age not have any other choice but to rely on nepotism for a job? There are a number of possible reasons, including inexperience, geographic location, or disability. However, many companies hire inexperienced young people, individuals often change locations, and many disabilities do not prohibit one from doing a variety of jobs. There is one condition, though, that almost always restricts one's choices: incompetence. For the sake of illustration, then, let's assume that the relative has to work for the founder's company because nobody else will hire him or her. This would mean a resentful founder hiring an incompetent relative—a recipe for conflict.

In Cell 3, the founder has a high level of continuance commitment to the relative, meaning that he or she sees no other choice but to hire the relative as a successor. This could be because no one else is available for or wants the job. Or, perhaps more common in today's world, continuance commitment could be due to "sunk costs," that is, the founder feels that so much time, effort, and money has been poured into the relative's potential development (paying for a son's or daughter's MBA, for example) that he or she perceives no other option except to have the relative lead the company. This creates a condition that I'm calling founder enmeshment: the entanglement of the founder in a circumstance of his or her own device. For instance, turning the company over to someone with a prestigious degree but little business acumen may be disastrous, regardless of how much time, effort, and money was expended on education. Yet the founder may find him- or herself knee-deep in the big muddy because such sunk costs make it difficult to justify to one's self or others a change of course—in this case a change of choice of successors (cf. Staw, 1976).

The remaining cells—4, 6, 7, and 9—are variations of those just described. Rather than discussing each cell, perhaps it is enough to reiterate that except in the case of affective commitment on the part of both founder and relative, there is a fair chance of dysfunctional conflict whenever a founder offers a relative a top management job. As implied by Proposition 3, there is one critical exception to this: when the relative truly is the most capable person for the position. Perhaps the relative took an early interest in the company and learned the ropes from the ground up, working in many jobs so as to thoroughly understand the organization. Perhaps the relative is proud enough to earn the right to the job by outworking and outlearning everyone else. In such an instance, the likelihood of conflict should be drastically less. A rational founder would not resent appointing such a relative successor nor would enmeshment be an issue when there is no reason to regret having the relative in the job. Incompetence becomes a nonissue and, assuming that the relative wants the job, resentment on his or her part would not be a problem. In this situation, due to existing personal ties, the commitments of the founder and relative to each other and to the organization may be higher than if a nonrelative were hired. It is possible that some employees or family members may experience conflict due to personal antagonisms, but widespread ill-will toward an outstanding, qualified leader is unlikely—even if he or she happens to share DNA with the founder. Thus, grooming potential familial successors to replace the founder is one way to obviate conflict, and there is a variety of literature addressing how grooming can be accomplished (for example, Oddou & Mendenhall, 1991; Zhang & Rajagopalan, 2006). The next section addresses in greater depth the topic of resolving nepotism conflicts.

Proposition 4: Dysfunctional conflict is more likely when two or more relevant parties are committed to different foci on the basis of incongruent values.

Proposition 5: When two relevant parties are affectively committed to each other the likelihood of dysfunctional commitment is lower than when other mindsets (shared or unshared) underlie commitment.

RESOLVING NEPOTISM CONFLICTS: RATIONAL SELF-INTEREST AND THE GOOD OF THE ENTERPRISE

One might legitimately argue that a founder has a legal and ethical right to hire or refuse to hire relatives as he or she sees fit. After all, the business belongs to the founder and, hence, is the founder's property. Within certain bounds, people may dispose of their property as they wish. Thus, other people (in this case family members, potential successors, and employees) generally do not have the right to the founder's business unless the founder relinquishes it to them. However, just because something is a right does not make it the right thing to do: one may have the right to burn all of his or her belongings but this act can be demonstrably wrong-headed from a variety of perspectives, not the least of which is enlightened self-interest.

Rational Self-Interest, Relevant Parties, and Nepotism

Lurking behind discussions of nepotism is the fundamental question: Is it ethical? To answer this question, one must have a tenable theory of ethics, and mine is Objectivism (Becker, 1998; Peikoff, 1991; Rand, 1964). Objectivist ethics are built on the central principle that, in order to live successfully, people require a code of values to guide their decisions and behavior. In particular, values that support one's life and well-being are ethical and those that do not are not. Hence, rational egoism simply means that the purpose of a moral code is to further, enhance, and protect one's life and, therefore, an individual should be the beneficiary of his or her moral code. From an Objectivist viewpoint, rationality is the greatest virtue because reason is our primary tool of life. That is, we don't have the biggest teeth or the sharpest claws, so we must use our minds to survive and thrive.

Self-interest, in this view, does not mean violating the rights of others or a lack of concern for other people. To the contrary, acting in concert with other ethical individuals, as in the exchange of values, is in the long-run best interests of a person. Note also that, unlike some theories of decision making and behavioral economics, Objectivism does not stipulate that to be rational one must be omnipotent or concerned only with material values. Human beings seldom have all the information relevant to a decision, and most rational people seek not only material values but psychological ones (e.g., a sense of achievement, joy in work, love of family and friends). Rather, Objectivism simply requires that a person assiduously applies reason when making choices. Other virtues such as benevolence, courage, honesty, fairness, independent thought, and productivity are corollaries of rationality because they are generally supportive of one's well-being. There are exceptions, of course, but discussion of these is beyond the scope of the chapter. For a more in-depth explication of Objectivist ethics, see Becker (1998, 2005), Locke and Becker (1998), Peikoff (1991), Kelley (1996), and Binswanger (1991).

Ultimately, then, the question of to what extent nepotism is good or bad boils down to the degree to which a given decision regarding a relative is rational or irrational. An example of a rational decision is hiring a relative because he or she is the most qualified, most trustworthy person for the position. Another, less commonly acknowledged reason would be that the founder does not wish to lose investments he or she has made in the enterprise. That is, if turning the company over to a nonfamily member means a monetary loss or forfeit of a psychological value (e.g., self-esteem or identity), nepotism in-and-of itself would not be irrational or unethical. Rather, the sum total of considerations pertinent to the decision must be weighed. Examples of applicable considerations favoring a nonfamily CEO include the need for advanced managerial skills (if no family members possess these), low cash flow, and compliance with equal opportunity guidelines; considerations favoring a family member CEO are prevention of external expropriation, potentially lower monitoring costs, and greater awareness of company culture (Hayajenh, Maghrabi, & Al-Dabbagh, 1994; Kaydo, 1998; Lin & Hu, 2007). Even a cursory analysis of such variables demonstrates the difficulty, if not impossibility, of drawing broad conclusions about the overall effectiveness or ethics of nepotism. In other words, when it comes to whether nepotism will lead to conflict (discussed in prior sections) or other possibly negative outcomes, a number of personal and situational moderators likely exist.

> Proposition 6: Nepotism is likely to decrease success of the enterprise and satisfaction of the parties when nepotistic decisions are made irrationally or in perceived violation of other ethical values such as honesty and fairness.
>
> Proposition 7: Nepotism is likely to decrease success of the enterprise and satisfaction of the parties when there is a need for advanced managerial skills not held by family members, little threat of external expropriation, and few monitoring costs associated with non-family professional hires.

Ethical values are also important with respect to directly resolving conflict. People are likely to develop trust with individuals of high versus low integrity (Ferrin, Kim, Cooper, & Dirks, 2007; Mayer, Davis, & Schoorman, 1995), primarily because high-integrity individuals are more honest, benevolent, and willing to use reason to solve problems and overcome disagreements (Becker, 2005). For example, assume that a retiring founder has made a rational decision, along the lines described earlier, to turn over the firm to his or her most qualified relative. Employees and other possible successors and family members might initially experience conflict due to a lack of understanding or misinterpretation of the founder's decision. However, if the founder is generally respected and trusted, the conflict need not be crippling or long term. Ideally the founder explained his or her rationale prior to the decision but, if not, an honest, thoughtful explanation may not be too late.

Even if some employees do not agree with the decision, they may accept it if they can see it was made for good reason and with some concern for their mutual interests. A key point, though, is that the founder's decision and explanation must actually be rational, honest, and so on. If instead it is a form of rationalization or impression management, the persuasion attempt is unlikely to succeed, at least in the long-run. As recent Ponzi schemes and other scams have demonstrated, even brilliant people cannot fool all the people all the time, and once a lack of integrity is detected, the results can be disastrous for all concerned. If nepotism is to succeed long-term in a given firm, the founder must not lie about or try to hide its existence. Similarly, the integrity of the successor and the nature of his or her pronouncements—and those of other relevant parties—can be expected to interact with conflict in determining the success of the firm and the satisfaction of the parties. Thus:

> Proposition 8: Integrity-relevant values, including rationality, benevolence, courage, honesty, independent thought, fairness, and productivity mitigate the effect of conflict on success of the enterprise and satisfaction of the parties. The greater the degree to which these values are held by relevant parties, especially the founder or key decision makers, the less likely that conflict will hurt the firm or irrevocably decrease satisfaction.

Commitment to the Enterprise as Mutual Self-Interest

Although integrity and related ethical values can be expected to ameliorate dysfunctional conflict, disagreements or quarrels about nepotism may still occur. Rational people, for instance, can disagree due to differences in information, divergent observations, or cognitive errors. Fortunately, there is another resolution to nepotistic conflict that may overcome these kinds of limitations: commitment to the enterprise.

Relevant parties who share a high level of commitment to the enterprise are likely to have less conflict and when conflict occurs, are less likely to allow it to damage the enterprise. This shared commitment is potentially profound because it reflects the pursuit of mutual self-interest and, hence, a genuinely collaborative effort. While mutual self-interest may at first sound different from rational self-interest, in a business setting the two are typically synonymous. Business involves numerous forms of trade—products for payment, work for wages, social exchanges among workers—and trade means helping one's self by helping others. Therefore, parties who share commitment to the enterprise are inclined to act in ways that benefit the firm and, thus, themselves. Avoiding dysfunctional conflict and effectively addressing it when it occurs are concrete cases of this process.

How can commitment to the enterprise be encouraged? The literature on organizational commitment provides many examples, including hiring people with certain characteristics, providing a positive workgroup climate, using effective human resource management procedures, and designing jobs to enhance motivation (Mathieu & Zajac, 1990). The integrity of the founder and the rest of management are also important because commitment to managers can rub off on the organization. Eisenberger and his colleagues have explained this phenomenon by reference to a concept they call supervisor–organization embodiment (SOE) (Eisenberger et al., 2010). SOE is the extent to which employees identify their supervisor with the organization, that is, the degree to which the supervisor represents the organization. When SOE is low, the supervisor is perceived as thinking and acting individually, largely apart from his or her role as an organizational agent. On the other hand, when SOE is high, employees see their supervisor as more of an agent, making decisions and taking action on behalf of the organization. One implication of this is that when SOE is high, commitment to the supervisor translates to commitment to the organization: the higher the commitment to the supervisor, the higher the commitment to the organization.

Applied to the context of nepotism, higher SOE (or FOE if the target is the founder) would mean more shared commitment to the enterprise, a greater sense of mutual self-interest and, hence, less fallout from dysfunctional conflict. This is especially true if the founder or other managers in fact embody the organization and foster commitment to themselves via competent leadership and trustworthy conduct. Part of effective leadership is reminding employees that "we're all in this together" and that conflict can be resolved via win–win solutions (Hauser & House, 2004). Certainly, nepotistic conflicts may still occur, but their effects are likely to be less severe when most employees trust key decision makers, feel strongly attached to the enterprise, and understand how their welfare is linked to the success of the enterprise. Any conflict that exists or remains may be seen as a storm to be weathered rather than a sinking ship from which to escape.

> Proposition 9: Mutual commitment to the enterprise moderates the effect of dysfunctional conflict on financial and personal outcomes such that as mutual commitment increases, the effects of conflict are less personal and severe.
>
> Proposition 10: The effects of dysfunctional conflict are further reduced when the founder embodies the organization, particularly when the founder is perceived as an effective, trustworthy leader.

GENERAL DISCUSSION

It seems that many people, including human resource managers, generally believe that nepotism is unethical and that it has negative effects on employees and business (Hayajenh et al., 1994; Prendergast & Taper, 1996). Nepotism can and perhaps often does have these characteristics, but I have argued that this need not always be the case. Rather, under some circumstances—as when the beneficiary relative is conscientious and agreeable, when important values are shared, and when commitments are compatible—conflict should not be an issue. Further, when dysfunctional conflict does occur, there are some situations—as when relevant parties have a high level of integrity, when the parties are highly committed to the enterprise, and the founder is a competent, trustworthy leader—where it may not severely damage the satisfaction of the parties or the success of the enterprise. Under these circumstances, the conflict may be functional, as in the case of an earnest debate about who should be the successor and why.

These notions are largely untested but deserve empirical investigation. To illustrate how the model in Figure 6.1 could be used to create concrete, testable hypotheses, I have offered several sample propositions throughout the chapter. With some effort, I suspect these could be developed into grounded, theoretically sound hypotheses worthy of research. Clever researchers could also build upon the model by identifying additional moderators, mediators, and dependent variables. For example, group cohesiveness could lead employees to respond more negatively or positively to nepotism depending on the group norm for commitment to the founder. That is, nepotism's effect on conflict may be moderated by group dynamics such as cohesiveness and norms. As another example, the effect of conflict on the success of the enterprise is almost certainly moderated by organizational variables (e.g., strategy) and environmental factors (e.g., number and nature of competitors). In terms of mediation, the effects of conflict, leadership, and commitment to the enterprise are probably mediated by more proximal motivational variables (e.g., employees' affect, cognitions, and goals). Finally, in addition to success of the enterprise and satisfaction of the parties, other potentially relevant outcomes include individual and unit-level performance (in-role and extra-role), withdrawal behaviors such as absenteeism and turnover and, perhaps most interesting, deviant behaviors (cf. Becker & Bennett, 2007).

One general implication of the model is that there are times when nepotism will lead to intractable, dysfunctional conflict. This could be because the personalities and values of relevant parties promote conflict, or differences in commitment profiles among the parties are antagonistic. In such cases, organizational change would be called for, as in replacing certain employees, attempting to alter people's foci or bases of commitment, or dissolving nepotistic practices. In a presumably less plausible scenario, there could be companies moving toward nepotism, perhaps seeking the human capital rewards discussed by Jones et al. (2008). Whether approaching or retreating from nepotism, the usual change models may prove helpful.

Selecting people who accept change, promoting education and communication, allowing some level of participation, and executing change fairly may help to counter resistance (Fedor, Caldwell, & Herold, 2006; Fiss & Zajac, 2006; Kotter & Schlesinger, 1979). Kotter's (1996) implementation steps also seem relevant and would involve actions such as creating a compelling reason for why nepotism is or is not needed, creating a corresponding vision, and reinforcing changes by demonstrating the links between the change and organizational success. Given the identity conflicts that may accompany nepotism (e.g., successor as child, heir, and boss), change models that address such conflicts may be particularly relevant (see Fiol, Pratt, & O'Connor, 2009). Beginning or ending nepotism is likely to be an emotionally charged, controversial event, so adhering to common organizational development values like respecting people, promoting trust and support, and deemphasizing hierarchical authority may be especially important. If internal politics and personalities do not support these kinds of change models and values, then an outside change agent may be needed.

In conclusion, nepotism may not be as bad as it is generally perceived, at least in the United States. On the other hand, there is ample room for serious conflict and related problems that can threaten the success of the enterprise and quality of life of the relevant parties. I have asserted that whether dysfunctional conflict occurs depends on characteristics and commitments of relevant parties and that, if dysfunctional conflict occurs, its effects depend on aspects of leadership, personal values of the parties, and commitment to the enterprise. Empirically studying these kinds of moderators, and nepotistic conflicts more generally, would deepen the understanding of nepotism in ways that personal opinion and even reasoned theorizing cannot.

REFERENCES

Allen, N. J., & Meyer, J. P. (1990). The measurement and antecedents of affective, continuance, and normative commitment to the organization. *Journal of Occupational Psychology, 63,* 1–18.

Amason, A. C. (1996). Distinguishing the effects of functional and dysfunctional conflict on strategic decision making: Resolving a paradox for top management teams, *Academy of Management Journal, 39,* 123–148.

Becker, T. E. (1992). Foci and bases of commitment: Are they distinctions worth making? *Academy of Management Journal, 35,* 232–244.

Becker, T. E. (1998). Integrity in organizations: Beyond honesty and conscientiousness. *Academy of Management Review, 23,* 154–161.

Becker, T. E. (2005). Development and validation of a situational judgment test of employee integrity. *International Journal of Selection and Assessment, 13,* 225–232.

Becker, T. E., & Bennett, R. (2007). Employee attachment and deviance in organizations. In J. Langan-Fox, C. Cooper, & R. Klimoski (Eds.), *Research companion to the dysfunctional workplace: Management challenges and symptoms* (pp. 136–151). Northampton, MA: Elgar.

Bellow, A. (2003). *In praise of nepotism.* New York: Doubleday.

Berg, M. B., Janoff-Bulman, R., & Cotter, J. (2001). Perceiving value in obligations and goals: Wanting to do what should be done. *Personality and Social Psychology Bulletin, 27,* 982–995.

Berkowitz, L., & Connor, W. H. (1966). Success, failure, and social responsibility. *Journal of Personality and Social Psychology, 4,* 664–669.

Binswanger, H. (1991). Volition as cognitive self-regulation. *Organizational Behavior and Human Decision Processes, 50,* 154–178.

Eisenberger, R., Karagonlar, G., Stinglhamber, F., Neves, P., Becker, T. E., Gonzalez-Morales, M. G., & Steiger-Mueller, M. (2010). Leader–member exchange and affective organizational commitment: The contribution of supervisor's organizational embodiment. *Journal of Applied Psychology, 95,* 1085–1103.

Fedor, D. B., Caldwell, S., & Herold, D. M. (2006). The effects of organizational change on employee commitment: A multilevel investigation. *Personnel Psychology, 59,* 1–29.

Ferrin, D. L., Kim, P. H., Cooper, C. D., & Kirks, K. T. (2007). Silence speaks volumes: The effectiveness of reticence in comparison to apology and denial for responding to integrity- and competence-based trust violations. *Journal of Applied Psychology, 92,* 483–908.

Fiol, C. M., Pratt, M. G., & O'Connor, E. J. (2009). Managing intractable identify conflicts. *Academy of Management Review, 34,* 32–56.

Fiss, P. C., & Zajac, E. J. (2006). The symbolic management of strategic change: Sensegiving via framing and decoupling. *Academy of Management Journal, 49,* 1173–1193.

Hauser, M., & House, R. J. (2004). Lead through vision and values. In E. A. Locke (Ed.), *Handbook of principles of organizational behavior* (pp. 257–273). Malden, MA: Blackwell.

Hayajenh, A. F., Maghrabi, A. S., & Al-Dabbagh, T. H. (1994). Assessing the effect of nepotism on human resource managers. *International Journal of Manpower, 16,* 60–67.

Jones, R. G., Stout, T., Harder, B., Levine, E., Levine, J., & Sanchez, J. I. (2008). Personnel psychology and nepotism: Should we support anti-nepotism policies? *The Industrial-Organizational Psychologist, 45*(3), 17–20.

Kaydo, C. (1998). Does nepotism work? *Sales and Marketing Management, 150,* 16.

Kelley, D. (1996). *Unrugged individualism: The selfish basis of benevolence.* Poughkeepsie, NY: Institute for Objectivist Studies.

Klein, H. J., Becker, T. E., & Meyer, J. P. (Eds.). (2009). *Commitment in organizations: Accumulated wisdom and new directions.* New York: Routledge.

Kotter, J. P. (1996). *Leading change.* Cambridge, MA: Harvard Business School Press.

Kotter, J. P., & Schlesinger, L. A. (1979). Choosing strategies for change. *Harvard Business Review, 57*(2), 106–114.

Lin, S. H., & Hu, S. Y. (2007). A family member or professional management? The choice of a CEO and its impact on performance. *Corporate Governance–An International Review, 15,* 1348–1362.

Locke, E. A. (2000). *The prime movers: Traits of the great wealth creators.* New York: American Management Association.

Locke, E. A., & Becker, T. E. (1998). Rebuttal to a subjectivist critique of an Objectivist approach to integrity in organizations. *Academy of Management Review, 23,* 170–175.

Locke, E. A., & Woiceshyn, J. (1995). Why businessmen should be honest: The argument from rational egoism. *Journal of Organizational Behavior, 16,* 405–414.

Lumsden, G., & Lumsden, D. (2000). *Communicating in groups and teams* (3rd ed.). Belmont, CA: Wadsworth.

Mathieu, J. E., & Zajac, D. M. (1990). A review and meta-analysis of the antecedents, correlates, and consequences of organizational commitment. *Psychological Bulletin, 108,* 171–194.

Mayer, R. C., Davis, J. H., & Schoorman, F. D. (1995). An interactional model of organizational trust. *Academy of Management Review, 20,* 709–734.

Meyer, J. P., Stanley, D. J., Herscovitch, L., & Topolnytsky, L. (2002). Affective, continuance, and normative commitment to the organization: A meta-analysis of antecedents, correlates, and consequences. *Journal of Vocational Behavior, 61,* 20–52.

Nepotism. (2001a). In E. J. Jewell & F. Abate (Eds.), *The new Oxford American dictionary.* New York: Oxford University Press.

Nepotism. (2001b). In F. C. Mish (Ed.), *Webster's dictionary* (10th ed.). Springfield, MA: Merriam-Webster.

Oddou, G. R., & Mendenhall, M. E. (1991). Succession planning for the 21st century: How well are we grooming our future business leaders? *Business Horizons, 34,* 26–34.

O'Reilly, C., & Chatman, J. (1986). Organizational commitment and psychological attachment: The effects of compliance, identification, and internalization on prosocial behavior. *Journal of Applied Psychology, 71,* 492–499.

Pace, R. C. (1990). Personalized and depersonalized conflict in small group discussions: An examination of differentiation. *Small Group Research, 21,* 79–96.

Peikoff, L. (1991). *Objectivism: The philosophy of Ayn Rand.* New York: Meridian.

Prendergast, C., & Taper, R. H. (1996). Favoritism in organizations. *Journal of Political Economy, 104,* 958–978.

Rand, A. (1964). *The virtue of selfishness: A new concept of egoism.* New York: New American Library.

Reichers, A. E. (1985). A review and reconceptualization of organizational commitment. *Academy of Management Review, 10,* 465–476.

Staw, B. (1976). Knee-deep in the big muddy: A study of escalating commitment to a chosen course of action. *Organizational Behavior and Human Performance, 16,* 27–44.

Van Offen, W., & De Cremer, D. (2007). Who cares about organizational justice? How personality moderates the effects of perceived fairness on organizational attachment. *European Journal of Work and Organizational Psychology, 16,* 386–406.

Vandenberghe, C. (2009). Organizational commitments. In H. J. Klein, T. E. Becker, & J. P. Meyer (Eds.), *Commitment in organizations: Accumulated wisdom and new directions* (pp. 99–135). New York: Routledge.

Vermunt, R., Van Knippenberg, D., Van Knippenberg, B., & Blaauw, E. (2001). Self-esteem and outcome fairness: Differential importance of procedural and outcome considerations. *Journal of Applied Psychology, 86,* 621–628.

Zhang, Y., & Rajagopalan, N. (2006). Grooming for the top post and ending the CEO succession crisis. *Organizational Dynamics, 35,* 96–105.

7

Nepotism Practices and the Work–Family Interface

Aline Masuda
EADA Business School

Michelle Visio
Missouri State University

When Mark Funkhouser was elected mayor of Kansas City, Missouri, his wife, Gloria Squitiro, who was also his former campaign manager, began working in a small desk next to his office as his personal assistant. Although Squitiro was working for free, her role of personal assistant to the mayor was not well received by the city hall employees. As a consequence, a "volunteer ordinance" was adopted banning relatives from working in the city hall on a regular basis. Nonetheless, this ordinance did not prevent Funkhouser from taking advantage of his wife's services. Because she was no longer allowed to enter the city hall, the mayor moved his weekly meetings with his top advisors to the library so that his wife could attend.

Although Funkhouser's behavior may resemble a type of nepotism, it could rather be viewed as a typical example of an employee's attempt to integrate work and family domains. As a result of societal changes, such as the increase in dual-career couples, and more women and older workers entering the workplace (Bond, Thompson, Galinsky, & Prottas, 2002), it is becoming more difficult for employees to conciliate work and family responsibilities. Hence, employees today are, more than ever, experiencing the burden of work–family conflict.

According to Greenhaus and Beutell (1985), work–family conflict (WFC) is defined as forms of interrole conflict in which role pressures from the work and family domains are mutually incompatible. Work–family conflict has negative consequences to employees and their organizations. For example, work–family conflict is related to lower job satisfaction, higher turnover intentions, more psychological strain, depression, and burn-out (Allen, Herst, Bruck, & Sutton, 2000; Byron, 2005; Ford, Heinen, & Langkamer, 2007; Kossek & Ozeki, 1998).

Given the increasing desire to reduce work–family conflict in organizations, scholars have begun to question the value of anti-nepotism policies for companies in the long run (Howard, 2008; Slack, 2001; Werbel & Hames, 1996). For example, Werbel and Hames (1996) argued that forbidding dual-career couples from working in the same organization prevents them from achieving greater personal and career coordination that might ease work–family conflict.

Additionally, although nepotism is often judged negatively in America, it is a cultural norm in other countries. As a result of globalization and business expansions across borders, anti-nepotism policies may be difficult to implement in countries where the culture does not support such practices, such as Asian countries where the boundary between work and family is blurred, and where "backdoor recruitment" strategies are preferred over recruiting based on job criteria (Yang, 2010). It may also be difficult to implement in countries where family-owned businesses play an important role in the economy. For example, according to the Instituto de la Empresa Familiar (Institute for Family Business) (2005) there are approximately 1.5 million family-owned businesses in Spain that employ approximately 9 million people. In the European Union, there are 17 million family-owned businesses that employ approximately 100 million people. Thus, implementing nepotism practices in some cultures may not make sense. This is consistent with claims that the successful implementation of managerial practices depends on the fit between cultural norms inherent in these practices and employee values (Kirkman & Shapiro, 1997).

In this chapter, we review the consequences of nepotism practices with regard to work–family conciliation. We frame our review based on work–family border theory (Clark, 2000) which describes the management of work and family roles as a continuum ranging from segmentation to integration. We structure the chapter by first describing work–family border theory and the role of nepotism practices in employees' ability to either integrate or segment both work and family domains. Second, we describe the positive and negative consequences of practices that allow integrating or segmenting of both work and family domains. Third, we report possible moderators between nepotism practices and the work–family interface, such as national culture, organization work–family culture, and personality variables. Last, we provide future direction to develop research on work–family conflict and nepotism practices.

WORK–FAMILY BOUNDARY THEORY AND NEPOTISM

After the Industrial Revolution, work and family activities became more segmented, since they were typically carried out "in different places, at different times, with different sets of people, and with different norms of behavior and expressed emotions" (Clark, 2001, p. 748). Since then, several theories have been postulated explaining relationships between the work and family domains, and describing their positive and negative consequences. Researchers taking a scarcity perspective to study work–family interface assume that resources, such as time and energy, are limited. As such, they argue that involvement in multiple roles leads to interrole conflict (Greenhaus & Beutell, 1985). Greenhaus and Beutell (1985) define different types of conflicts: (a) strain-based conflict, which happens when stress experienced in one domain spills over into the other domain; (b) time-based conflict, which occurs when time spent at work limits the use of time in the other domain; and (c) behavior-based conflict, which describes how behaviors from one domain can be used and enacted in the other domain. These types of conflict are bidirectional in nature (Greenhaus & Beutell, 1985). Specifically, work influences family roles and vice versa (Frone, 2003).

Recently, researchers have taken a more expansive approach to study work–family interface, acknowledging that energy is expandable and that participation in multiple roles can have several benefits to employees (Greenhaus & Powell, 2006; Grzywacz & Butler, 2005). According to Greenhaus and Powell (2006), individuals can experience work–family enrichment (WFE), which is defined as "the extent to which experiences in one role improve the quality of life in the other role" (p. 73). Like work–family conflict, work–family enrichment is viewed as bidirectional in nature. That is, work can provide positive elements to family and vice versa. Research has shown that work–family enrichment and work–family conflict are independent constructs that could be experienced concurrently (Frone, 2003).

Clark's work–family border theory can be used to explain both work–family conflict and enrichment. Work–family border theory draws from Nippert-Eng's (1996) work to describe how individuals manage the boundaries between work and family roles to achieve better work–family balance. According to Nippert-Eng, individuals enact boundary management strategies in a continuum ranging from segmentation to integration. A person who fully integrates both domains tends to blend work and family activities, blurring the distinction between work and family roles. A person who is more likely to segment both work and family domains tends to keep elements of work domain separate from elements of family domain.

Clark (2000) uses the concept of borders to explain the different strategies that individuals take to manage work and family domains. Individuals can use physical borders (i.e., rules about how to manage *space* used for activities linked to both domains), temporal borders (i.e., rules on how to manage *time* between two domains), and psychological borders (i.e., rules that determine how to manage *emotions and thinking*) to either integrate or segment these roles. Clark further explains that these borders can either be high in permeability, which is the extent to which these borders are weaker, allowing elements of one domain to spill over to others (e.g., friends from work participate in your leisure and family activities), and flexibility, which is the extent to which these borders will either expand or contract (e.g., you work at home).

If we take the earlier example, Funkhouser's physical, temporal, and psychology borders can be characterized as permeable, because he allowed one element of his family life (e.g., his wife) to enter into his work domain. One could also characterize his borders as flexible if he has the freedom to choose the time, location, and when he discusses work. For example, scheduling a meeting at the library shows flexibility.

Managing the Work–Family Interface With Nepotism

Because nepotism involves family members working in the same organization, it may allow more border permeability and flexibility between work and family domains. This may have consequences for the way individuals manage the work–family interface. People can experience negative or positive consequences from their strategies for participating in work and family roles. Let us take the example of the dual-career relocation dilemma. Imagine a dual-career couple who worked in different companies. Their lives may be more segmented, such that the spouses work in different locations, develop different friendships, have different bosses, and avoid talking about work when they are at home. In this case, a segmented approach is taken to managing both work and family domains. This approach may be effective for preventing work–family conflict, such that employees may avoid the spillover of negative emotions from one domain to another. However, it may be ineffective if the employee wants to achieve synergies between work and family domains. (We will discuss the consequences of strategies to both work–family conflict and work–family enrichment later.)

Then, the wife receives a compelling job offer, which requires moving to a different country. Consequently, her spouse has to quit work to follow her to another country. This situation poses several challenges to the organization and the employee. First, the organization may lose the opportunity to hire the best qualified employee for the position if it does not provide assistance to the employee's spouse. This may occur because an employee's willingness to relocate is related to the spouse's employment-related issues (Eby & Russell, 2000; Kirschenbaum, 1991). Second, the employee may decide to take the job and the spouse may choose to follow, even if the company does not provide any help. In this case, the employee may suffer from stress and concerns regarding her spouse's professional future. Given the evidence showing that spouse employment-related issues are important predictors of employee and spouse relocation adjustment (Lawson & Angle, 1994; Pellico & Stroh, 1997), this stress could cause potential conflict between husband and wife, which could be carried into the workplace. Third, the company may choose to provide assistance by providing resources to the spouse of the employee so he can find a job in the country (Eby et al., 2002). This benefit may lessen the probability of work–family conflict. Last, if the employee is qualified and works in a similar industry to the spouse, the company may consider offering a position to the employee's spouse. This way, the company does not lose its best qualified employee, and the employee will not sacrifice family well-being.

By offering a job to the spouse, the company will also influence the way this employee manages her work and family border (e.g., she and the spouse will now share colleagues, the company, and perhaps bosses). This strategy may help this employee to reduce work–family conflict by giving her flexibility that will enable her to fulfill both work and family responsibilities. For example, by sharing more time with her spouse, she might experience less time-based work–family conflict.

The aforementioned example illustrates a possible positive consequence of nepotism practices. However, advocates of anti-nepotism practices argue that nepotism may instead promote work–family conflict. For example, some researchers claim that a family dispute could be disruptive by interfering with the employee's ability to perform the job (Reed & Cohen, 1989). However, Howard (2008) argues that "implementing policies and rules in the workplace always results with benefits and consequences, and anti-nepotism policies and no-spouse rules are no different" (p. 35). He further argues the consequences of implementing anti-nepotism policies and no-spouse rules might be greater than their potential benefits. Next we review the literature on practices that integrate work–family domains to stipulate when these nepotism practices could ease work–family conflict and improve enrichment.

BOUNDARY INTEGRATION AND SEGMENTATION AND THE WORK–FAMILY INTERFACE

Boundary Integration and Segmentation and Work–Family Conflict

Researchers have argued that organizational policies can reflect different values regarding segmentation and integration of work and family roles (Rau & Hyland, 2002; Rothbard, Phillips, & Dumas, 2005). For example, Rau and Hyland (2002) argue that flexible working arrangements (FWAs), which are defined as "employer provided benefits that permit employees some level of control over when and where they work outside of the standard workday" (Lambert, Marler, & Gueutal, 2008, p. 107), fall closer to the integration pole of the segmentation and integration continuum. This is because FWA, like flextime and telecommuting, enable flexibility in both spatial and temporal boundaries, which allows employees to integrate multiple roles. For example, by telecommuting, one can work at home while fulfilling the role of parent. Onsite childcare is another organizational benefit that allows employees to integrate work and family roles (Ashforth, Kreiner, & Fugate, 2000; Kossek, Noe, & DeMarr, 1999; Nippert-Eng, 1996; Rau & Hyland, 2002). Research has shown that these policies are related to an organization's ability to attract, motivate, and retain employees (Batt & Valcour, 2003).

Scholars have identified at least two types of FWA: time flexibility (e.g., flextime, compressed working weeks) and space flexibility (e.g., telecommuting). FWAs are implemented by organizations to enable employees to cope with family and work responsibilities (Lee, MacDermid, & Buck, 2002).

Although there is evidence that FWA availability is negatively related with work–family conflict, the results have been uneven (see Allen & Shockley, 2009, and Kelly et al., 2008, for reviews). While some studies have shown that perceived schedule flexibility and telecommuting are negatively related to work–family conflict (Anderson, Coffey, & Byerly, 2002; Gajendran & Harrison, 2007; Hammer, Allen, & Grigsby, 1997; Kossek, Lautsch, & Eaton, 2006), other studies have not (Batt & Valcour, 2003; Mesmer-Magnus & Viswesvaran, 2005). For example, Byron's (2005) meta-analysis showed an effect size for flexibility with work–family conflict, whereas Mesmer-Magnus and Viswesvaran's (2005) meta-analysis did not. Some researchers have explained that flextime and telecommuting allow employees greater work and family integration (for example, Raghuram & Wiesenfeld, 2004), whereas other scholars state that the use of certain FWAs allows permeability of work and family boundaries (Standen, Daniels, & Lamond, 1999), which could potentially intensify conflict. Based on these studies, it is important to identify potential moderators between FWA and work–family conflict. In fact, Shockley and Allen (2007) have already demonstrated that the relationship between work interfering with family (WIF) and FWA is stronger for women who have greater family responsibility than for women who have less family responsibility. This shows that these policies may be more useful for some individuals than for others.

Similar to FWA, nepotism policies may enable employees to better manage their borders by integrating both work and family domains. For example, dual-career couples working at the same company may be able to spend more time together during lunch breaks or coffee breaks, thus reducing time-based work–family conflict. However, working at the same company with a spouse allows permeability of work and family boundaries, which could potentially intensify conflict. This is because, just like telecommuting, when an employee shares a workspace with a spouse, or other nuclear family member (e.g., in the same organization), it is more likely that the elements of one domain will transfer to another domain (e.g., stress). For example, in the case of Funkhouser, it is possible that having a disagreement with his wife because of work issues may lead to a personal disagreement or conflict.

Allowing nepotism in organizations may also pose unique challenges to the employee who was hired because of her status. For example, the employee may experience more stress and pressure if she is hired because of her family status (e.g., daughter of an important person within the organization). The stress generated from being related to an important company member may be transferred to the family domain. Take the case of Jean Sarkozy, the 23-year-old son of French President Nicolas Sarkozy. In October 2009, Jean Sarkozy renounced a bid to head an important public agency that oversees Paris's business district after he was accused of nepotism. He did not want the public to think that his potential victory was due to his affiliation with Nicolas Sarkozy. Hence, a person who is hired because of a family association may experience different performance expectations, which may lead to stress that can be transferred to the family domain.

Boundary Integration and Work–Family Enrichment

In addition to decreasing WFC through integration of the two domains, nepotism in organizations may also produce positive synergies between work and family roles. The permeability of work and family boundaries, which may occur when family members work together at the same company, could provide opportunities to transfer resources from one domain to another. According to Greenhaus and Powell's (2006) theoretical framework of work–family enrichment, an employee experiences enrichment when resources gained in one of her roles (e.g., wife) promote improved performance in another role (e.g., worker). In their model, resource generation enables improved performance in the other role via two paths: an instrumental path or an affective path. Greenhaus and Powell identified a number of resources that influence the work–family enrichment process. For example, the employee can gain *skills* (e.g., interpersonal skills), *social-capital resources* (e.g., networking from spouse's professional network), and *material resources* (e.g., share a car to go to work together) in one role (i.e., from being a spouse) that can be transferred to another role (e.g., worker) and *psychological resources* (e.g., emotional support). Greenhaus and Powell argue that the resources an employee gains in her family role (e.g., knowledge shared from a romantic partner) may directly improve her work role (e.g., knowledge learned can be directly used to improve performance at work) or may indirectly produce positive affect (e.g., improving knowledge leading to higher satisfaction, positive mood), which in turn benefits the employee at work.

A recent meta-analysis reported several positive consequences of work–family enrichment to employees. Specifically, McNall, Nicklin, and Masuda (2010) conducted a meta-analysis with 25 studies and found that employees who experienced some form of work–family enrichment were more satisfied with their job, more committed, more satisfied with their family, and reported better physical and mental health.

Nepotism practices that allow integration of work–family roles may improve work–family enrichment by facilitating transfer of resources from one role to another. A study has shown policies that allow integration of family and work roles such as flexible work arrangements (i.e., flextime and compressed workweek) related positively to work–family enrichment (McNall, Masuda, & Nicklin, 2010). Specifically, McNall, Masuda, and Nicklin (2010) showed that individuals working in companies offering FWA were more likely to experience work–family enrichment, and in turn, WFE was related to both higher job satisfaction and lower turnover intention.

Like FWA, nepotism practices may lead to work–family enrichment by promoting opportunities for employees to gain and transfer resources between different roles in family and work domains. For example, when dual-career couples share the same company, colleagues, and work environment, one partner will be more able to provide emotional support related to problems encountered at work (i.e., emotional resources) and may have more opportunities to provide this support, given that they will be more likely to spend time together. For example, they may be likely to share a ride going and coming from work (i.e., physical resources—car) and may be more likely to share knowledge gained from the work when communicating. Perhaps the reason that some individuals want to share the work environment with their family members is to benefit from synergies between work and family roles. In the case of Funkhouser, it is clear that his wife provided him with several resources that he could use to facilitate his performance as mayor. Whether performance was facilitated, in this case, is yet to be determined.

Figure 7.1 illustrates how nepotism practices may allow employees to either integrate or segment work–family roles. Integration and segmentation could influence employees' probability of experiencing work–family conflict and enrichment.

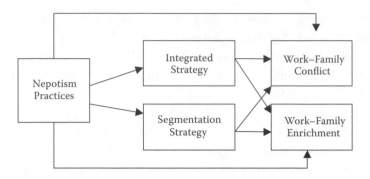

FIGURE 7.1
Nepotism practices on the work–family interface: The role of integration and segmentation strategies.

POSSIBLE MODERATORS OF NEPOTISM PRACTICES AND WORK–FAMILY CONFLICT AND ENRICHMENT

As suggested earlier, nepotism practices may have costs and benefits (Howard, 2008). Similar to FWA, the relationship between nepotism practices and WFC or WFE may depend on several moderators. In particular, research on integration and segmentation has shown that the fit between individual desire for integration and segmentation moderates the relationship between access to policies that help manage boundaries, on one hand, and job satisfaction and commitment, on the other (Rothbard et al., 2005). Some individuals may prefer segmentation because it allows them to preserve and develop each role more completely. Further, segmentation between work and family roles may prevent employees from experiencing negative spillover of emotions from one domain to the other (Edwards & Rothbard, 2000; Hall & Richter, 1988). For example, by implementing a segmentation rule, such as not checking e-mails at home, the employee may prevent the reading of stressful work e-mail at home, thus preserving her mood. Also, by segmenting work and family roles, employees are likely to avoid interruptions, focusing only on the salient role (Ashforth et al., 2000; Rothbard, 2001; Rothbard & Edwards, 2003). Last, employees may seek segmentation to cope with differing expectations or norms for behavior in the two domains (Hewlin, 2003).

Rothbard et al. (2005) argue that whereas some prefer segmenting, others may prefer integration. Blending role boundaries enables some people to accommodate their multiple identities in the workplace (Meyerson & Scully, 1995), preventing the tension that can arise from holding competing roles. For these individuals, greater integration between work and family roles may provide the necessary flexibility to fulfill both work and family responsibilities simultaneously. Integration does reduce the effort needed to transition back and forth between roles (Ashforth et al., 2000). For example, while working at home, a person is capable of doing laundry while writing a report for work.

A study by Chen, Powell, and Greenhaus (2009) demonstrated the importance of fit between organizational practices and individual desires as a means to predict work–family conflict and work–family positive spillover. Specifically, Chen et al. showed that employees were less likely to experience time-based and strain-based work–family conflict when their preferences toward integration or segmentation were met by their organizations. They also found that when employees' preferences for work-to-family segmentation were met, employees were more likely to experience work-to-family instrumental positive spillover. Based on these findings, it is possible that the consequences of nepotism practices to outcome variables such as work–family conflict or work–family enrichment may depend on the fit between individuals' desire to segment or integrate and the policy.

These results showed that, among other factors, individual variables may moderate the effects of nepotism practices on work–family conflict and enrichment. In the following sections, we review other possible characteristics that may serve as moderators among nepotism practices, permeability of boundaries, and perceptions of work–family conflict or enrichment. For example, demographic variables, including gender, marital status, parental status, and relationship between family members within an organization may serve as moderators. Dispositional or personality characteristics, such as the Big Five factors of openness to experience, conscientiousness, agreeableness, extraversion, and neuroticism, show some promise as moderators. Other dispositional variables, such as locus of control, attachment style, and life role values have been found to influence the degree to which individuals experience work–family conflict or enrichment, suggesting them as moderators of the relationship between nepotism practices and work–family enrichment or conflict.

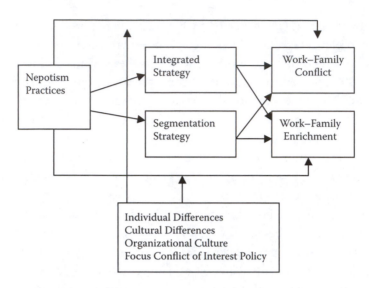

FIGURE 7.2
Nepotism practices on work–family conflict and enrichment and proposed moderators.

Last, contextual variables, such as organizational and national culture, may effect implementation of policies to improve work and family enrichment and ease work–family conflict. Figure 7.2 illustrates these moderators. Next we elaborate on these potential moderators.

Demographic Variables

Gender

Although there is mixed support for gender differences in work–family conflict (Allen et al., 2000; Byron, 2005; Eby, Casper, Lockwood, Bordeaux, & Brinley, 2005), gender may be an important moderator. In a meta-analysis examining antecedents of work–family conflict, Byron (2005) found that male employees had slightly higher levels of work interfering with family (WIF) and female employees had slightly higher levels of family interfering with work (FIW), though the difference between males and females was very small. Further, gender was a moderator in a meta-analysis examining the outcomes of work–family enrichment (McNall, Nicklin, & Masuda, 2010). Specifically, work–family enrichment was more strongly related to job satisfaction and life satisfaction when the sample included more female participants.

Because anti-nepotism polices are more likely to affect women adversely (Howard, 2008), it is likely that gender will operate as a moderator in the relationship between nepotism policies and work–family conflict.

Parental and Marital Status

In general, work–family conflict is higher among those with children at home (Eby et al., 2002). Byron (2005) found the combination of parental status and gender was important for explaining the relationship between job stress and WIF and FIW. Byron found no difference between married and single employees; however, the combination of marital status with parental status is an important moderator. Similarly, with gender, when there were more parents in the sample, mothers experienced more WIF and FIW than fathers. When there were fewer parents in the sample, men experienced more WIF and FIW. Last, single parents had more WIF and FIW compared to married parents.

Relationship Between Working Family Members

The relationship between working family members may contribute to work–family conflict or work–family facilitation. Very little quantitative research exists examining the relationship of family members working with each other (Halbesleben & Wheeler, 2007), but we speculate the closer the relationship between family members, the more likely the relationship will influence someone's perception of conflict or facilitation. Spouses or partners working together, an adult child working with a parent, or siblings working together may experience more family dynamics in the workplace compared to distant relatives working together.

Working with family members may provide social support, which will reduce the perception of work–family conflict (Carlson & Perrewé, 1999). However, more important than the type of relationship between family members is the way individuals manage these relationships. As described earlier, family members who work together choose to either segment or integrate their borders. For example, although spouses work in the same company, they may choose to avoid talking about work when having lunch together. Hence, it is possible that if borders are permeable between work and family domains, family members working together may experience more spillover from work and family. However, they may choose to segment domains and prevent negative spillover.

Disposition or Personality Variables

Personality affects how people interpret and react to situations, so it makes sense that researchers include personality as a variable in work–family studies. There is considerable evidence showing that the dimension of neuroticism (Goldberg, 1992; McCrae & Costa, 1990) explains employees' experience of work–family conflict (Aryee, Srinivas, & Tan, 2005; Gryzwacz & Marks, 2000; Rantanen, Pulkkinen, & Kinnunen, 2005; Wayne, Musisca, & Fleeson, 2004). Male and female employees with high levels of neuroticism are more likely to report WIF and FIW (Ayree et al., 2005; Gryzwacz & Marks, 2000; Rantanen et al., 2005; Wayne et al., 2004). The findings are mixed for the other Big Five traits and the work–family interface. Some researchers have found a negative correlation between agreeableness and work–family interference (Bruck & Allen, 2003; Wayne et al., 2004); others have not (Rantanen et al., 2005). Mixed results have been found for conscientiousness as well (Bruck & Allen, 2003; Rantanen et al., 2005; Wayne et al., 2004). Given the role of personality traits in work–family studies, it is important that researchers continue to investigate the five dimensions until a clear pattern emerges as to how the different dimensions may hinder or facilitate employees' ability to balance their work and family life.

Other dispositional factors that show a relationship with work–family balance include locus of control (Andreassi & Thompson, 2007), attachment style (Sumer & Knight, 2001), life role values (Carlson & Kacmar, 2000), and core self-evaluations (Boyar & Mosely, 2007). Andreassi and Thompson (2007) found internal locus of control was negatively related to both WIF and FIW, and positively related to positive spillover between work and family. Sumer and Knight (2001) reported that employees with preoccupied attachment style indicated greater negative spillover from family to work than those with a secure or dismissing style. In addition, those with a preoccupied attachment style were less likely to use a segmentation strategy compared to the three other attachment styles. Carlson and Kacmar (2000) found that people who value work over family reported more FIW, and people who value family over work reported greater WIF. Boyar and Mosley (2007) examined the relationship between work–family conflict and a constellation of personality traits referred to as *core self-evaluation*, which includes self-esteem, locus of control, self-efficacy, and emotional stability. Core self-evaluation was negatively related to the perception of FIW and WIF (Boyar & Mosley, 2007).

Given the role of personality traits in the work–family interface, it is possible that personality plays a moderating role on the effects of nepotism practices on work–family conflict and work–family enrichment. For example, a person high in neuroticism will probably experience more work–family conflict when working with their family members. This is because people high in neuroticism experience high levels of negative affect, which could potentially spillover between work and family when boundaries are blurred. On the other hand, individuals high on internal locus of control may be more able to manage boundaries even in situations where work and family roles are integrated, such as in the situation where they work with a spouse. In this case, individuals high in internal locus of control may be less likely to experience work–family conflict when working under nepotism practices. Additionally, a person with high internal locus of control may be more capable of seeking opportunities to create synergies between work and family roles when working under nepotism practices. In turn, these individuals may be more likely to experience work–family enrichment.

The moderating role of personality variables on nepotistic practice and the work–family interface has never been explored. However, given the important role of personality on work–family interface, we encourage further exploration of personality as a potential moderator of nepotism practices and the work–family interface. Determining whether some of these personality traits relate to work family boundary management, and dealing with the challenges of balancing work and family in nepotistic organizations are core areas for future research.

Contextual Variables

Besides personal variables, contextual variables may moderate the effect of nepotism policies and work–family enrichment or conflict. Next we review three potential contextual moderators: national culture, organizational culture, and the scope of nepotism practices.

National Culture

National culture is an important variable because it cannot only determine nepotism practices, but it could possibly moderate the relationship between nepotism practices and the work–family interface. The concept of collectivism and individualism (I–C) may be a potential moderator of the effects of anti-nepotism practices and work–family conflict or enrichment. I–C is the extent to which a culture prioritizes group goals and interpersonal ties over individual goals (Triandis, 1995). For example, in Asian countries, which are characterized as more collectivistic societies, nepotism may be the norm. According to Yang (2010), Chinese managers tend to hire relatives, friends, and also tend to use employee referrals as a recruiting strategy. Taiwan's human resources management (HRM) practices are rooted in collectivism where close social connections (e.g., *guanxi*) are preferred over others. Korean firms tend to hire blue-collar workers from a pool of family and friends of current employees. Yang (2010) explains that these practices are commonly called "backdoor recruitment," in contrast with the "open door recruitment" strategy, which is based on job criteria. From an organizational perspective, employees' friends and family members provide a good pool of job candidates. This is because this pool promotes a social network built on trust. Based on the same philosophy, some Japanese firms encourage intraorganizational marriage (Steinhoff & Tanaka, 1994).

Beside collectivism and individualism, researchers have argued that other cultural values may play an important role in determining work–family conflict (Masuda & McNall, 2010). For example, Schwartz's (1999) cultural value orientation of embeddedness versus autonomy may be a potential moderator between accessibility to nepotism practices and work–family conflict or enrichment. According to Schwartz's (2008) theory, individuals in countries with a value orientation toward embeddedness tend to place more importance on values such as social order, respect for traditions, and family security versus values such as curiosity, broadmindedness, creativity (intellectual autonomy), pleasure, exciting life, and varied life (affective autonomy).

Schwartz (1999) argues that national values are related to work perceptions. For example, people in countries with an autonomous orientation are more likely to perceive work as central to their identity compared with people in countries with an orientation toward embeddedness values. This value orientation may lead to different perceptions regarding the acceptance of certain work policies. For example, in embedded countries, where family values are more important, anti-nepotism values may be received with some resistance. On the other hand, in autonomous countries where intellectual autonomy and merit are priorities, anti-nepotism practices may be more easily embraced and promoted. These values may also influence one's likelihood to experience stress when working in a company that adopts nepotism practices. For example, the wife of a director who received a job because of her family status may experience less pressure in India (i.e., orientation toward embeddedness) than in The Netherlands (i.e., orientation toward autonomy). As a consequence, one will experience more work–family conflict in autonomous rather than in embedded cultures.

Organizational Work–Family Culture

Offering benefits to help employees balance their work and family life is not sufficient to create a family-friendly work environment if employees are reluctant to use them (Allen, 2001; Kossek et al., 1999; Thompson, Beauvais, & Lyness, 1999). Employees will not use benefits, services, and policies if there are norms in the workplace that encourage working long hours (Blair-Loy & Wharton, 2002), if it is expected that employees put work ahead of family (Thompson et al., 1999), and if employees are penalized for using those services (Judiesch & Lyness, 1999). For employees to use benefits there must be an existing work culture that is concerned about employees' nonwork life (Andreassi & Thompson, 2004). Thompson et al. (1999) referred to this type of culture as work–family culture and defined it as "the shared assumptions, beliefs, and values regarding the extent to which an organization supports and values the integration of employees' work and family lives" (p. 394). Thompson et al. assert that work–family culture is comprised of three dimensions: (a) organizational time demands, (b) career consequences for using work–family benefits, and (c) managerial support. *Organizational time demands* refer to the amount of time employees are expected to work and expectations that work takes a higher priority than nonwork life. *Career consequences for using work–family benefits* pertain to positive or negative consequences associated with using benefits and services or allowing nonwork issues to spill over into the workplace. *Managerial support* refers to the extent to which managers and supervisors support the use of work–family benefits and services and are sensitive to employees' nonwork lives. Other researchers suggest similar components of work–family culture (Clark, 2001; Kirchmeyer, 1995; Kossek, Colquitt, & Noe, 2001; Kossek et al., 1999), but, generally, they all point to a family supportive work environment. If the environment is unsupportive, employees will perceive greater work–family conflict (Breaugh & Frye, 2008; Lapierre et al., 2008).

Nepotism practices may be more likely to be adopted by companies with a culture that embraces work–family integration. Additionally, nepotism practices may lead to lower work–family conflict when the culture is characterized by the shared belief that these practices have potential benefits to employees and the organization. Hence, working with a family member in a company where some managers and colleagues have negative perceptions toward this arrangement may be stressful to employees. This can lead to higher probability of experiencing work–family conflict. Hence, organizational culture is an important factor that should be explored in future studies examining nepotism practices on the work–family interface.

Focused Conflict of Interest Policy

Another possible moderator is the type of anti-nepotism practice companies adopt. For example, Howard (2008) suggested that companies could benefit from implementing what he called focused conflict of interest policies. These are policies that allow hiring family members only under certain conditions. For instance, family members may be employed or considered for a position only if they are not working under the supervision of another family member. Focusing the policy would diminish the conflict of interest. The company may also limit the policy by considering or employing members only when working in different departments. Figure 7.2 illustrates how the aforementioned variables could play a role in the relationship between nepotism practices and the work–family interface.

CONCLUSIONS AND RECOMMENDATIONS FOR FUTURE RESEARCH

In this chapter, we drew from Clark's work–family border theory to explain possible consequences of reconsidering anti-nepotism practices in organizations as a way to help employees to conciliate both work and family responsibilities. The theory postulates that individuals manage work and family boundaries along a continuum of high integration to high segmentation. According to this model, an individual's boundaries can be high or low on permeability and flexibility, and these characteristics define levels of integration and segmentation. Researchers have argued that, although the flexibility and permeability of a role boundary might prevent interrole conflict by allowing the individual to change roles when necessary (for example, an employee working in the same company with a spouse may be able to have coffee with the spouse to discuss any personal issues and then return to work), it could also "exacerbate conflict by creating confusion among the individual and members of his or her role sets as to which role is or should be most salient" (Ashforth et al., 2000, p. 475).

Because nepotism allows family members to work at the same company, it may influence employees' role permeability and flexibility. Hence, nepotism practices could have either positive or negative consequences for individuals who are trying to prevent role conflict.

Our review showed there is a lack of empirical studies examining the effects of anti-nepotism or nepotism practices on the interface between work and family. The lack of empirical research is problematic for several reasons. First, because of social demographic changes, such as more dual-career couples entering the workplace (for example, Bond, Thompson, Galinsky, & Prottas, 2002), employees are demanding flexibility to cope with work and family demands. Second, with the increasing number of dual-career couples, employees are faced with a relocation dilemma and often one person has to sacrifice his or her career for the other or has to move with the spouse. In this case, the company is faced with the challenge of helping with employee adjustment. Last, the world is increasingly globalized and such practices are widely used in several countries in Asia. For this reason, it is beneficial for both practitioners and researchers to better understand the consequences of introducing nepotism practices in their organizations. Like other practices that address integration of roles (e.g., FWA), nepotism practices could have potential benefits to employees' satisfaction and commitment to the organization by allowing them to better manage work and family boundaries, and to reduce conflict between work and family roles. However, by increasing boundary flexibility, it may create confusion and conflict, as in the case of an employee who is enacting both the father and boss roles.

Hence, we encouraged further investigation of moderators of the potential effect of nepotism practices on work family conflict and enrichment. Drawing from the literature on work–family conflict, enrichment and FWA, we proposed that the extent to which nepotism practices may have a beneficial effect on work–family conflict or enrichment may be partly due to the national context, organizational context, personal characteristics, and even the scope of the practice adopted by the organization.

As of now, we can only conclude that nepotism practices could be remedies for the work–family conflict problems or catalysts that accelerate interrole conflict. Further, we suggest that these practices could provide employees opportunity to create synergies between both roles by experiencing work–family enrichment. However, no conclusions can be reached given the paucity of empirical research in this area. We hope that this chapter will encourage the development of empirical studies examining the effects of nepotism practices in organizations. We believe it is worth reexamining the use of anti-nepotism policies, especially in countries where family ties are given considerable weight. We suggest that the focused conflict of interest policy suggested by Howard (2008) could be a solution to some work–family problems that employees are facing (e.g., the relocation problem often faced by dual-career couples).

REFERENCES

Allen, T. D. (2001). Family-supportive work environments: The role of organizational perceptions. *Journal of Vocational Behavior, 58*, 414–435.

Allen, T. D., Herst, D. E. L., Bruck, C. S., & Sutton, M. (2000). Consequences associated with work-to-family conflict: A review and agenda for future research. *Journal of Occupational Health Psychology, 5*, 278–308.

Allen, T. D., & Shockley, K. M. (2009). Flexible work arrangements: Help or hype? In D. R. Crane & E. J. Hill (Eds.), *Handbook of families and work: Interdisciplinary perspectives* (pp. 265–284). Lanham, MD: University Press of America.

Anderson, S., Coffey, B. S., & Byerly, R. (2002). Formal organizational initiatives and informal workplace practices: Links to work–family conflict and job-related outcomes. *Journal of Management, 28*, 787–810.

Andreassi, J. K., & Thompson, C. A. (2007). Dispositional and situational sources of control: Relative impact on work–family conflict and positive spillover. *Journal of Managerial Psychology, 22*, 722–740.

Aryee, S., Srinivas, E. S., & Tan, H. H. (2005). Rhythms of life: Antecedents and outcomes of work–family balance in employed parents. *Journal of Applied Psychology, 90*, 123–146.

Ashforth, B. E., Kreiner, G. E., & Fugate, M. (2000). All in a day's work: Boundaries and microrole transition. *Academy of Management Review, 25*, 472–491.

Batt, R., & Valcour, P. M. (2003). Human resources practices as predictors of work–family outcomes and employee turnover. *Industrial Relations, 42*, 189–220.

Blair-Loy, M., & Wharton, A. (2002). Employees' use of work–family policies and the workplace social context. *Social Forces, 80*, 813–845.

Bond, J. T., Thompson, C. A., Galinsky, E., & Prottas, D. (2002). *Highlights of the National Study of the Changing Workforce.* New York: Families and Work Institute.

Boyar, S., & Mosley, D. (2007). The relationship between core self-evaluations and work and family satisfaction: The mediating role of work–family conflict and facilitation. *Journal of Vocational Behavior, 71*, 265–281.

Breaugh, J. A., & Frye, N. K. (2008). Work–family conflict: The importance of family-friendly employment practices and family supportive supervisors. *Journal of Business Psychology, 22*, 345–353.

Bruck, C. S., & Allen, T. D. (2003). The relationship between Big Five personality traits, negative affectivity, type A behavior, and work–family conflict. *Journal of Vocational Behavior, 63*, 457–472.

Byron, K. (2005). A meta-analytic review of work–family interference and its antecedents. *Journal of Vocational Behavior, 67*, 169–198.

Carlson, D. S., & Kacmar, K. M. (2000). Work–family conflict in the organization: Do life role values make a difference? *Journal of Management, 26*, 1031–1054.

Carlson, D. S., & Perrewé, P. L. (1999). The role of social support in the stressor-strain relationship: An examination of work–family conflict. *Journal of Management, 25*, 513–540.

Clark, S. C. (2000). Work/family border theory. *Human Relations, 53*, 747–770.

Clark, S. C. (2001). Work cultures and work/family balance. *Journal of Vocational Behavior, 58*, 348–365.

Chen, Z., Powell, G. N., & Greenhaus, J. H. (2009). Work-to-family conflict, positive spillover, and boundary management: A person–environment fit approach. *Journal of Vocational Behavior, 74*, 82–93.

Eby, L. T., Casper, W. J., Lockwood, A., Bordeaux, C., & Brinley, A. (2005). Work and family research in IO/OB: Content analysis and review of the literature (1980–2002). *Journal of Vocational Behavior, 66*, 124–107.

Eby, L., Douthitt, S., Perrin, T., Noble, C., Atchley, K., & Ladd, R. (2002). Managerial support for dual-career relocation dilemmas. *Journal of Vocational Behavior, 60*(3), 354–373.

Eby, L. T., & Russell, J. E. A. (2000). Predictors of employee willingness to relocate for the firm: A multiorganization study of 872 married couples. *Journal of Vocational Behavior, 57*, 42–61.

Edwards, J. R., & Rothbard, N. P. (2000). Mechanisms linking work and family: Clarifying the relationship between work and family constructs. *Academy of Management Review, 25*, 178–199.

Ford, M. T., Heinen, B. A., & Langkamer, K. L. (2007). Work and family satisfaction and conflict: A meta-analysis of cross-domain relations. *Journal of Applied Psychology, 92*, 57–80.

Frone, M. R. (2003). Work–family balance. In J. C. Quick & L. E. Tedrick (Eds.), *Handbook of occupational health psychology* (pp. 143–162). Washington, DC: American Psychological Association.

Gajendran, R. S., & Harrison, D. A. (2007). The good the bad and the unknown about telecommuting: Meta-analysis of psychological mediators and individual consequences. *Journal of Applied Psychology, 92*, 1524–1541.

Goldberg, L. R. (1992). The development of markers for the Big-Five factor structure. *Psychological Assessment, 4*, 26–42.

Greenhaus, J. H., & Beutell, N. J. (1985). Sources of conflict between work and family roles. *Academy of Management Review, 10*, 76–88.

Greenhaus, J. H., & Powell, G. N. (2006). When work and family are allies: A theory of work–family enrichment. *Academy of Management Review, 31*, 72–92.

Gryzwacz, J. G., & Butler, A. B. (2005). The impact of job characteristics on work-to-family facilitation: Testing a theory and distinguishing a construct. *Journal of Occupational Health Psychology, 10,* 97–109.

Gryzwacz, J. G., & Marks, N. F. (2000). Reconceptualizing the work–family interface: An ecological perspective on the correlates of positive and negative spillover between work and family. *Journal of Occupational Health Psychology, 5,* 111–126.

Halbesleben, J. R. B., & Wheeler, A. R. (2007). The costs and benefits of working with those you love: A demand/resources perspective on working with family. In P. L. Perrewé & D. C. Ganster (Eds.), *Exploring the work and non-work interface: Research in occupational stress and well-being* (Vol. 6, pp. 119–169). Greenwich, CT: Elsevier.

Hall, D. T., & Richter, J. (1988). Balancing work life and home life: What can organizations do to help? *The Academy of Management Executive, 2,* 212–223.

Hammer, L., Allen, E., & Grigsby, T. (1997). Work–family conflict in dual-earner couples: Within-individual and crossover effects of work and family. *Journal of Vocational Behavior, 50,* 185–203.

Hewlin, P. (2003). And the award for best actor goes to …: Facades of conformity in organizational settings. *Academy of Management Review, 28*(4), 633–642.

Howard, J. L. (2008). Balancing conflicts of interest when employing spouses. *Employee Responsibilities and Rights Journal, 20,* 29–43.

Instituto de la Empresa Familiar. (2005). *Estudio sobre la profesionalización de la Empresa Familiar.* Available at http://www.iefamiliar.com/biblioteca/documentos/Doc.129.pdf.

Judiesch, M., & Lyness, K. (1999). Left behind? The impact of leaves of absence on managers' career success. *Academy of Management Journal, 42,* 641–651.

Kelly, E. L., Kossek, E. E., Hammer, L. B., Durham, D., Bray, J., Chermack K., … Kaskubar, D. (2008). Getting there from here. Research on the effects of work–family initiatives on work–family conflict and business outcomes. *The Academy of Management Annals, 2,* 305–349.

Kirchmeyer, C. (1995). Managing the work–nonwork boundary: An assessment of organizational responses. *Human Relations, 48,* 515–536.

Kirkman, B. L., & Shapiro, D. L. (1997). The impact of cultural values on employee resistance to teams. Toward a model of globalized self-managing work team effectiveness. *Academy of Management Review, 22,* 730–757.

Kirschenbaum, A. (1991). The corporate transfer: Origin and destination factors in the decision to change jobs. *Journal of Vocational Behavior, 38,* 107–123.

Kossek, E. E., Colquitt, J. A., & Noe, J. A. (2001). Caregiving decisions, well-being, and performance: The effects of place and provider as a function of dependent type and work–family climates. *Academy of Management Journal, 44,* 29–44.

Kossek, E., Lautsch, B., & Eaton, S. (2006). Telecommuting, control, and boundary management: Correlates of policy use and practice, job control, and work–family effectiveness. *Journal of Vocational Behavior, 68*(2), 347–367.

Kossek, E. E., Noe, R. A., & DeMarr, B. J. (1999). Work–family role synthesis: Individual and organizational determinants. *International Journal of Conflict Management, 10,* 102–129.

Kossek, E. E., & Ozeki, C. (1998). Work–family interference, policies, and the job-life satisfaction relationship: A review and directions for organizational behavior–human resources research. *Journal of Applied Psychology, 83,* 139–149.

Lawson, M. B., & Angle, H. L. (1994). When organizational relocation means family relocation: An emerging issue for strategic human resource management. *Human Resource Management, 22*, 33–54.

Lambert, A. D., Marler, J. H., & Gueutal, H. G. (2008). Individual differences: Factors affecting employee utilization of flexible work arrangements. *Journal of Vocational Behavior, 73*, 107–117

Lapierre, L. M., Spector, P. E., Allen, T. D., Poelmans, S., Cooper, G. L., O'Driscoll, … Kinnunen, U. (2008). Family-supportive organization perceptions, multiple dimensions of work–family conflict, and employee satisfaction: A test of model across five samples. *Journal of Vocational Behavior, 73*, 92–106.

Lee, M. D., MacDermid, S. M., & Buck, M. L. (2002). Reduced-load work arrangements: Response to stress or quest for integrity of functioning? In D. L. Nelson & R. J. Burke (Eds.), *Gender, work stress, and health* (pp. 169–190). Washington, DC: American Psychological Association.

Masuda, A. D., & McNall, L. A. (2010). A conceptual framework for understanding work–family conflict and policy implementation across countries. In N. Chinchilla, M. Las Heras, & A. D. Masuda (Eds.), *Balancing work and family: A practical guide to help organizations meet the global workforce challenge* (pp. 23–35). Amherst, MA: HRD Press.

McCrae, R. R., & Costa, P. T. (1990). *Personality in adulthood.* New York: Guilford Press.

McNall, L. A, Masuda, A. D., & Nicklin, J. M. (2010). Flexible work arrangements and job satisfaction/turnover intentions: The mediating role of work-to-family enrichment. *Journal of Psychology: Interdisciplinary & Applied, 144*, 1–21.

McNall, L. A., Nicklin, J. M., & Masuda, A. D. (2010). A meta-analytic review of the consequences associated with work–family enrichment. *Journal of Business and Psychology, 25*(3), 381–396. doi: 10.1007/s10869-009-9141-1

Mesmer-Magnus, J., & Viswesvaran, C. (2005). Convergence between measures of work-to-family and family-to-work conflict: A meta-analytic examination. *Journal of Vocational Behavior, 67*, 215–232.

Meyerson, D., & Scully, M. (1995). Tempered radicalism and the politics of ambivalence and change. *Organization Science, 6*(5), 585–600.

Nippert-Eng, C. E. (1996). *Home and work.* Chicago: University of Chicago Press.

Pellico, M. T., & Stroh, L. K. (1997). Spousal assistance programs: An integral component of the international assignment. *New Approaches to Employee Management, 4*, 225–241.

Raghuram, S., & Wiesenfeld, B. (2004). Work–nonwork conflict and job stress among virtual workers. *Human Resource Management, 43*(2), 259–277.

Rantanen, J., Pulkkinen, L., & Kinnunen, U. (2005). The Big Five personality dimensions, work–family conflict, and psychological distress: A longitudinal view. *Journal of Individual Differences, 26*, 155–166.

Rau, B. L., & Hyland, M. M. (2002). Role conflict and flexible work arrangements: The effects on applicant attraction. *Personnel Psychology, 55*(1), 111–136.

Reed, C. M., & Cohen, L. J. (1989). Anti-nepotism rules: The legal rights of married co-workers. *Public Personnel Management, 18*, 37–44.

Rothbard, N. P. (2001). Enriching or depleting? The dynamics of engagement in work and family roles. *Administrative Science Quarterly, 46*, 655–684.

Rothbard, N. P., & Edwards, J. (2003). Investment in work and family roles: A test of identity and utilitarian motives. *Personnel Psychology, 56*(3), 699–730.

Rothbard, N. P., Phillips, K. W., & Dumas, T. Y. (2005). Managing multiple roles: work–family policies and individuals' desires for segmentation. *Organizational Science, 16,* 243–258.

Schwartz, S. (1999). A theory of cultural values and some implications for work. *Applied Psychology: An International Review, 48,* 23–47.

Schwartz, S. H. (2008). *Cultural value orientations: Nature and implications of national differences.* Moscow: Publishing House of SU HSE.

Shockley, K. M., & Allen, T. D. (2007). When flexibility helps: Another look at the availability of flexible work arrangements and work–family conflict. *Journal of Vocational Behavior, 71*(3), 479–493.

Slack, C. (2001, September). Breeding success. *MBA Jungle,* pp. 82–88.

Standen, P., Daniels, K., & Lamond, D. (1999). The home as a workplace: Work–family interaction and psychological well-being in telework. *Journal of Occupational Health Psychology, 4,* 1–15.

Steinhoff, P. G., & Tanaka. K. (1994). Women managers in Japan. In N. J. Adler & D. N. Izraeli (Eds.), *Comparative frontiers: Women managers in a global economy* (pp. 79–100). Cambridge, MA: Blackwell Publishers.

Sumer, H. C., & Knight, P. A. (2001). How do people with different attachment styles balance work and family? A personality perspective on work–family linkages. *Journal of Applied Psychology, 86,* 653–663.

Thompson, C. A., Beauvais, L. L., & Lyness, K. S. (1999). When work–family benefits are not enough: The influence of work–family culture on benefit utilization, organizational attachment, and work–family conflict. *Journal of Vocational Behavior, 54,* 392–415.

Triandis, H. C. (1995). *Individualism and collectivism.* Boulder, CO: Westview.

Wayne, J. H., Grzywacz, J. G., Carlson, D. S., & Kacmar, K. M. (2007). Work–family facilitation: A theoretical explanation and model of primary antecedents and consequences. *Human Resource Management Review, 17,* 63–76.

Wayne, J. H., Musisca, N., & Fleeson, W. (2004). Considering the role of personality in the work family experience: Relationships of the big five to work–family conflict and facilitation. *Journal of Vocational Behavior, 64,* 108–130.

Werbel, J. D., & Hames, D. S. (1996). Anti-nepotism reconsidered: The case of husband and wife employment. *Group and Organization Management, 21,* 365–379.

Yang, N. (2010). The work–family relationship in China: Cultural tradition, socioeconomic changes, and policy implications. In N. Chinchilla, M. Las Heras, & A. D. Masuda (Eds.), *Balancing work and family: A practical guide to help organizations meet the global workforce challenge* (pp. 157–175). Amherst, MA: HRD Press.

8

Nepotism and Leadership

Ketan H. Mhatre
Claremont McKenna College

Ronald E. Riggio
Claremont McKenna College

Heidi R. Riggio
California State University, Los Angeles

Consider these two cases of nepotism and leadership:

- England's King Edward II was arguably England's worst monarch. His father, Edward I (called "Longshanks"; both are depicted in the movie *Braveheart*), taught the young Edward statesmanship and warcraft from an early age. However, Edward II showed little interest in war or government, instead focusing on boating and craftmaking. He was considered by the court to have very poor leadership qualities. When Edward I died suddenly, Edward II ascended the throne. He was soon accused of giving too much authority and power to his friends, led his troops in the worst defeat in the history of the English army, and was abandoned by his wife for her lover (the two later led a successful invasion of England). Edward II was forced to abdicate his throne (to his 14-year-old son) and was subsequently murdered.
- Legendary Southern California burger chain, In-N-Out Burger, has been a family-held company for decades. When founder Harry Snyder died in 1976, leadership of the growing company passed to the younger son, Rich, instead of the older son Guy (who had problems with substance abuse). Rich, even at 24, was quite experienced, having worked his way up in the company. When Rich was killed in a plane crash, keeping the company in the family was difficult,

and the leadership was reluctantly given to Guy, despite his drug problems. When Guy died of a drug overdose, the company looked past seasoned nonfamily In-N-Out executives and brought back the 79-year-old mother, Esther. When Esther passed away, control of the company passed to the Snyder's only grandchild, the 23-year-old daughter of Rich. A lawsuit over control of the company from a long-time vice president ended in the Snyder family keeping control of the business with the young granddaughter in charge.

There is an obvious link between nepotism and leadership. For millennia, leadership of tribes, kingdoms, and nations has been transferred from parent to offspring or other kin within the extended family unit. Traditionally, in many societies, leader succession was seen as a birthright. Yet, leader succession continues to favor relatives even in modern times. Consider the case of leader succession in democratic societies or in business. In U.S. politics, spouses have been appointed to complete senate and congressional terms (for example, Muriel Humphrey Brown, Mary Bono). Children of politicians are often given inside tracks to political appointments and automatic party support as candidates (for example, the Kennedy and Bush political dynasties). In small businesses, leader succession often remains in the family (although there is admittedly a sense of "ownership," in family-held businesses).

The goal of this chapter is to shed light on the enduring link between nepotism and leadership—a link that has not received sufficient attention in the research literature. Our aim is to take a closer look at the phenomenon of nepotism and how it operates and exerts its control within a leadership context. We plan to achieve this aim by bringing to the forefront some of the underlying mechanisms through which this control is exerted. In the process, we will seek answers to questions, such as: What are the evolutionary, cognitive, and relational antecedents of nepotism? How do these antecedents function to propagate the practice of nepotistic leadership? What are the potential pitfalls and benefits associated with nepotistic leadership practices in organizations? What are the mediating processes through which such nepotistic practices tend to exert an influence on critical leadership outcomes? And finally, what lessons can we draw from the latest advances in leadership research to inform contemporary leaders about methods to lead organizations that have deeply entrenched nepotistic values and practices? It is our belief that seeking answers to questions such as these is the crucial first step toward gaining a better understanding of how nepotism and leadership work hand in hand.

A logical first step in any endeavor of such nature and magnitude is to provide working definitions of the constructs involved in the intended exploration. However, before we do that, there are a few issues regarding the conceptualization of nepotism that deserve further clarification. The first issue involves the establishment of a set of criteria that dictate whether a particular act qualifies as a nepotistic practice. Specifically, what are the necessary and sufficient conditions for a practice to qualify as nepotistic? Is all promotion of kin members necessarily nepotistic? Does promoting a kin member when all other things are equal (for instance, hiring a member of kin when all candidates for a job—including the kin member—are equally competent and qualified) constitute an act of nepotism?

Not all promotion of kin members is necessarily nepotistic. If a kin member exceeds standards set by the organization (not merely those of the leader), and is evaluated by other organizational members and separate organizations as exceptional, the fact of kin membership itself does not indicate biased acts of nepotism. In such a case, kin membership becomes an irrelevant issue because, theoretically, the focus is on the competence and qualifications of the kin member versus his or her kin membership. However, in reality, it could be difficult (if not impossible) for a leader to objectively and rationally focus on the competence and qualifications of a kin member and not let kin membership affect decision making. According to Fiske and Taylor (1991), a leader's perceptions regarding a son's or daughter's (or other relatives') skills, talents, and abilities are inherently more biased than judgments of unrelated persons, because they are intertwined with powerful emotions and based on more extended, extensive interpersonal interactions and experiences. This seems to suggest that the determination of whether a particular act is nepotistic depends heavily on the extent to which the decision maker (individual or a group) has succeeded in eliminating personal biases from decision making and has resorted to equitable principles while making the decision.

A second issue that needs attention is whether promoting a kin member when all things are equal constitutes an act of nepotism. So, for example, if all candidates for a particular job are equally competent and are equally qualified, would giving preference to a kin member constitute an act of nepotism? This is a very critical question because it allows us to examine the "unfair" component associated with the conceptualization of nepotism. To seek a satisfactory response to this question, one has to evaluate whether equity has been sacrificed. It could be argued that, when all the candidates are equally competent and qualified, it may seem unfair to the nonkin members if preference is given to kin membership.

In such a case, the normative leadership focus should be on pursuing an additional set of neutral criteria that would enable fair decision making instead of relying on kin membership to make a choice. A decision made on the basis of the new criteria, which would be equally applicable to all candidates, kin members or otherwise, would constitute a fair decision. On the other hand, if a decision is made based on kin membership, there is a chance that it may receive a negative response from some organizational members. It is also possible that such a decision will be welcomed and may meet with a positive response. Speculation about these outcomes depends on a number of contingencies and situational factors, and needs to be empirically validated by future research. However, given our focus on authentic leadership (Avolio & Gardner, 2005), which involves leaders practicing balanced processing (i.e., objectively analyzing data before making decisions and putting aside personal feelings and biases), and internalized moral perspective (i.e., adhering to internal moral standards and values, and acting consistently with those), we suggest that leaders pursue an additional set of neutral criteria and not rely on kin membership to make the final decision.

There could be potential benefits associated with giving preference to kin members when all things are equal. For example, when all the candidates for a particular position are equally qualified and when it is difficult to make a decision based on the current criteria of selection, going with a family member may have its advantages. One example of such an advantage would be access to the social capital and social networks that the family member may have but which the nonkin members may lack. This may prove to be a critical asset and may make the kin member better suited for the job. Additionally, if the kin member is the son or daughter of a highly successful leader, then he or she may enjoy instantaneous trust and commitment from organizational stakeholders as a result of the kin's relationship with the leader. However, such benefits remain speculative, and their nature and magnitude need to be explored further through empirical research.

A third issue that requires additional clarification is the distinction between nepotism and perceptions of nepotism. Perceptions of nepotism can exist in the absence of an act of actual nepotism and vice versa. For example, even though a leader may not have committed an act of nepotism by hiring the most capable candidate (who just happened to be a relative), it may still be perceived to be an act of nepotism by the leader's followers and by other organizational stakeholders. Such perceptions of nepotism may affect organizational culture, structure, and other bottom-line performance variables. Alternately, an extremely charismatic and a well-liked leader may indulge in nepotistic practices and still manage to avoid creating perceptions of nepotism among his or her followers. In such cases, actual nepotism and perceptions of nepotism may or may not refer to the same thing. Thus, care needs to be taken while hypothesizing the relationships among constructs associated with nepotism and leadership.

Given that our exploration of nepotism is embedded within the context of leadership, our definition of nepotism assumes a more specific tenor, one that reflects a reciprocal influence of the leadership context in which it is rooted. We define nepotism as *unfair displays of favoritism by a leadership source (i.e., an individual leader, a group, or an organization) that are based on kinship*. Such displays can take the forms of both overt, explicit, and observable phenomena (e.g., hiring of a close relative by a leader) and implicit acts of favoritism (e.g., allocation of greater psychological resources by a leader to projects associated with members of his or her kin). Several researchers have attempted to define and conceptualize nepotism in the past. For instance, Simon, Clark, and Tifft (1966) defined nepotism as "the bestowal of patronage by reason of relationship regardless of merit" (p. 344). Bellow (2003) described nepotism as "favoritism based on kinship" (p. 11) and Jones et al. (2008) argued that nepotism involved the use of family influence for employing relatives. Our definition draws heavily from these prior conceptualizations and, by embedding nepotism within a broader context of leadership, paves the way for the introduction of a whole new nomological network that can potentially augment our understanding of both nepotism and leadership.

An important aspect of this definition of nepotism is that inequity and nepotism often go hand in hand. We contend that unfairness is an integral part of nepotism and, as far as authentic leadership is concerned (Avolio & Gardner, 2005; more on authentic leadership later), there is no such thing as "good nepotism," as has been alluded to in the existing literature (Bellow, 2003). For example, when a leader hires a son or a daughter to an important position in an organization on the basis of kinship disregarding (fully or partially) the qualifications required for that position and failing to consider other more qualified candidates, then that constitutes an act of nepotism. On the other hand, by our definition, when a leader hires the best candidate for the position based on skills, talents, and abilities, and the selected individual happens to be the leader's son or daughter, then that does not constitute an act of nepotism.

How, then, do we know whether a leader's decision was equitable, even if the outcome may or may not appear to be so? How can we determine if a leader has made his or her decision based on a candidate's skills, talents, and abilities without letting the aspect of kin membership influence the decision in any way, shape, or form? These are critical questions and that makes it difficult to determine whether a decision was equitable. As stated earlier, Fiske and Taylor (1991) suggested that a leader's perceptions regarding kin members' skills, talents, and abilities are inherently more biased than judgments of unrelated persons. This seems to suggest that a leader can hire a kin member as a result of a biased or faulty decision without being aware of the bias and set a precedent for nepotistic practices in his or her organization without intending to do so.

The remaining chapter will be divided into three sections. In the first section, we provide a brief account of the current state of research on nepotism and leadership. Next, we explore some causal determinants of nepotism in leadership. We begin with an examination of nepotism from an evolutionary perspective and attempt to offer explanations for its existence and apparent prevalence from an inclusive fitness and kin selection perspective. Next, we examine nepotism through a cognitive lens and highlight the potential role of certain heuristics and biases (e.g., principle of least effort) in the origin and practice of nepotism. We also examine the influence of trust dynamics, power, and characteristics of the setting or context (e.g., crisis situations) on the emergence of nepotistic practices by leaders. In presenting this section, our aim is to provide an account of some of the personal, relational, and contextual antecedents of nepotism and thus lay the foundation for an in-depth understanding of the mechanisms by which nepotism has an impact on leadership and leadership effectiveness.

In the second section, we focus on the processes by which nepotism influences leadership and its effectiveness. Specifically, we suggest that the influence of nepotism on leadership effectiveness is mediated by the effect that perceptions of nepotism have on the attitudes and actions of followers, which in turn become the key predictors of the effectiveness of the "nepotized" leader (i.e., someone who is made a leader through perceived nepotism). We also examine the role played by perceptions of nepotism in informing perceptions of a breach of procedural justice and the subsequent impact of such a breach on the formation of undesirable attitudes among followers. Next, we shift our attention to the effects of moderators such as organizational type (viz, work organizations versus social organizations, public organizations versus private organizations, etc.), organizational culture, and leader personality attributes (e.g., charisma, authenticity, integrity, and so forth) on the relationship between perceptions of nepotism and follower attitudes and actions. Last, we attempt to establish a link between nepotism and leadership effectiveness by looking at specific individual-level outcomes of follower motivation, satisfaction, commitment, and performance, and their subsequent impact on broad organizational level outcomes.

In the third and final section, we utilize existing research on authentic leadership (Avolio & Gardner, 2005) to provide a normative account of behaviors that can be used for avoiding, minimizing, or negating the ill effects of nepotism perceptions. Specifically, we focus on empirically validated behaviors associated with authentic leadership that emphasize the establishment of equitable organizational protocols, transparent leader–follower relationships, trust, and an organizational culture geared toward learning. Additionally, we provide insights into the process by which authentic leaders can successfully lead in organizations that have deeply entrenched nepotistic values and practices, thus laying the foundation for leadership initiatives to effectively negotiate the issue of nepotism in ways that do not deter organizational performance. Finally, we suggest avenues for future research to explore the constructs of nepotism and leadership in further detail by providing a set of broad research questions for empirical validation.

CAUSAL DETERMINANTS OF NEPOTISM

Research on nepotism can be characterized as emerging at best. There have been a few attempts at providing descriptive accounts of its nature and how it is manifested in past and present societies (Bellow, 2003). Additionally, some researchers have attempted to empirically verify the effects of nepotism (and perceptions of nepotism) on leadership. For instance, Kets de Vries (1993) interviewed 300 executives associated with family-controlled firms and contrasted the advantages and the disadvantages of family firms. Werbel and Hames (1996) examined attitudes toward paired employees (i.e., dual-career couples working for the same organization) and found that spouse employment status, supervisory role, gender, and organizational size determined the extent to which paired employees were perceived negatively by others. Padgett and Morris (2005) explored the consequences of nepotism in the hiring process and found that perceptions of nepotism yielded judgments of inequity, and individuals known to have benefited through nepotistic actions were viewed less favorably than individuals believed to have been hired on merit. Arasli and Tumer (2008) found that nepotism, cronyism, and favoritism were important causes of job stress in the workplace (with nepotism's effect being the greatest) and were also responsible for reduced levels of satisfaction.

Such findings have helped organizational and social scientists obtain a better understanding of some of the causes, effects, and the underlying mechanisms of nepotism. However, a systematic theoretical representation of the antecedents of the construct, of how it tends to influence social psychological processes such as those associated with leadership, and how such processes in turn influence subsequent leadership outcomes has been conspicuous by its absence. In spite of the rapid evolution of leadership research, few would disagree that nepotism and its effects have not been adequately theorized and empirically studied, and that there is a void that begs to be filled. In the following section, we aim to take the first step toward filling that void by outlining some of the evolutionary, cognitive, relational, and contextual antecedents of the practice of nepotism.

EVOLUTIONARY DETERMINANTS OF NEPOTISM

Evolutionary theorists view nepotism (and many other social behaviors) (Wilson, 1975) as resulting from the idea of *inclusive fitness*, that organisms include the survival and reproduction of genetic relatives as part of their own individual "reproductive fitness" (classically defined as producing offspring as a way of genetic survival) (Hamilton, 1964a, 1964b). Because the survival and success of related individuals increase the likelihood that our genes will survive in some way (because related individuals are likely to reciprocate help and support we provide to them), we are more likely to provide resources and to behave "altruistically" toward related individuals than to unrelated individuals. Hamilton (1964a) argues that our assistance to a relative depends on the costs of the behavior and whether they are greater than the benefits for the other individual, with benefits outweighing costs more and more as genetic relatedness of the helper and help recipient increases. As such, we are more likely to provide help to relatives more closely related to us, particularly offspring. Such helping behaviors toward relatives and other characteristics that in some way benefit kin are thus supported evolutionarily (Smith, 1964).

Sociobiologists define nepotism as "the dispensing of benefits to relatives other than offspring or other direct descendants" (Alexander, 1979, pp. 45–46). The dispensing of benefits to offspring is merely called *parenting* within sociobiological approaches (Alexander, 1979), so providing resources more commonly and abundantly to offspring than to non-relatives (our definition of nepotism, which involves the idea of biased preferences to all relatives, including offspring) is perfectly natural and really the main point of any organism's existence—the survival of genes themselves (Dawkins, 1976). Kin supportive behaviors like nepotism are called *kin altruism* (Smith, 1964), and are described as phenotypically altruistic (apparently self-sacrificing) but genotypically selfish (a genetic purpose of promoting gene survival) (Alexander, 1979). Whether we are talking about food and shelter or wealth and power, including ownership of parents' property or a leadership position in a business organization, providing for offspring and relatives is evolutionarily advantageous and normative, not exceptional in any way. While we do differ somewhat from sociobiology in our definitions of nepotism (particularly in terms of the appropriateness and advantages of such behaviors depending on context and social norms), sociobiological research on parental investment, and delay of dispersal in particular provide insight into understanding when leaders are nepotistic (or when people become leaders through the practice of nepotism).

If providing resources to offspring is so advantageous to us, why do we not live with our parents throughout our own adulthood? Certainly, a multitude of macro- and microlevel situational processes influence family structures and living patterns, particularly culture (Berry & Georgas, 2009).

Sociobiological research on parental investment indicates that devotion of resources to any one offspring will depend on associated costs, including the ability to invest in other offspring (Trivers, 1972, 1974). The ability to invest in any one offspring is diminished by the number of offspring present in the household, and it is difficult to maintain investment in any one offspring over long periods of time into adulthood. Thus offspring are likely to leave the parental household once they reach the age of self-sufficiency. Research on parental investment indicates that even when parents attempt to follow equity or fairness principles in their treatment of their children by distributing resources equally among them, certain children (namely, middleborns) are disadvantaged because they are rarely if ever the sole child in the household and thus never experience a period of time where they are the sole recipients of parental investment (Hertwig, Davis, & Sulloway, 2002).

Parents may intentionally overinvest in one offspring who shows particular promise or who is particularly valued; indeed, parental differential treatment is rather common (Brody, Copeland, Sutton, Richardson, & Guyer, 1998; Kowal, Kramer, Krull, & Crick, 2002), particularly in cultures where firstborn children are more highly valued and in cultures where boy children are valued more than girl children (McHale, Updegraff, Shanahan, Crouter, & Killoren, 2005; Tsai, 1998). Leaders who are nepotistic are likely to choose particular offspring over others in bequeathing leadership positions or extensive power and resources to offspring. For example, historically, sons have been favored over daughters and firstborns have been assigned to higher positions in terms of birthright (the practice of *primogeniture*) (Hrdy & Judge, 1993). There are evolutionary reasons for this practice as well. Paternity certainty is higher for a firstborn child. If a couple is paired long enough to reproduce multiple offspring, it stands to reason that the male partner would be most certain of his paternity of the firstborn child, possibly conceived in a relatively short period of time. Absolute certainty about the paternity of subsequent children borne by the female partner would require her sexual fidelity to the single male partner over time. As relationship length increases, there are simply more opportunities for other men to father laterborn children. If firstborn sons are lacking in character or ability, parents are likely to select a laterborn child as a main inheritor of power or of an organizational leadership position (as in the case of In-N-Out Burger, where the firstborn son was addicted to drugs and incapable of taking a leadership role in the organization).

In addition to the costs to parents of maintaining investment in off-spring until adulthood, offspring are likely to leave the parental household when they become mature enough for sexual reproduction; sociobiologists call this *dispersal* (Emlen, 1995). Offspring leave the natal territory (the family of origin and household) to improve access to potential mates because of incest restrictions and because potential mates attracted by sexually mature offspring can lead to interfamilial aggression in competition for those mates (Emlen, 1995). Although there is very little research on people, research on many different animal species indicates that sometimes animals engage in *delay of dispersal*, where offspring delay leaving the natal territory in search of mates (Ekman, Baglione, Eggers, & Griesser, 2001). Although offspring may delay leaving the nest for many reasons—including lack of available quality habitats (Brown, 1969), lack of potential mates (Rowley, 1981), and great risks associated with dispersal (Emlen, 1982)—recent research indicates that offspring are especially likely to delay dispersal when the natal territory is rich in resources. That is, sexually mature offspring are most likely to stay with parents when parents provide a high-quality environment; as the quality of the resources provided by parents increases, the motivation to remain with the family and inherit those resources also increases (Emlen, 1995). Studies of animals indicate that family groups will live together (with offspring delaying dispersal) in a particular territory for longer periods of time, over generations, when the environment is rich in resources (Brown, 1987), and that offspring living in such high-quality natal environments are more particular and choosy (Emlen, 1995, p. 8094) in their selection of potential mates. Inheritance of breeding positions, which involves family maintenance of control of group reproduction and the number of sexually mature males allowed into a territory over time, has also been documented in numerous animal species (Brown, 1987; Stacey & Koenig, 1990).

The implications of delay of dispersal for nepotism among people is clear; extended nepotism (favoring kin over others) is especially likely when the family group has substantial resources, including wealth and power. Simply put, wealthy, powerful families are much more likely to be nepotistic than families with little power and wealth. Royal families live together and hand off thrones and crown jewels to each other; they do not distribute such rich resources to nonrelatives and the family is not likely to disperse, but is likely to live together in close proximity, including upon offspring marriage. They are certainly also very choosy in terms of selection of marital partners. By extension, when a family has control over an organization, top leadership and executives are more likely to be nepotistic than are employees who have little control over the organization. Although modern Western societies discourage nepotistic behaviors as "unfair" or "biased," based on strong cultural beliefs in the Protestant work ethic, particularly in the United States (Furnham, 1990), nepotism among the powerful is typical. In fact, there is little apparent reaction on the part of the powerless to nepotistic practices by those in charge (based simply on observation of the ease with which George W. Bush was accepted by the American public as a "fair" presidential candidate). Thus, whereas those of lower socioeconomic status and relatively little social standing are encouraged by Western cultural norms to pull up your boot straps, work hard, and earn position and power, the wealthy and powerful within those same cultures feel perfectly free to practice blatant nepotism, perhaps because it is truly in our nature (or in the nature of our selfish genes) to do so.

COGNITIVE HEURISTICS AND NEPOTISM

The foray into an examination of cognitive heuristics and biases as potential determinants of nepotism provides for an interesting extension to the evolutionary antecedents of nepotism described earlier. At the heart of the process lies the concept of *categories* and the process of categorization. Categories are defined as "mental representations of the classes or groups of events/things/people that help us to structure our knowledge" and categorization is a process by which we place an object, person, or an event into a group of familiar things (Moskowitz, 2005, p. 111). People tend to categorize objects (or people and events) because it saves them from the need to expend extra effort to figure out the exact nature of the stimulus each time they encounter it. It allows them to make sense out of the stimulus and make predictions about what to expect from the stimulus in a relatively efficient (and oftentimes inaccurate) manner, thus reducing the complexity associated with the environment facing them. The utilization of such mental shortcuts has roots in the principle of limited capacity and the principle of least effort (Allport, 1954) outlined next.

The principle of limited capacity (Moskowitz, 2005) states that individuals are bounded in their mental abilities. They have a finite quota of cognitive resources to expend on the literally infinite amount of stimuli they encounter on a day-to-day basis. Given this apparent deficit, it becomes imperative to develop mechanisms that allow sense making in a way that is practical and efficient. Categorization of external stimuli expedites the process of sense making and decision making. Moreover, according to the principle of least effort (Allport, 1954) individuals seek to maximize their outcomes "with the least amount of work possible" (p. 175).

Two heuristics in particular, the representative heuristic and the availability heuristic, can help explain how cognitive shortcuts tend to be responsible for leaders indulging in acts of nepotism and the subsequent formation of perceptions of nepotism within an organization. The representative heuristic can be described as "a rule whereby categorization is made based on overt appearance" and where individuals make decisions about the probabilities that govern relationships between objects (i.e., people and categories) based on the extent to which one is representative of the other (Moskowitz, 2005, p. 142). So, for example, if a successful leader is on the verge of hiring someone for a position that requires the incumbent to have good leadership skills, he or she is bound to make inferences regarding his or her offspring's leadership abilities based on his or her own. Thus, even though there may be other candidates who are more qualified and capable than the leader's own offspring, the leader's decision to hire may be significantly affected by the representative heuristic and he or she may choose to follow the principle of least effort (consciously or otherwise) to reduce the cognitive expenditure associated with making a hiring decision.

The availability heuristic, on the other hand, can be described as a phenomenon whereby individuals make a judgment based on what they can remember or what comes to mind quickly rather than the complete set of data. It is a heuristic "that associates the ease of retrieval of information with the frequency with which this information is encountered and the probability that this information is true" (Moskowitz, 2005, p. 148). Reverting back to the earlier example, a leader may make a decision to hire his or her offspring because he or she may be able to recall his or her offspring's leadership experience, abilities, and talents in much more vivid detail versus those of the other candidates, thus introducing an element of bias in the decision-making process and resulting in an act of nepotism. In sum, nepotism could be viewed as an outcome of cognitive/information processing "laziness."

RELATIONAL DETERMINANTS OF NEPOTISM

Trust Dynamics

The concept of trust plays a significant role in the process of leadership. The benefits accrued when trust is present in a leader–follower relationship offer substantial incentives for leaders to strive to gain the trust of their followers. There have been several different conceptions of trust in the research literature. In an integrative model presented by Mayer, Davis, and Schoorman (1995), trust was defined as the "willingness of a party to be vulnerable to the actions of another party based on the expectation that the other will perform a particular action important to the trustor, irrespective of the ability to monitor or control that other party" (p. 712). Another conception of trust offered by Rousseau, Sitkin, Burt, and Camerer (1998) views trust as the "psychological state comprising the intention to accept vulnerability based upon positive expectation of the intentions of behavior of another" (p. 395). A common thread that can be seen running through the different conceptions of trust is that the trustor is willing to make himself or herself vulnerable to the trustee. Such willingness to be vulnerable has been shown to result in a lot of positive leadership outcomes. For instance, trust in coaches has been found to result in increased performance of basketball teams (Dirks, 2000). Davis, Schoorman, Mayer, and Tan (2000) found that trust in restaurant general managers was positively related to bottom-line sales and profits. Dirks and Ferrin (2002) performed a meta-analysis of the effect of trust in leadership on various organizational outcomes and found that trust in leadership was associated with increased commitment, belief in information, organizational citizenship behaviors, greater satisfaction with the leaders, and greater intentions to stay. Empirical research on trust is quite eloquent regarding the benefits that accrue when leaders enjoy the trust of their followers.

Trust does not exist or happen in a vacuum. There is a series of preconditions that a leader has to satisfy to gain the trust of his or her followers. Butler (1991) used a grounded theory approach and outlined 10 conditions of trust from prior research. They were availability, competence, consistency, fairness, integrity, loyalty, openness, overall trust, promise fulfillment, and receptivity. Thus, for a leader to gain the trust of followers, he or she has to fulfill most if not all of these conditions. Then and only then would the leader be able to reap the rewards associated with high levels of leader–follower trust. Moreover, fulfilling these conditions would require a leader to invest a lot of time and resources in the process, and the resulting outcome (followers' trust) would be a relatively uncertain event in the distant future. What if there was a shortcut that yielded instantaneous trust?

Nepotism offers the perfect shortcut to "buy" trust instantaneously without having to do the hard work associated with "earning" trust. As evidenced in the principle of least effort (Allport, 1954) where individuals tend to maximize their outcomes with the least amount of work possible, leaders have a lot to gain by surrounding themselves with individuals who trust them from the outset. One way of doing this is to hire relatives with whom they have an already established trustworthy relationship. This saves them a lot of time and energy on two fronts. First, they are spared from the effort of looking for a suitable person to assume the roles and responsibilities in question. This frees up a great deal of time and resources that can be diverted toward other avenues. Second, leaders do not have to invest energy in activities associated with trust-building initiatives. They already (think they) know the person. They are aware of the strengths and weaknesses of the person and enjoy the luxury of a ready-made relationship with the person, which seems like a bargain for the price they pay. The overall process becomes much more efficient with the added benefit of greater reliability. This adequately explains the role of trust dynamics in initiating acts of nepotism by leaders. It is therefore not surprising that 95% of all American businesses are family owned or controlled, along with about 40% of the Fortune 500 companies (Bellow, 2003).

Power, Influence, and Nepotism

It is difficult to envision any process of leadership without paying sufficient attention to the concepts of power and influence. Of the several different ways in which leadership has been conceptualized by scholars over the past 100 years, one element that is common across almost all of them is the existence of an intentional influence exercised by a source (i.e., a person or a group of people) over other people to "guide, structure, and facilitate activities and relationships in a group or an organization" (Yukl, 2006, p. 3). Such influence lies at the heart of any leadership process, and to be an effective leader it is important to be able to successfully influence people to work toward a common set of objectives and goals.

Power on the other hand is defined as the "capacity of one party (the agent) to influence another party (the target)" (Yukl, 2006, p. 146). Its nature determines the success of leadership influence attempts. Yukl (2006) outlined three outcomes of leadership influence, namely, commitment, compliance, and resistance. Commitment is described as a psychological state in which followers are in internal agreement with a decision or a request from their leaders. They make an honest and sincere effort to carry out the request or partake in the decision because they believe in it, identify with it, and have internalized it. Compliance was described as an outcome in which followers are willing to do what leaders ask them to do but are rather indifferent about it. Their actions are not characterized by enthusiasm because they may not be totally convinced that the leader's decision or request is the best thing to do. Finally, resistance was described as an outcome in which followers are opposed to leaders' requests or decisions, and they actively try to avoid carrying them out.

Follower commitment has been shown to be related to positive leadership outcomes. If the followers are committed to the leader or to the cause advocated by the leader, it leads to a greater recruitment of effort from them, which significantly enhances the probability of achieving success. On the other hand, if followers are resistant to leaders' influence attempts, very little gets accomplished and it may be characterized as a failure of leadership. Thus, from a leadership perspective, it is very crucial for a leader to wield the right kind of power and to be able to engineer influence attempts in a manner that ensures commitment.

The question of how the pursuit of power may lead to acts of nepotism could be answered quite effectively through the mechanisms associated with the social exchange theory of leadership. The social exchange theory of leadership (Hollander, 1958, 1980) provides an explanation for how power can be gained and lost. According to the social exchange theory, followers accord status and power to leaders after evaluating the leader's contribution to group or organizational goals. Additionally, when leaders exhibit good judgment, they gain idiosyncratic credits and are allowed a greater amount of latitude to deviate from nonessential group norms. Such accumulation of idiosyncratic credits not only takes a long time, it also involves considerable investment of psychological and financial resources by the leader. However, by resorting to acts of nepotism, leaders can utilize existing idiosyncratic credits and can save on expenditures of time and cognitive processing. By hiring members of their kin, leaders succeed in creating an instantaneous network of followers or colleagues over which they have power and who can be influenced relatively easily. Thus, pursuit of efficiency (through unfair means), again, becomes responsible for the prevalence of nepotism in organizations.

It is interesting to note that nepotism may be more likely to occur when the level of power (and wealth) is greater. Powerful individuals, such as leaders (business, political, or others), may be reluctant to lose their strong power base (Kipnis, 1976). Therefore, they strive to maintain familial control over their power resources. Indeed, there is some evidence that the more power individuals have, the more likely they are to engage in self-serving behavior (Mitchell, Hopper, Daniels, Falvy, & Ferris, 1998), so one can imagine that the greater the power, the greater the tendency toward nepotism in the selection of successors.

CONTEXTUAL DETERMINANTS OF NEPOTISM

The process of leadership oftentimes does not allow the luxury of operating under optimal conditions and within the most favorable of contexts. Leaders are frequently faced with crisis situations that compel them to act outside their zone of comfort and make tough decisions in a rapid manner. James and Wooten (2005) defined crisis as "any emotionally charged situation that, once it becomes public, invites negative stakeholder reaction and thereby has the potential to threaten the financial well-being, reputation, or survival of the firm or some portion thereof" (p. 142). They classified crises into two broad categories: sudden crises and smoldering crises. Sudden crises were described as "those unexpected events in which the organization has virtually no control and perceived limited fault or responsibility" (James & Wooten, 2005, p. 142). For example, natural disasters, terrorist attacks, plant explosions, and workplace violence could be classified as sudden crises. Smoldering crises, on the other hand, were described as "those events that start out as small, internal problems within a firm, become public to stakeholders and, over time, escalate to crisis status as a result of inattention by management" (p. 143). For example, product defects, rumors/scandals, workplace safety issues, and so forth, could be characterized as smoldering crises.

Events in a crisis situation frequently occur (or are perceived to occur) more rapidly than those during normal times. The environment is generally characterized by confusion, indecision, and the individuals facing the crisis may or may not be prepared to deal with the rigors of the situation. The potential risks associated with making an incorrect decision are sufficiently large to add to the already emotionally charged environment. Time, in such situations, is at an absolute premium and leaders bear the added onus of having to lead under extreme pressure. Also, under such circumstances, followers expect their leaders to be more assertive, directive, and decisive (Mulder & Stemerding, 1963), and to exhibit initiative in defining the problem at hand, formulating a solution, and leading the group's response to the crisis.

James and Wooten (2005) described building a foundation of trust, and making wise and rapid decisions as two important competencies for successful leadership in crises. Given that time is scarce, it becomes necessary for leaders to successfully build an environment of trust as quickly as they possibly can. As described in the previous section, nepotism offers the perfect solution for leaders who are willing to divorce equity in favor of bottom-line outcomes. By hiring members of their kin, leaders can be assured that they are surrounded by individuals who they can trust, and thus save them the added time and resources that go into trust-building initiatives. Additionally, because of the rapidly evolving context as a result of the prevailing crisis, leaders are forced to make quick decisions. So, when faced with a hiring decision, they find it easier to tap into the social kinship network with which they are familiar, leading to nepotism. This seems to conform with findings that have shown that leaders in crisis situations tend to use less consultation with their followers (Mulder, De Jong, Koppelaar, & Verhage, 1986); exercise more power; and are more directive, autocratic, and goal oriented (Mulder, Ritsema van Eck, & De Jong, 1970).

NEPOTISM AND LEADERSHIP: UNDERLYING MEDIATING MECHANISMS

Nepotism and perceptions of nepotism tend to exert an impact on organizational outcomes through multiple pathways. When organizational citizens or followers of a leader witness an act of nepotism, they may experience a breach of an implicit psychological contract that lays at the foundation of any well-functioning and equitable organization. It tends to have an adverse effect on many fronts. First and foremost, a display of nepotistic behavior by a leader sends a clear signal that equity as an organizational value can potentially be compromised without any reprisal. For example, when a leader hires a member of his or her kin by disregarding other more qualified candidates, it sets a precedent for the future implying that other things besides honest and intelligent efforts are acceptable means to get ahead in the organization. Such precedents may set organizational norms that suggest that compromising on quality is tolerable. Additionally, this could spark a contagion of sorts, where the ill effects of such actions are reflected in organizational decision making. For example, if the top leader of an organization is seen exhibiting not only nepotism, but also cronyism (favoritism based on group membership), the middle-level leaders could adopt a similar rationale for decisions regarding, for example, choosing vendors. Because favoritism is seen as an implicitly accepted norm, vendors who are related to the chief decision makers or those belonging to the in-group may receive undue preference. This may lead to significant problems and may be an important reason for leadership failure.

Second, the establishment of counterproductive norms can violate procedural justice expectations of organizational citizens. Leventhal (1980) outlined four criteria that people utilize to determine which procedures are fair or unfair. He suggested that for people to experience a perception of fairness during a decision-making process, the procedures associated with the decision-making process should be consistent across persons, should be able to make accurate use of all the available information, should be in line with fundamental morals and ethical values, and should represent the core concerns and values of the individuals that would be affected by the decision. Blatant acts of nepotism by top-level organizational leaders or even the existence of the perceptions of nepotism among organizational citizens tends to violate all four of these criteria, leading to a breach of procedural justice expectations.

Such breaches of procedural justice expectations, if experienced on a regular basis, could potentially lead to reduced levels of follower motivation. If the followers feel that their hard work is not going to matter, they will be less inclined to give full effort to their roles and responsibilities. Moreover, low levels of follower motivation could potentially impact the extent to which they are committed to their jobs, their leader, and their organization. This could trigger a chain reaction, with the outcomes being reduced job satisfaction, reduced intentions to stay, and finally an increase in organizational turnover. This does not augur well for any organization that wishes to remain stable and profitable. Principles of effective leadership dictate that a substantial amount of initiative and effort need to be expended toward making sure that procedural justice expectations are met.

As previously noted, evidence suggests that nepotism, cronyism, and favoritism are associated with high levels of job stress and low levels of job satisfaction (Arasli & Tumer, 2008). Additionally, individuals who have benefited from acts of nepotism are viewed less favorably than individuals who are perceived to have been hired on the basis of merit (Padgett & Morris, 2005). Such perceptions can potentially result in the formation of an organizational culture that is deficient in trust. Organizational trust has been shown to be one of the most important foundations of a well-functioning organization. Low levels of trust combined with the absence of general overall cohesiveness as a result of leader nepotism could potentially affect intermediary outcomes such as organizational citizenship behaviors and helping behaviors. These have been shown to predict organizational success, meaning that perceptions of nepotism may detract from core organizational performance.

It is clear that nepotism occurs in all kinds of organizations, but the perception of nepotism may change depending on the type of organization or sector. As noted earlier, in the business world, particularly in privately held companies (much like in monarchist governments), there is a belief system about birthright—a *right* to keep the ownership/leadership of the company (or the crown) in the family. This notion of birthright may be diminished somewhat when companies go public and ownership passes to shareholders. In the leadership of democratic governments, there is less acceptance of nepotism, but of course, the notion of political family dynasties suggests that among voters there is some acceptance of keeping governmental control and power "in the family." In nonelected leadership positions in government, there would be less tolerance of nepotism (imagine the questions that would be raised by a school principal or city manager who hired relatives). The perception of nepotism in the nonprofit sector might be less clear. One can imagine that many nonprofit organizations are like startup business enterprises, with a founder dedicated to solving some social problem or ill. In these instances, there may be greater acceptance of placing relatives in positions of leadership; but not so in larger or older nonprofits that are more detached from the founder.

Regardless of the type of organization, the perception of nepotism is important for leadership effectiveness. From a leadership perspective, an important issue might be acceptance or tolerance for nepotism. Tolerance for nepotism can be seen as an individual difference variable, or a group or cultural-level construct. Tolerance for nepotism refers to how accepted nepotism, as we have defined it (unqualified relative chosen as leader over more qualified nonrelatives), is by an individual or group. If followers, for example, are more tolerant of nepotism, they are more accepting of nepotistic decisions in leader succession and less likely to object. Likewise, in certain groups or cultures, there may be greater acceptance of nepotism in leader succession or selection. Tolerance for nepotism as an individual difference is likely related to other traditional belief systems, such as authoritarianism, dogmatism, and social dominance orientation (Christie, 1991).

In cultures or systems that are accepting of and tolerant of nepotism, it may be easier to keep leadership within the family. Yet, this clashes with egalitarian ideals and with best practices in leadership, which both argue the importance of merit (e.g., experience, qualifications) in leader selection or succession. In the United States, there appears to be ambivalent tolerance of nepotism. Although the culture respects the right of family-owned businesses to put control and leadership into the hands of family members, instances like the fight for control of In-N-Out Burger between inexperienced family members and experienced executives suggests such ambivalence. Nonrelative employees appeared to feel some sense of ownership of their work organization and disagreed with the idea that family members should hold control regardless of their experience and regardless of the outcomes for the organization. This suggests a sense that decisions in leader selection and succession in U.S. organizations should be merit based.

NEPOTISM AND AUTHENTIC LEADERSHIP

There is growing concern about the quality of leadership, and particularly about leader ethics and authenticity in business, government, and elsewhere (Gardner, Avolio, & Walumbwa, 2005). Numerous authors have called for greater attention to ethical leadership issues (Ciulla, 1998). Nepotism, as we have defined it (viz, unfair displays of favoritism by a leadership source that are based on kinship), can be considered a form of "unethical" or at the very least "inauthentic" leader behavior. Hiring an unqualified relative over a more qualified nonrelative is, simply put, a bad leadership practice. In an effort to understand how leaders can and should work to prevent nepotism in leader selection or succession, we rely on a recent model of "authentic leadership" (Walumbwa, Avolio, Gardner, Wernsing, & Peterson, 2008).

In part, authentic leadership involves leaders who possess "greater self-awareness and self-regulated positive behaviors" (Luthans & Avolio, 2003, p. 243). The four components that constitute the construct of authentic leadership are (a) leader self-awareness, (b) relational transparency, (c) balanced processing, and (d) internalized moral perspective (Walumbwa et al., 2008). Leaders with these qualities may be more likely to resist nepotistic tendencies and do the right thing in selecting leaders and successors in their organizations. In the following section, we will use these dimensions to explore the processes through which authentic leaders are able to avoid engaging in nepotistic behaviors as well as successfully operate in organizations that have firmly entrenched nepotistic values and practices.

The first component of authentic leadership is *self-awareness*. It involves a leader's clear self-perception—a recognition of one's strengths and limitations. It also involves an understanding of how one's behavior impacts others. Self-aware leaders will resist the temptation to engage in nepotism, fully understanding that one does no favors for the unqualified relative who is placed in the position of leadership. Moreover, the self-aware leader realizes that unfair displays of favoritism based on kinship could potentially have an adverse impact on organizational members and on the performance of the organization itself.

The second component of authentic leadership is *relational transparency*. It involves presenting one's true self to others and openly expressing thoughts and feelings to them. It also involves openly sharing information (versus indulging in secrecy and obfuscation) and creating close bonds that are based on intimacy and trust. An authentic leader therefore is clear about feelings—"I would like to keep control of this organization in the family, but I realize that more capable persons will likely lead more effectively"—and communicates them to followers. Relational transparency, and the trust that it tends to build in followers, will be particularly important if the leader decides that a relative is indeed the most qualified person for the leadership position. Under such circumstances, it will help combat perceptions of nepotism when the selected kin member is the best choice.

The third component of authentic leadership is *balanced processing*. It is critical to all forms of good leader selection and is particularly important in combating nepotism. Balanced processing involves objectively analyzing data before making decisions and putting aside personal feelings and biases, such as denials, exaggerations, distortions, private knowledge, and ignorance of internal experiences. It is called balanced processing (and not unbiased processing) because "humans are inherently flawed and biased as information processors, particularly when it comes to processing self relevant information" and allows authentic leaders to "make accurate and balanced self assessments, as well as social comparisons" (Gardner, Avolio, Luthans, May, & Walumbwa, 2005, p. 356). If the leader engages in this form of analysis, particularly in leader selection, nepotism is avoided simply because the best qualified individual is eventually chosen.

The fourth and final component of authentic leadership is *internalized moral perspective*. It allows authentic leaders to indulge in "an ethical and transparent decision-making process whereby authentic leaders develop and draw on reserves of moral capacity, efficacy, courage, and resiliency to address ethical issues and achieve authentic and sustained moral actions" (Avolio & Gardner, 2005, p. 324). It suggests that a leader is guided by internal moral standards and values, and acts consistently with those. The authentic leader is concerned about the various organizational stakeholders and what is good for them and the organization. As a result, an authentic leader would resist nepotism because it is inconsistent with his or her own moral standards.

It seems quite clear that leader authenticity would combat nepotism. Perhaps more important, though, authentic leadership may combat perceptions of nepotism when none exists. There are many instances when selection of a kin member may be the correct choice (see Bellow, 2003), and it is these instances where leader authenticity may be particularly good for the organization.

As stated previously, about 95% of all American businesses are family owned or controlled along with about 40% of the Fortune 500 companies (Bellow, 2003). Given this apparent widespread potential for nepotism in American business, it becomes critical that leadership models, such as the authentic leadership model, provide normative accounts of ways and means by which leaders can successfully lead in nepotistic environments.

Authentic leaders can act as agents of change and be able to lead successfully in a nepotistic environment or organization in three ways. First, by inculcating a strong sense of self-awareness within themselves as well as within their peers and their followers, authentic leaders can generate a better collective understanding of how nepotism and perceptions of nepotism can have an impact on different organizational elements and outcomes. By generating such a shared sense of understanding, authentic leaders can prepare their followers and colleagues to deal with any persisting or anticipated ill effects as a result of prevailing nepotistic practices. Second, authentic leaders can initiate the process of transforming a nepotistic organization into an organization that values and practices equitable and fair procedures by advocating adherence to a positive moral perspective. By providing a new moral backbone to a nepotistic environment, authentic leaders will be able to realign the values and practices prevalent in the organization, and set the course toward the creation of a culture that gives preference to qualifications, hard work, and experience versus membership to a particular group. Third, authentic leaders can ensure fairness in decision making by putting in place mechanisms that objectively evaluate the decision-making process through multiple methods and sources. They can use standardized procedures to assess everyone objectively and information from multiple sources can be evaluated by multiple decision makers to ensure that the process of decision making is fair and involves minimal bias. And finally, authentic leaders can ensure fairness in decision making by making the decision-making process completely transparent. By practicing and promoting relational transparency, they can create a transparent organizational culture where organizational citizens focus on achieving openness and truthfulness in their relationships with each other. This would ensure that every concerned stakeholder in the decision would have knowledge regarding how the decision was made and will have the opportunity to raise red flags in case the decision-making process indicates a departure from equitable principles. This is likely to result in an environment where information is communicated and shared openly, and there are high levels of interpersonal trust and commitment among organizational citizens.

NEPOTISM AND LEADERSHIP: A RESEARCH AGENDA

Given the importance of nepotism in the specific area of leadership, it is quite surprising that there is not more research on the topic. What follows are suggested avenues for research building from our review of nepotism and its relationship with leadership.

First and foremost, we need to *develop a better understanding of the definition, and identification, of nepotism.* We have suggested a definition of nepotism that focuses on unqualified relatives being selected for positions of organizational leadership. There may be more subtleties to the construct of nepotism, and the actual measurement of nepotism as we have defined it may be difficult to achieve (i.e., what constitutes "unqualified").

We need to *distinguish between nepotism and perceived nepotism, and understand the dynamics of each* construct. Although nepotism may or may not exist in the selection of a leader, it is the perception of nepotism by stakeholders in the organization that can affect important work outcomes, such as motivation, organizational commitment, satisfaction with the leadership, and bottom-line variables (e.g., productivity/performance, and voluntary absenteeism and turnover).

A key aspect of perceptions of nepotism is what we are referring to as tolerance for nepotism, which is construed as an individual-level and group- or culture-level variable. Individuals and cultures with low tolerance for nepotism are likely to react more negatively to nepotism (or perceived nepotism) in the selection of leaders. Those with high tolerance for nepotism may be largely unaffected by nepotism in the leader selection process and show little variance in their behavior regardless of who leads them.

Integration of nepotism into all aspects of leadership research is needed. We are quite excited about the wide-open field of research opportunities in the study of nepotism. As in other aspects of leadership, we can imagine studying a variety of precursors to nepotism in leader selection or succession. For instance, do constructs related to tolerance of nepotism—social dominance orientation, authoritarianism, traditional values—predict who will be more or less likely to be nepotistic? Will situational elements, such as crises (as we have previously discussed), increase the incidence of nepotism? What are other contingencies associated with the practice of nepotism?

What about *sex differences in nepotism*? Are perceptions of nepotism more likely to emerge if the chosen relative is male rather than female? Are men more likely to engage in nepotism? Given the paucity of women leaders in business and government, is there lesser or greater tolerance when nepotism involves men versus women? How are stakeholders' perceptions of nepotism colored by gender?

Another interesting question to explore would be what if the nepotized leader's organization succeeds or fails. Would failure on the part of a nepotized leader be judged more harshly than failure by a nonnepotized leader? On the other hand, would success on the part of a nepotized leader be discounted in comparison with success on the part of a nonnepotized leader? Also, to what extent can a nepotized leader enjoy the support, commitment, trust, and loyalty of his or her followers following a failure in comparison with a non-nepotized leader? These are some interesting questions that future research must address if we are to have a better understanding of how nepotism and leadership work hand in hand.

Finally, what will happen if the research spotlight shines on nepotism, as we have defined it, in the workplace? Will the public begin to rethink the general acceptance of nepotistic decisions in organizations (e.g., family-owned businesses) and will this have an impact on future leader selection decisions? The research possibilities are truly abundant.

REFERENCES

Alexander, R. D. (1979). *Darwinism and human affairs.* Seattle: University of Washington Press.

Allport, G. W. (1954). *The nature of prejudice.* Cambridge, MA: Addison-Wesley.

Arasli, H., & Tumer, M. (2008). Nepotism, favoritism, and cronyism: A study of their effects on job stress and job satisfaction in the banking industry of north Cyprus. *Social Behavior and Personality, 36*(9), 1237–1250.

Avolio, B. J., & Gardner, W. L. (2005). Authentic leadership development: Getting to the root of positive forms of leadership. *Leadership Quarterly, 16*, 315–318.

Bellow, A. (2003). *In praise of nepotism: A natural history.* New York: Doubleday.

Berry, J. W., & Georgas, J. (2009). An ecocultural perspective on cultural transmission: The family across cultures. In U. Schönpflug (Ed.), *Cultural transmission: Psychological, developmental, social, and methodological* (pp. 95–125). New York: Cambridge University Press.

Brody, L. R., Copeland, A. P., Sutton, L. S., Richardson, D. R., & Guyer, M. (1998). Mommy and daddy like you best: Perceived family favoritism in relation to affect, adjustment, and family process. *Journal of Family Therapy, 20*(3), 269–291.

Brown, J. L. (1969). Territorial behavior and population regulation in birds. *Wilson Bulletin, 81*, 293–329.

Brown, J. L. (1987). *Helping and communal breeding in birds.* Princeton, NJ: Princeton University Press.

Butler, J. K. (1991). Toward understanding and measuring conditions of trust: Evolution of conditions of trust inventory. *Journal of Management, 17*, 643–663.

Christie, R. (1991). Authoritarianism and related constructs. In J. P. Robinson, P. R., Shaver, & L. S. Wrightsman, (Eds.), *Measures of social psychological attitudes* (pp. 501–571). San Diego, CA: Academic Press.

Ciulla, J. (1998). *Ethics, the heart of leadership.* Westport, CT: Quorum Books.

Davis, J. H., Schoorman, F. D., Mayer, R. C., & Tan, H. H. (2000). The trusted general manager and business unit performance: Empirical evidence of a competitive advantage. *Strategic Management Journal, 21*, 563–576.

Dawkins, R. (1976). *The selfish gene.* Oxford, UK: Oxford University Press.

Dirks, K. T. (2000). Trust in leadership and team performance: Evidence from NCAA Basketball. *Journal of Applied Psychology, 85*, 1004–1012.

Dirks, K. T., & Ferrin, D. L. (2002). Trust in leadership: Meta-analytic findings and implications for research and practice. *Journal of Applied Psychology, 87*, 611–628.

Ekman, J., Baglione, V., Eggers, S., & Griesser, M. (2001). Delayed dispersal: Living under the reign of nepotistic parents. *The Auk: Perspectives on Ornithology, 118*, 1–10.

Emlen, S. T. (1982). The evolution of helping, I: An ecological constraints model. *American Naturalist, 119*, 29–39.

Emlen, S. T. (1995). An evolutionary theory of the family. *Proceedings of the National Academy of Science USA, 92*, 8092–8099.

Fiske, S. T., & Taylor, S. E. (1991). *Social cognition* (2nd ed.). New York: McGraw-Hill.

French, J., & Raven, B. H. (1959). The bases of social power. In D. Cartwright (Ed.), *Studies of social power* (pp. 150–167). Ann Arbor, MI: Institute of Social Research.

Furnham, A. (1990). A content, correlational, and factor analytic study of seven questionnaire measures of the Protestant work ethic. *Human Relations, 43*, 383–399.

Gardner, W. L., Avolio, B. J., Luthans, F., May, D. R., & Walumbwa, F. O. (2005). "Can you see the real me?" A self-based model of authentic leader and follower development. *The Leadership Quarterly, 16*, 343–372.

Gardner, W. L., Avolio, B. J., & Walumbwa, F. O. (Eds.). (2005). *Authentic leadership theory and practice: Origin, effects, and development.* Oxford, UK: Elsevier.

Hamilton, W. D. (1964a). The genetical evolution of social behavior, I. *Journal of Theoretical Biology, 7*, 1–16.

Hamilton, W. D. (1964b). The genetical evolution of social behavior, II. *Journal of Theoretical Biology, 7*, 17–52.

Hertwig, R., Davis, J. N., & Sulloway, F. J. (2002). Parental investment: How an equity motive can produce inequality. *Psychological Bulletin, 128*, 728–745.

Hollander, E. P. (1958). Conformity, status, and idiosyncrasy credit: *Psychological Review, 65*, 117–127.

Hollander, E. P. (1980). Leadership and social exchange processes. In K. J. Gergen, M. S. Greenberg, & R. H. Willis (Eds.), *Social exchange: Advances in theory and research* (pp. 343–354). New York: Plenum Press.

Hrdy, S. B., & Judge, D. S. (1993). Darwin and the puzzle of primogeniture: An essay on biases in parental investment after death. *Human Nature, 4*, 1–45.

James E. H., & Wooten, L. P. (2005). Leadership as (un)usual: How to display competence in times of crisis. *Organizational Dynamics, 32*(2), 141–152.

Jones, R. G., Stout, T., Harder, B., Levine, E., Levine, J., & Sanchez, J. I. (2008). Personnel psychology and nepotism: Should we support anti-nepotism policies. *The Industrial Organizational Psychologist, 45*, 17–20.

Kets de Vries, M. F. (1993). The dynamics of family controlled firms: The good and the bad news. *Organizational Dynamics, 21*(3), 59–71.

Kipnis, D. (1976). *The powerholders.* Chicago: University of Chicago Press.

Kowal, A., Kramer, L., Krull, J. L., & Crick, N. R. (2002). Children's perceptions of the fairness of parental preferential treatment and their socioemotional well-being. *Journal of Family Psychology, 16*, 297–306.

Leventhal, G. S. (1980). What should be done with equity theory? New approaches to the study of fairness in social relationships. In K. J. Gergen, M. S. Greenberg, & R. H. Willis (Eds.), *Social exchange: Advances on theory and research.* New York: Plenum Press.

Luthans, F., & Avolio, B. J. (2003). Authentic leadership: A positive developmental approach. In K. S. Cameron, J. E. Dutton, & R. E. Quinn (Eds.), *Positive organizational scholarship: Foundations of a new discipline* (pp. 241–258). San Francisco, CA: Berrett-Koehler

Mayer, R. C., Davis, J. H., & Schoorman, F. D. (1995). An integrative model of organizational trust. *Academy of Management Journal, 20*(3), 709–734.

McHale, S. M., Updegraff, K. A., Shanahan, L., Crouter, A. C., & Killoren, S. E. (2005). Siblings' differential treatment in Mexican-American families. *Journal of Marriage and Family, 67,* 1259-1274.

Mitchell, T. R., Hopper, H., Daniels, D., Falvy, J. G., & Ferris, G. R. (1998). Power, accountability, and inappropriate actions. *Applied Psychology: An International Review, 47,* 497–517.

Moskowitz, G. B. (2005). *Social cognition: Understanding self and others.* New York: Guilford Press.

Mulder, M., De Jong, R. D., Koppelaar, L., & Verhage, J. (1986). Power, situation, and leaders' effectiveness: An organizational study. *Journal of Applied Psychology, 71,* 566–570.

Mulder, M., Ritsema van Eck, J. R., & De Jong, R. D. (1970). An organization in crisis and non-crisis conditions. *Human Relations, 24,* 19–41.

Mulder, M., & Stemerding, A. (1963). Threat, attraction to group, and need for strong leadership. *Human Relations, 16,* 317–334.

Padgett, M. Y., & Morris, K. A. (2005). Keeping it "all in the family": Does nepotism in the hiring place really benefit the beneficiary? *Journal of Leadership and Organizational Studies, 11*(2), 34–45.

Rousseau. D. N., Sitkin, S. B., Burt, R. S., & Camerer, C. (1998). Not so different after all: A cross-discipline view of trust. *Academy of Management Review, 23,* 393–404.

Rowley, I. (1981). The communal way of life in the Splendid Wren, *Malurus splendens. Zeitschrift für Tierpsychologie, 55,* 228–267.

Simon, R. J., Clark, S. M., & Tifft, L. L. (1966). Of nepotism, marriage and the pursuit of an academic career. *Sociology of Education, 39,* 344–358.

Smith, J. M. (1964). Group selection and kin selection. *Nature, 201,* 1145–1147.

Stacey, P. B., & Koenig, W. B. (Eds.). (1990). *Cooperative breeding in birds: Long-term studies of ecology and behavior.* Cambridge, UK: Cambridge University Press.

Trivers, R. L. (1972). Parental investment and sexual selection. In B. Campbell (Ed.), *Sexual selection and the descent of man, 1871–1971* (pp. 136–179). Chicago: Aldine.

Trivers, R. L. (1974). Parent–offspring conflict. *American Zoologist, 14,* 249–264.

Tsai, W. H. (1998). *Marriage and the family: The sociology of family.* Taipei, Taiwan: Wu-Nan Publishing.

Walumbwa, F. O., Avolio, B. J., Gardner, W. L., Wernsing, T. S., & Peterson, S. J. (2008). Authentic leadership: Development and validation of a theory-based measure. *Journal of Management, 34*(1), 89–126.

Werbel, J. D., & Hames, D. S. (1996). Anti-nepotism reconsidered: The case of husband and wife employment. *Group and Organization Management, 21*(3), 365–379.

Wilson, E. O. (1975). *Sociobiology: The new synthesis.* Cambridge, MA: Harvard University Press.

Yukl, G. (2006). *Leadership in organizations.* Upper Saddle River, NJ: Prentice-Hall.

9

The Cultural Boundary of Managing Nepotism

Guillermo Wated
Barry University

Juan I. Sanchez
Florida International University

Nepotism refers to the preferential treatment provided to others (e.g., relatives, friends, acquaintances) by an agent in a position of power when such preferential treatment is motivated by the beneficiary's relationship with the agent rather than by merit (Conway, 2004; Jones, 2006; Padgett & Morris, 2005; Singell & Thomton, 1997). The benefits of nepotism range from favorable evaluations leading to wage increases to preferential hiring. From a merit-based perspective, this practice may be regarded as unethical since it involves the abuse of one's position in the interest of one's family or one's in-group, thereby leading to transgressions of both procedural and distributive justice (Colquitt, Greenberg, & Zapata-Phelan, 2005). Such transgressions may provoke withdrawal or, possibly worse, incite counterproductive behavior among the least favored employees.

This negative view of nepotism has led several authors to include it among other forms of corruption like bribery and extortion (for example, Alatas, 1999; Schnudel, 2009). Nevertheless, not everyone shares this negative view of nepotism. For instance, it has been argued that some degree of preferential treatment toward in-group members may promote all-encompassing values of trust and solidarity, thereby fostering corporate cultural environments that are personal and warm (Welch & Welch, 2006).

Regardless of whether one sees it in a negative light, nepotism seems to be a widespread phenomenon that is very much alive in organizations (He, 2005; Jones, 2004). For instance, Lentz and Laband (1990) suggested that nepotism is practiced in admissions to medical school. Werbel and Hames (1996) examined the perceptions of small-business employees toward paired employees (dual-career couples) who work for the same organization. Arasli, Bavik, and Ekiz (2006) investigated the impact of nepotism on job satisfaction, intention to quit, and word-of-mouth reputation among Turkish Cypriot hotel employees in Northern Cyprus. Furthermore, Bellow (2003) suggested that several sectors of the American society, including the movie industry and the political class, have effectively embraced nepotism; for example, Albert Gore Jr., George W. Bush, Jeb Bush, Jane Fonda, Michael Douglas, and Gwyneth Paltrow are all successful second-generation politicians and actors.

Despite its allegedly widespread existence, few studies have researched the phenomenon of nepotism at the organizational level (for example, Arasli et al., 2006; Arasli & Tumer, 2008). Even though such studies have yielded some evidence of the relationship between nepotism and work-related outcomes, there does not seem to be a well-accepted theoretical framework providing insight into the antecedents of nepotism.

We contend that cultural values allow for a better understanding of nepotism. For instance, in the case of Latin America, it can be argued that dominant cultural values such as collectivism may predispose individuals to favor nepotism. Individualism–collectivism (I–C) refers to the relationship between the individual and society, with individualism pertaining to societies with loose ties among individuals, whereas collectivism characterizes societies in which individuals form cohesive in-groups (Hofstede, 1980). This emphasis on interdependence among in-group members in collectivistic societies may in turn trigger an employment decision mechanism that promotes in-group favoritism. According to social identity theory, members of one's in-group tend to be perceived in more favorable terms and assumed to have more desirable traits than those of the out-group (Tajfel, 1984). Furthermore, humans tend to make decisions that favor in-group members regardless of their fairness or discriminatory nature (Turner, Brown, & Tajfel, 1979). In fact, Gudykunst et al. (1992) found that members of collectivist cultures make stronger distinctions between in- and out-group members than those in individualist cultures.

The model presented here is an attempt to better understand the interplay between cultural background and managers' tolerance of nepotism in the relatively homogeneous context of Latin America. Managers' actions send a powerful message to all organizational stakeholders, thereby playing a key role in shaping the norms that regulate organizational members' behavior. However, dominant cultural values alone cannot explain a phenomenon as complex as nepotism. We argue that managers' attitudes, social norms, attributions, and goals interact with regionally dominant cultural values to shape managers' decisions to tolerate preferential treatment of certain stakeholders based on personal relations. Accordingly, this chapter aims at integrating different theoretical perspectives into a comprehensive model explaining how dominant cultural values are a driving force at the core of tolerance toward nepotism. But our aim is not simply to make a theoretical contribution to our understanding of the phenomenon of nepotism, but also to provide a set of pragmatic recommendations intended to balance an organization's need to minimize the impact that nepotism may have on those who are affected by it, with the need to preserve the role of culturally acceptable local relationships that assist corporations in the accomplishment of their global objectives.

As stated earlier, nepotism is a universal phenomenon. Yet, we chose the Latin American region as the setting to present our model not only because its relatively cultural homogeneity but also because of the alleged persistent of nepotism in less developed countries (Hayajenh, Maghrabi, & Al-Dabbagh, 1994). In particular, Latin American history has been characterized by the persistent and intense presence of a wide range of corruption-like behaviors, which, like nepotism, are believed to limit economic development, social change, and welfare (Gaviria, 2001). As early as the year 1813, while battling for independence against Spain, Simón Bolívar already recognized the impact of corruption on the public interest by issuing a decree stipulating the death penalty for corrupt public officials (Coronel, 2006). The continued presence of such practices in Latin America is illustrated by the 1999–2000 Ecuadorian banking crises. Analysts agree that the collapse of the Ecuadorian banking system was partly due to bankers' predispositions to give high-risk loans to well-connected political and business figures of their inner circle ("Ecuador Economy," 2000). Corrupt banking practices in Ecuador precipitated the failure of 16 banks, which controlled 70% of the country's deposits. The collapse of the financial system eventually led to the replacement of the 115-year-old national currency, the sucre, with the U.S. dollar. It was not a mere coincidence that Transparency International ranked Ecuador as the most corrupt country in Latin America in the year 2000 ("Optimism After," 2000).

In a more recent example, teachers across Mexico went on strike blocking highways and seizing government property as they protested against a federal education reform aiming to end practices associated with nepotism (Lloyd, 2008). Upon retirement, Mexican teachers working for government schools customarily passed their jobs to their children or sold their appointments, in some instances for as much as $6,000. This practice has been blamed for fueling corruption in the educational system and is regarded as a relic from the past when teaching was considered to be a trade rather than a profession (Lloyd, 2008).

The president of Venezuela, Hugo Chávez, has been accused of allowing his family members to accrue unusual power: his younger brother is the mayor of his hometown, his father heads its surrounding state (Barinas), another of his brothers holds the job of secretary of state for the state of Barinas (a position specially created for him by the president), still another brother supervises the government's construction projects, and yet another of his brothers has been appointed by the president to serve at the Venezuelan Embassy in Canada and in Cuba (Romero, 2007). Despite the fact that combating such practices has been a stated priority of Chávez's administration (Coronel, 2006), Venezuela ranks among the most corrupt countries in Latin America and the world (Transparency International, 2009). In spite of all of these facts, Chávez's government continues to enjoy impressive levels of popular approval, with rates as high as 70% since his election in 1999 (Grant, 2008).

In Bolivia, a 12-year old boy became the world's youngest professional soccer player when his father (the team's coach) allowed him to play in a first division match during the final 9 minutes (Carroll, 2009). The boy earned a standing ovation from the fans after being injured during the game; accusations of nepotism were dismissed by the father who stated his contentment with his decision.

To summarize, the model presented here proposes that culture predisposes managers to favor nepotism. More specifically, we propose that an emphasis on interdependence among in-group members in collectivistic societies may be triggering an employment decision mechanism that promotes nepotism. Furthermore, we argue that managers' culturally driven desire to maintain group cohesiveness influences their attitudes, social norms, attributions and goals, and shapes their tolerance toward nepotism. Latin America was used as the context to present our model given its relative cultural homogeneity and the alleged persistence of the phenomenon in the region. In the following section, we provide a road map for the chapter by presenting a brief outline of its content.

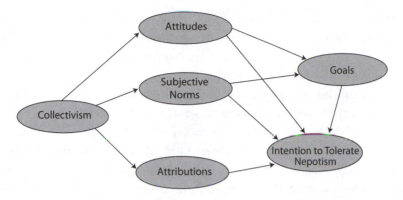

FIGURE 9.1
Model predicting managers' tolerance toward nepotism.

CHAPTER OVERVIEW

We begin by outlining a process model (see Figure 9.1) that explains managerial tolerance toward employees' acts of preferential treatment to select stakeholders by shedding light onto the cultural characteristics that may indirectly drive this phenomenon. We then draw from several theories, including the theory of planned behavior, attribution theory, and stakeholder theory to identify variables that seemingly influence managers' intentions to tolerate nepotism. In line with Ajzen's (1991) theory of planned behavior (TPB), we maintain that a manager's intention to tolerate nepotism in an organization is determined by the manager's attitudes, subjective norms, and perceived behavioral control. As Ajzen noted, "the theory of planned behavior is, in principle, open to the inclusion of additional predictors if it can be shown that they capture a significant proportion of the variance in intention or behavior after the theory's current variables have been taken into account" (p. 199). Consequently, we expand Ajzen's notion of perceived behavioral control by examining it in the context of Heider's (1958) attribution theory. Specifically, attribution theory further expands on the notion of control by distinguishing between internal (i.e., caused by the person) and external (i.e., caused by the context) attributions. We argue that the distinction between internal and external attributions can fruitfully enrich the role of perceived behavioral control, particularly for collectivist societies. In collectivist societies, individuals are especially attentive to external causes of behavior (Hofstede, 1984). Therefore, in collectivist societies, nepotism should be better understood in light of both internal and external factors.

The integration of theories proposed here is then further enriched by incorporating the role of managerial goals into the model. Jensen's (2001) enlightened stakeholder theory emphasizes the formulation of managerial goals that encourage long-term organizational value maximization, while attending to all legitimate stakeholders' demands. Indeed, goals provide direction to intention (Locke & Latham, 1990); yet, goal setting can in turn be influenced by individuals' beliefs as well as societal values (Steers & Sanchez-Runde, 2002). Hence, our model also incorporates the role that culture may play in attitude and norms formation as related to setting of managers' objectives. Finally, practical implications are discussed regarding the effectiveness of organizational procedures, such as anti-nepotism policies intended to curtail the practice of nepotism, the impact that nepotism may have on employees who do not benefit from it, and culturally sensitive ways to deal with nepotism in organizations within the Latin American context.

CULTURAL VALUES AS ANTECEDENTS OF ATTITUDES, NORMS, AND ATTRIBUTIONS IN PREDICTING MANAGERIAL TOLERANCE TOWARD NEPOTISM

Societies develop different cultural solutions to basic problems due to idiosyncrasies in their physical, historical, and socioeconomic situation. These factors impact not only the way individuals relate to one another but also their decision-making process (Kluckhohn & Strodtbeck, 1961; Vitell, Nwachukwu, & Barnes, 1993). For instance, all societies deal with more or less pronounced differences in the distribution of resources across their members. Societies with an uneven distribution of wealth tend to house cultures that accept such differences, whereas societies with a burgeoning middle-class adhere to cultures that advocate more egalitarian values. Accordingly, dominant cultural values also represent part of the environment that an individual manager must filter, through his or her experience and education, to arrive at a decision (Wines & Napier, 1992).

In particular, Hofstede's (1980) cultural construct of I–C is commonly associated with ethics research, and it has proven to be useful in capturing the relationship between culture and a number of behaviors (Bernardi, Witek, & Melton, 2009; Hofstede, 1984; Trompenaars, 1994). For instance, Wagner (1995) examined the influence of I–C on the level of cooperation in groups, whereas Gomez, Kirkman, and Shapiro (2000) used it to predict in- and out-group team members' evaluations. Similarly, we propose that the I–C dimension also influences intentions to tolerate nepotism as predicted by attitudes, subjective norms, and attributions. It seems that collectivists have a greater tendency to attribute actors' behavior to external factors than individualists do (Lu, Rose, & Blodgett, 1999). Furthermore, collectivists tend to have a more positive attitude toward in-group than out-group members and adhere to social norms that foster in-group membership and favoritism (Leung & Bond, 1984). As stated earlier, nepotism refers to the preferential treatment provided to relatives or peers, and relatives and peers are indeed regarded as members of the in-group (Tajfel, 1982). Therefore, there are reasons to believe that the I–C dimension will play an important role in managers' intentions to tolerate nepotism.

In collectivist cultures, people value group solidarity and stable friendships (Kim, Triandis, Kagitcibasi, Choi, & Yoon, 1994). People also tend to belong to a few select in-groups, such as family and friendship circles, with whom duties and obligations are critically intertwined (Triandis, Bontempo, Villareal, Asai, & Lucca, 1988). Furthermore, members of the out-group are perceived to possess more undesirable traits, such as dishonesty, than members of the in-group, which further impacts the way individuals relate to each other (Judd, Ryan, & Parke, 1991; Lambert, 1995; Linville & Fischer, 1993). Due to the stability of these in-groups, collectivists have a tendency to discriminate against out-group members in favor of in-group members (Triandis et al., 1988). For example, some studies have shown that people in collectivist countries give more generous reward allocations to recipients who are deemed in-group members (Leung & Bond, 1984).

The fact that collectivists generally favor their in-group is well illustrated by a Latin American saying: *A los amigos todo, a los enemigos nada, al extraño la ley* ("Everything for my friends, nothing for my enemies, the law for strangers"). Davila and Elvira (2005) specifically note that in Latin America, work is seen as the means to one goal, that of providing a "good quality of life for the employee's family" (p. 15). Furthermore, the

Economist Intelligence Unit reported that less than 20% of the population in Argentina, Brazil, Venezuela, and Peru, and just over 20% in Mexico and Chile feel they can trust people ("Latin America," 2008). These levels are in sharp contrast with those gauged in Europe, North America, and Asia where they range from 30% to 70%. Thus, it seems fair to conclude that Latin American managers are, on the average, more likely to hold a positive attitude toward the appointment of relatives, friends, or political associates, regardless of their merits, than managers from less collectivist regions. Their attitude would presumably be based on the belief that such appointment will not only benefit a member of the employee's in-group, but also ensure the appointment of a trustworthy incumbent. The same principles would apply to the perception of subjective norms, that is, these managers will also believe that those important to them would be equally sympathetic to their family and friends.

In the context of attributions, the making of internal or external attributions is also heavily influenced by cultural factors such as the I–C dimension (Hofstede, 1984). Collectivists place a high value on interpersonal harmony and interdependence (Markus & Kitayama, 1991). These values suggest that one's behavior is principally determined by factors other than the actor himself or herself. On the other hand, individualists place a high value on autonomy, competitiveness, independence, individual achievement, and self-sufficiency (Gudykunst, 1998), which should lead them to make internal attributions. In fact, Wated and Sanchez (2005) found a positive relationship between collectivism and external attributions about bribery among Ecuadorian managers. Therefore, there are reasons to believe that collectivist managers will attribute favoritism toward family and friends to allegedly legitimate factors, such as group solidarity, rather than internal factors, such as egotistic goal pursuit or a self-centered orientation.

Furthermore, both Hofstede (1991) and Triandis (1995) pointed out that collectivists are more sensitive to their environments. In contrast, individualists are more self-centered than collectivists and, unlike collectivists, they expect the environment to be sensitive to them (Chiu, 1972). This finding further suggests that collectivistic managers will be more prone to recognize the external benefits of nepotism than those who endorse individualistic principles. Moreover, several streams of research in cross-cultural settings also suggest that I–C is related to the attribution of internal and external causes of nepotism. First, in the academic achievement area, Stevenson and Stieger (1992) concluded that, whereas collectivistic East

Asians associated achievement with context-specific factors, individual-istic Americans associated achievement with internal dispositions. In the marketing arena, Lu et al. (1999) found that people in collectivistic nations seem to place greater value on fellow employees' interests than people in individualistic countries do.

Culture may indeed play a role as an antecedent of nepotism by impact-ing managers' attitudes, subjective norms, and attributions. Nevertheless, we also need to understand the mechanisms through which attitudes, sub-jective norms, and attributions impact managers' intentions. Thus, the next section relies on Ajzen's (1991) TPB in order to highlight the role that atti-tudes, subjective norms, and attributions may play in determining manag-ers' intentions to tolerate the practice of nepotism in organizations.

THE THEORY OF PLANNED BEHAVIOR: THE ROLE OF ATTITUDES, SUBJECTIVE NORMS, AND ATTRIBUTIONS IN PREDICTING MANAGERIAL INTENTION TO TOLERATE NEPOTISM

The goal of the theory of reasoned action and its successor, the theory of planned behavior, is to provide a model to better understand and pre-dict human behavior (Ajzen, 1991). Fishbein and Ajzen (1975) stated that the best predictor of behavior (i.e., whether the action is going to be per-formed or not) is the strength of the intention to perform it. According to Francis et al. (2004), this proposed use of intention as a proximal measure of behavior is one of the most important contributions of the TPB model. It allows the use of the model, despite the fact that there is no perfect rela-tionship between intention and actual behavior, to gauge the effectiveness of interventions in the absence of measures of actual behavior (Francis et al., 2004).

Given that our proposed model is a modified extension of Ajzen's (1991) TPB, the present model can allow us to also gain insight into managers' intentions to tolerate nepotism in organizations. For such purposes, the TPB is best suited to predict the occurrence of specific, intentional behav-iors that are defined in terms of target, action, context, and time (Francis et al., 2004). For instance, the behavior "tolerating employees' prefer-ential treatment of in-group members in hiring decisions" has a target (the employee), an action (tolerating preferential treatment of in-group members), a context (hiring decisions), and an implicit time (at work). In addition, the degree of specificity of the behavior has to correspond to the predictors of the behavior in question (including intention). That is, both predictors and criterion need to adhere to the principle of compatibility in order for the model to accomplish predictive relevance (Ajzen & Fishbein, 1977). According to the principle of compatibility, all measures in a given questionnaire (including the measure of intention) should refer to the same level of generality (Fishbein, 1967). For example, presenting a measure of attitudes toward tolerance of nepotism in general and a measure of intentions to tolerate nepotism in terms of a specific job-related decision such as hiring "in the same questionnaire" would violate the principle of compatibility. Nonetheless, the model can also be used to predict more general behaviors, such as tolerance of preferential treatment of in-group members for overall job-related decisions, provided that the principle of compatibility is observed (Francis et al., 2004).

According to the theories of reasoned action and planned behavior (Ajzen, 1991; Ajzen & Fishbein, 1980; Fishbein & Ajzen 1975), behavioral intention is jointly determined by three factors: the attitude, the subjective norm, and the perceived behavioral control toward the behavior. The attitude toward the behavior, Ajzen and Fishbein (1980) explained, refers to the person's belief that performing the behavior is acceptable or unacceptable. For example, some managers may think that allowing employees to provide preferential treatment to certain stakeholders is an acceptable means of doing business. The subjective norm aspect deals with the social pressure individuals experience regarding whether to perform the behavior. In this case, a manager's belief that most people important to him or her think he or she should allow employees to provide preferential treatment to perceived in-group members will also influence the manager's behavior.

Perceived behavioral control is the individual belief about available resources and opportunities that increase or reduce the difficulty of performing the behavior (Ajzen & Madden, 1986). Ajzen's (1985, 1987, 1991) dimension of perceived behavioral control implies that the manager's impression of how much control the employee had over the behavior will influence the managers' intentions to discipline such an employee. Coincidentally, attribution theory also explains human behavior in terms of perceived behavioral control. However, attribution theory goes one step beyond and distinguishes between internal and external aspects of behavioral control.

Heider (1958) suggested that observers can explain actors' behavior in terms of internal (i.e., caused by the person) or external (i.e., caused by the context) factors. The degree to which a cause is perceived to be under the control of an actor (i.e., an internal cause) has implications for the observer's expectations and future behavior (Weiner, 1986). Specifically, if the observer considers an actor's negative behavior to be the result of uncontrollable external causes, the observer tends to interpret the actor's behavior more positively. On the other hand, if the observer considers an actor's negative behavior to be the result of controllable internal causes, the observer has the tendency to construe the actor's behavior in a rather negative light. For instance, Green and Mitchell (1979) asserted that leaders would reprimand subordinates' actions that led to failure most severely when subordinates were perceived to have high control over a situation. Similarly, managers who perceive their followers' acts of nepotism to be the result of internal causes may also tend to punish it more severely than those who perceive it to be the result of external causes. In other words, managers who perceive employees' practices of nepotism to be caused by external factors such as group solidarity (e.g., helping an unemployed family member) may be more tolerant of such employee behavior than those who perceive it to be caused by internal factors such as personal gain (e.g., charging the family member a specific amount of money in return for the favor).

Despite the role that attitudes, subjective norms, and attributions may play in intentions to tolerate nepotism, there may be other factors that influence managers' decisions to engage in nepotism. As Locke and Latham (1990) stated, goals provide direction to intention, and accounting for their contribution may help to further expand the model. In the following section, we elaborate on the role that managerial goals may play in the prediction of intentions to tolerate nepotism by incorporating stakeholder theory into the model.

THE IMPACT OF ATTITUDES AND NORMS ON GOAL SETTING AND MANAGERIAL TOLERANCE TOWARD NEPOTISM IN THE CONTEXT OF STAKEHOLDER THEORY

According to stakeholder theory, managers' decisions should fit the interests of all legitimate organizational stakeholders, including governments, investors, political groups, suppliers, customers, trade associations, employees, and communities (Donaldson & Preston, 1995). In other words, managerial activities are or should be directed toward obtaining the resources and monetary benefits that will best serve the diverse stakeholders' interests. Yet, scandals involving nepotism are prevalent in today's organizations worldwide (He, 2005; Jones, 2004). For instance, the director of Spain's National Intelligence Center (CIN) recently resigned after accusations of appointing friends and family to government jobs ("Spain's Spy Chief," 2009).

Jensen (2001) explained that stakeholder theory itself may be responsible for managerial failure in delivering value to stakeholders. Managers experience conflicting demands when attempting to meet the multiple objectives of the diverse stakeholders. Without the clarity of a clear goal, managers derail in their attempt to create value for organizations. For instance, a general manager may tolerate a human resources director's decision to hire a family member in an effort to service the economic interest of other workers yet fail to address the impact of the decision on the overall organization's interests. Jensen proposes a revised corporate objective function, the enlightened stakeholder theory, which identifies long-term market value maximization as the organization's ultimate objective. While keeping in mind all stakeholders' interests, managers are held accountable for the long-term sum of all company values including equity, financial claims, warrants, and preferred stock, thereby avoiding conflicting stakeholder demands.

According to Jensen (2001), the enlightened stakeholder theory is "the business equivalent of the Hippocratic Oath" (p. 8). Namely, efforts need to be directed toward establishing measurable managerial goals that deter managers from servicing the interest of a particular group. Accordingly, goals informed by enlightened stakeholder theory's principles direct managers' behavior toward overall value-seeking decisions, which ultimately enable the generation of social welfare. Indeed, goal-setting theory maintains that goals are intended behaviors that influence performance (Locke & Latham, 1990). Nevertheless, the formation of those goals is influenced by the belief systems of individuals, as well as societal values and norms (Steers & Sanchez-Runde, 2002). For instance, a manager's negative attitude toward the preferential treatment of in-group members in hiring decision may trigger the formation of goals that encourage generation of overall social welfare through merit-based principles. Therefore, we propose that attitudes toward nepotism and subjective norms will influence managers' setting of target objectives, which in turn will influence managers' intention to discipline an employee who has favored an in-group member.

PRACTICAL IMPLICATIONS

Nepotism may be perceived by some as a discriminatory practice against out-group members, and it may even considered to be a form of corruption (for example, Alatas, 1999; Schnudel, 2009). And in such instances, organizational practices may need to be repositioned to restore the uneven distribution of resources. Yet, cultural values such as I–C are deeply ingrained in individuals and, as a result, are difficult to change (Kostova & Zaheer, 1999). To achieve change, managers may need to resort to managerial practices that fit rather than clash with dominant values to achieve both attitudinal and normative changes (Osland & Bird, 2000; Weick, 1995). At the heart of nepotism is the implied duty to favor in-group members. Managers may need to redefine the concept of in-group for employees in the context of value maximization for the entire company. Managers should signal that, even though the organization will look after the employee's in-group, the latter is broadly redefined as the organization and its stakeholders in their entirety, and not just the employee's close circle of friends and family. The benefits of this broader definition of in-group should also be clarified to ensure employee buy-in. For instance, Gomez (2004) suggested involving family members in company programs and events to aid employees in redefining their definition of in-group.

Employee orientation, training, and other forms of socialization should probably focus on making the employee proud of being part of the organizational family. According to social identity theory, individual identification with a specific group can indeed help individuals feel pride in this group (Tajfel, 1982). Therefore, when employees see the organization as their in-group, they will have a more positive predisposition to support and engage in decisions that benefit the organization as a whole. Researchers studying Latin America (Gomez, 2004; Gomez et al., 2000; Stephens & Greer, 1995) argue that transferring the employees' and managers' feeling of family to the company can funnel the collectivistic mentality to benefit the organization. For instance, companies in many developing countries use training as a reward or corporate perk, and not just a chance to develop new skills (Drost, Frayne, Lowe, & Geringer 2002). In Mexico, managers thought that training and career development implied that the employee had been embraced as a true in-group member in whose long-term development the organization was genuinely interested.

Organizational attention to managerial attributions that discourage counterproductive practices may also help in hindering the practice of nepotism. As proposed by the present model, managers who attribute employees' behavior to internal causes, such as helping an unemployed family member, may be more tolerant of such employee behavior than those who perceive it to be caused by internal factors, such as personal gain. As Gomez and Sanchez (2005) stated, the HR task is to ensure organizational success by developing human capital according to mission-critical practice guidelines. Therefore, organizations may want to focus on changing managers' perceptions by (a) establishing rules and regulations that explicitly prohibit the practice of nepotism, (b) establishing visible procedures to enforce those rules and regulations, and (c) highlighting that anti-nepotism rules and regulations apply at all organizational levels without exceptions. After all, implementing organizational interventions to change managerial attributions may prove to be easier than trying to change a deeply rooted cultural value such as collectivism.

On the other hand, employees who perceive themselves as victims of nepotism may find it valuable to engage in networking outside of their in-group. According to the contact hypothesis, increased contact among members of different groups under favorable conditions may be effective in reducing misconceptions among them (Pettigrew, 1981). Similarly, increasing contact with people from different groups may increase a particular employee's ability to have his or her knowledge, skills, and abilities recognized by outside members. Attending meetings of, for instance, trade associations, chambers of commerce, or volunteer groups may provide the favorable conditions needed for individuals to expand their social circle. By allowing others to get to know them, employees can forge new friendships and membership in other groups, thereby expanding their employment opportunities.

CONCLUSIONS

The model presented here integrates several research streams to provide insight into the process through which Latin American managers may become tolerant toward the preferential treatment provided by employees to in-group members. We maintain that Hofstede's (1980) cultural construct of I–C serves as a catalyst to Latin American managers' attitudes, subjective norms, and attributions. Furthermore, the model proposes that both attitudes and subjective norms will influence managers' setting of acceptable target objectives that either encourage or hinder nepotism. More specifically, we maintain that managers will be more likely to discipline an employee who has favored a perceived in-group member when they (a) have a negative attitude toward nepotism, (b) perceive social pressure by relevant others to enforce meritocracy, (c) attribute the employee's behavior to internal causes, and (d) set goals that encourage value maximization through meritocracy.

Future models may also explore the role of personality factors in managers' tolerance of nepotism. McCrae (2001) found that individualistic cultures tend to have higher mean levels of extroversion and openness to experience than collectivistic cultures. These results were contrary to expectations and violated national stereotype outlooks suggesting a positive relationship between collectivism and extroversion. Nevertheless, the results provided valuable insight into how personality traits interact with culture in shaping people's lives. McCrae noted that cultural context shapes the influence of personality on behavior, so that two individuals in opposite cultural environments (e.g., collectivistic versus individualistic), but with similar personalities traits (e.g., both high on extroversion), can react differently to a particular situation. For instance, McCrae explained that an outgoing Frenchman and a talkative Korean can share the same extroverted traits; yet the behavioral expression of such tendency may be bound to their cultural context. Similarly, managers who exhibit extroverted traits in a collectivist context may engage more in interaction with members of their in-group than of the out-group and may be less likely to be interested in learning about out-group members. Subsequently, they will be more willing to tolerate preferential treatment of recognizable in-group members than of unfamiliar out-group constituents. On the other hand, managers who exhibit extroverted traits in an individualistic environment may engage in interactions with members of both the in-group and the out-group. Consequently, they will be less willing to tolerate preferential treatment of in-group members. As Triandis et al. (1988) stated, "people in individualist cultures are very good at meeting outsiders, forming new in-groups, and getting along with new people"

(p. 325). On the other hand, collectivists are more likely to associate with members of their own group and discount out-group members. McCrae in fact suggested that collectivistic institutions may essentially arise as a survival mechanism to compensate for the lack of interaction with others at the individual level.

Finally, the purpose of our model is not to suggest that the practice of nepotism in Latin America leads to more or less effective organizational functioning, nor to argue that nepotism is more or less ethically acceptable in certain regions. It merely provides a path to guide such interventions as deemed appropriate by the organization's constituents. The tolerance level for nepotism is a social construction that needs to fit rather than clash with dominant cultural values (Osland & Bird, 2000; Weick, 1995). Therefore, the notion that management practices may be modified needs to be in accordance to the needs of organizations as well as individuals who benefit or are affected by the practice of nepotism. In instances where preferential treatment to relatives or friends in employment practices is negatively impacting employees' job satisfaction (for example, Arasli & Tumer, 2008), nepotism may need to be ruled out. On the other hand, nepotism may be encouraged when preferential treatment toward in-group members promotes culturally appropriate personal and warm corporate environments as proposed by Welch and Welch (2006).

REFERENCES

Ajzen, I. (1985). From intentions to actions: A theory of planned behavior. In J. Kuhl & J. Beckman (Eds.), *Action–control: From cognition to behavior* (pp. 11–39). Heidelberg, Germany: Springer.

Ajzen, I. (1987). Attitudes, traits, and actions: Dispositional prediction of behavior in personality and social psychology. In L. Berkowitz (Ed.), *Advances in experimental social psychology* (Vol. 20, pp. 1–63). New York: Academic Press.

Ajzen, I. (1991). The theory of planned behavior. *Organizational Behavior and Human Decisions Processes, 50,* 170–211. DOI: 10.1016/0749-5978(91)90020-T

Ajzen, I., & Fishbein, M. (1977). Attitude-behavior relations: A theoretical analysis and review of empirical research. *Psychological Bulletin, 84,* 888–918. DOI: 10.1037/0033-2909.84.5.888.

Ajzen, I., & Fishbein, M. (1980). *Understanding attitudes and predicting social behavior.* Englewood Cliffs, NJ: Prentice-Hall.

Ajzen, I., & Madden, T. J. (1986). Prediction of goal-directed behavior: Attitudes, intentions, and perceived behavioral control. *Journal of Experimental Social Psychology, 22,* 453–474. DOI: 10.1016/0022-1031(86)90045-4.

Alatas, S. H. (1999). *Corruption and the destiny of Asia.* Englewood Cliffs, NJ: Prentice-Hall.

Arasli, H., Bavik, A., & Ekiz, E. (2006). The effects of nepotism on human resource management: The case of three, four and five star hotels in Northern Cyprus. *International Journal of Sociology and Social Policy, 26*, 295–308. DOI: 10.1108/01443330610680399.

Arasli, H., & Tumer, M. (2008). Nepotism, favoritism and cronyism: A Study of their effects in job stress and job satisfaction in the banking industry of North Cyprus. *Social Behavior and Personality, 36*, 1237–1250. DOI: 10.2224/sbp.2008.36.9.1237.

Bellow, A. (2003, July/August). In praise of nepotism. *The Atlantic*. Retrieved from http://www.theatlantic.com/doc/200307/bellow.

Bernardi, R. A., Witek, M. B., & Melton, M. R. (2009). A four-country study of the associations between bribery and unethical actions. *Journal of Business Ethics, 84*, 389–403. DOI: 10.1007/s10551-008-9715-2.

Carroll, R. (2009, July 23). Bolivian boy of 12 becomes youngest professional footballer: Despite accusations of nepotism because his father is coach, boy says he is "happiest man in the world" after his debut. *Guardian.co.uk*. Retrieved from http://www.guardian.co.uk/world/2009/jul/23/youngest-footballer-bolivia.

Chiu, L. H. (1972). A cross-cultural comparison of cognitive styles in Chinese and American children. *International Journal of Psychology, 8*, 235–242. DOI: 10.1080/00207597208246604.

Colquitt, J. A., Greenberg, J., & Zapata-Phelan, C. (2005). What is organizational justice? A historical overview. In J. Greenberg & J. A. Jason (Eds.), *Handbook of organizational justice*. Mahwah, NJ: Lawrence Erlbaum Associates.

Conway, B. (2004). The new nepotism. *Public Interest, 154*, 130.

Coronel, G. (2006). Corruption, mismanagement, and abuse of power in Hugo Chávez's Venezuela. *Center for Global Liberty and Prosperity: Development Policy Analysis, 2*, 1–23.

Davila, A., & Elvira, M. M. (2005). Culture and human resources management in Latin America. In M. M. Elvira & A. Davila (Eds.), *Managing human resources in Latin America* (pp. 3–24). New York: Routledge.

Donaldson, T., & Preston, L. E. (1995). The stakeholder theory of the corporation: Concepts, evidence and implications. *Academy of Management Review, 20*, 65–91.

Drost, E. A., Frayne, C. A., Lowe, K. B., & Geringer, J. M. (2002). Benchmarking training and development practices: A multi-country comparative analysis. *Human Resource Management, 41*, 6–86. DOI: 10.1002/hrm.10020.

Ecuador economy hurting, warmly switches to the dollar. (2000, June 1). *The Boston Globe*, p. A1.

Fishbein, M. (1967). Attitude and the prediction of behavior. In M. Fishbein (Ed.), *Readings in attitude theory and measurement* (pp. 477–492). New York: Wiley.

Fishbein, M., & Ajzen, I. (1975). *Belief, attitude, intention, and behavior*. Reading, MA: Addison-Wesley.

Francis, J. J., Eccles, M. P., Johnston, M., Walker, A., Grimshaw, J., Foy, R., ... Bonetti, D. (2004). *Constructing questionnaires based on the theory of planned behavior: A manual for health services researchers*. Newcastle upon Tyne, UK: Center for Health Services Research.

Gaviria, A. (2001). Assessing the effects of corruption and crime on firm performance. *Emerging Markets Review, 3*, 245–268.

Grant, W. (2008). Local elections test Chávez support. *BBC News*. Retrieved from http://news.bbc.co.uk/2/hi/americas/7733690.stm.

Green, S. G., & Mitchell, T. R. (1979). Attributional processes of leaders in leader-member interactions. *Organizational Behavior and Human Performance, 23*, 429–458. DOI: 10.1016/0030-5073(79)90008-4.

Gomez, C. (2004). The influence of environmental, organizational, and HRM factors on employee behaviors in subsidiaries: A Mexican case study of organizational learning. *Journal of World Business, 39*, 1–11. DOI: 10.1016/j.jwb.2003.08.006.

Gomez, C., Kirkman, B. L., & Shapiro, D. L. (2000). The impact of collectivism and in-group/out-group membership on the evaluation generosity of team members. *Academy of Management Journal, 43*, 1097–1106.

Gomez, C., & Sanchez, J. I. (2005). HR's strategic role within MNC: Helping build social capital in Latin America. *International Journal of Human Resource Management, 16*, 2189–200. DOI: 10.1080/09585190500298438.

Gudykunst, W. B. (1998). Individualistic and collectivistic perspectives on communication: An introduction. *International Journal of Intercultural Relations, 22*, 107–134. DOI: 10.1016/S0147-1767(98)00005-4.

Gudykunst, W. B., Gao, G., Schmidt, K., Nishida, T., Bond, M. H., Leung, K., … Barraclough, R. A. (1992). The influence of individualism collectivism, self-monitoring, and predicted-outcome value on communication in in-group and out-group relationships. *Journal of Cross-Cultural Psychology, 23*, 196–213. DOI: 10.1177/0022022192232005.

Hayajenh, A. F., Maghrabi, A. S., & Al-Dabbagh, T. H. (1994). Research note: Assessing the effect of nepotism on human resource managers. *International Journal of Manpower, 15*, 60–67. DOI: 10.1108/EUM0000000003933.

He, W. (2005). Introduction: Kinship and family in international context. *International Journal of Sociology and Social Policy, 25*, 1–8. DOI: 101108/01443330510791108.

Heider, F. (1958). *The psychology of interpersonal relations.* New York: Wiley.

Hofstede, G. (1980). *Culture's consequences: International differences in work-related values.* Beverly Hills, CA: Sage.

Hofstede, G. (1984). The cultural relativity of the quality of life concept. *Academy of Management Review, 9*, 389–398. DOI: 10.2307/258280.

Hofstede, G. (1991). *Cultures and organizations: Software of the mind.* London: McGraw-Hill.

Jensen, M. C. (2001). Value maximization, stakeholder theory, and the corporate objective function. *Journal of Applied Corporate Finance, 14(3)*, 8–21. DOI: 10.1111/j.1745-6622.2010.00259.x.

Jones, R. (2004). [Review of the book *In praise of nepotism: A natural history*, by A. Bellow]. *Personnel Psychology, 57*, 550–553.

Jones, R. G. (2006). Corporate ethics. In *Encyclopedia of industrial and organizational psychology*. Thousand Oaks, CA: Sage.

Judd, C. M., Ryan, C. S., & Parke, B. (1991). Accuracy in the judgment of in-group and out-group variability. *Journal of Personality and Social Psychology, 61*, 366–379. DOI: 10.1037/0022-3514.61.3.366.

Kim, U., Triandis, H. C., Kagitcibasi, C., Choi, S., & Yoon, G. (1994). *Individualism and collectivism.* Thousand Oaks, CA: Sage.

Kluckhohn, F., & Strodtbeck, F. (1961). *Variations in value orientations.* Evanston, IL: Row, Peterson.

Kostova, T., & Zaheer, S. (1999). Organizational legitimacy under conditions of complexity. The case of multinational enterprises. *Academy of Management Review, 24*, 64–81.

Lambert, A. J. (1995). Stereotypes and social judgments: The consequences of group variability. *Journal of Personality and Social Psychology, 68*, 388–403. DOI:10.1037/0022-3514.68.3.388.

Latin America politics: Corruption's taint. (2008, October 1). *The Economist Intelligence Unit.* Retrieved from http://proquest.umi.com.ezproxy.barry.edu/pqdweb?did=1587934331&sid=15&Fmt=3&clientId=18082&RQT=309&VName=PQD.

Lentz, B. F., & Laband, D. N. (1990). Why so many children of doctors become doctors: Nepotism versus human capital transfer. *Journal of Human Resources, 24,* 396–413.

Leung, K., & Bond, M. H. (1984). The impact of cultural collectivism on reward allocation. *Journal of Personality and Social Psychology, 47,* 793–804. DOI: 10.1037/0022-3514.47.4.793.

Linville, P. W., & Fischer, G. W. (1993). Exemplar and abstraction models of perceived group variability and stereotypicality. *Social Cognition, 11,* 92–125.

Lloyd, M. (2008, October 12). For Mexico's teachers, jobs are things to inherit or sell, and they're on strike to keep it that way: Standardizing gets tested. *Houston Chronicle.* Retrieved from http://www.chron.com/disp/story.mpl/moms/6054921.html.

Locke, E. A., & Latham, G. P. (1990). *A theory of goal setting and task performance.* Englewood Cliffs, NJ: Prentice-Hall.

Lu, L. C., Rose, G. M., & Blodgett, J. G. (1999). The effects of cultural dimensions on ethical decision making in marketing: An exploratory study. *Journal of Business Ethics, 18,* 91–105. DOI: 10.1023/A:1006038012256.

Markus, H. R., & Kitayama, S. (1991). Culture and the self: Implications for cognition, emotion, and motivation. *Psychological Review, 98,* 224–253. DOI: 10.1037/0033-295X.98.2.224.

McCrae, R. R. (2001). Trait psychology and culture: Exploring intercultural comparisons. *Journal of Personality, 69,* 819–846. DOI: 10.1111/1467-6494.696166.

Optimism after the chaos: U.S. dollar, oil prices bring measure of stability to Ecuador's finances. (2000, November 7). *The Miami Herald,* p. 1C.

Osland, J. S., & Bird, A. (2000). Beyond sophisticated stereotyping: Cultural sensemaking in context. *Academy of Management Executive, 14,* 65–77.

Padgett, M. Y., & Morris, K. A. (2005). Keeping it all in the family: Does nepotism in the hiring process really benefit the beneficiary? *Journal of Leadership and Organizational Studies, 11*(2), 34–45. DOI: 10.1177/107179190501100205.

Pettigrew, T. G. (1981). Extending the stereotype concept. In D. L. Hamilton (Ed.), *Cognitive processes in stereotyping and intergroup behavior* (pp. 303–331). Hillsdale, NJ: Erlbaum.

Romero, S. (2007, February 18). Chávez family dogged by nepotism claims. *The New York Times.* Retrieved from http://www.nytimes.com/2007/02/18/world/americas/18iht-venez.html.

Schnudel, C. J. W. (2009). Corruption and bilateral aid: A dyadic approach. *Journal of Conflict Resolution, 52,* 507–526. DOI: 10.1177/0022002708316646.

Singell, L. D., & Thomton, J. (1997). Nepotism, discrimination and the persistence of utility-maximizing, owner operated firms. *Southern Economic Journal, 63*(4), 904–920.

Spain's spy chief quits after nepotism accusations. (2009, July 2). *Reuters India.* Retrieved from http://in.reuters.com/article/worldNews/idINIndia-40764720090702.

Steers, R. M., & Sanchez-Runde, C. J. (2002). Culture, motivation, and work behavior. In M. J. Gannon & K. L. Newman (Eds.), *The Blackwell handbook of principles of crosscultural management* (pp. 190–216). Bodmin, UK: MPG Books.

Stephens, G. K., & Greer, C. R. (1995). Doing business in Mexico: Understanding cultural differences. *Organizational Dynamics, 24,* 39–55. DOI: 10.1016/0090-2616(95)90034-9.

Stevenson, H. W., & Stieger, J. W. (1992). *The learning gap: Why our schools are failing and what we can learn from Japanese and Chinese education.* New York: Summit Books.

Tajfel, H. (1982). *Social identity and intergroup relations.* Cambridge, UK: Cambridge University Press.

Tajfel, H. (1984). Social psychology of intergroup relations. *Annual Review of Psychology, 33,* 1–39. DOI: 10.1146/annurev.ps.33.020182.000245.

Transparency International. (2009). *Global corruption report*. Retrieved from http://www.transparency.org/publications/gcr/gcr_2009.

Triandis, H. C. (1995). *Individualism and collectivism*. Boulder, CO: Westview Press.

Triandis, H. C., Bontempo, R., Villareal, M. J., Asai, M., & Lucca, N. (1988). Individualism and collectivism: Cross-cultural perspectives on self-in-group relationships. *Journal of Personality and Social Psychology, 54*, 323–338. DOI: 10.1037/0022-3514.54.2.323.

Trompenaars, F. (1994). *Riding the waves of culture: Understanding cultural diversity in global business*. New York: McGraw Hill.

Turner, J. C., Brown, R. J., & Tajfel, H. (1979). Social comparison and group interest in in-group favoritism. *European Journal of Social Psychology, 9*, 187–204.

Vitell, S. J., Nwachukwu, S. L., & Barnes, J. H. (1993). The effects of culture on ethical decision making: An application of Hofstede's typology. *Journal of Business Ethics, 12*, 753–760. DOI: 10.1007/BF00881307.

Wagner, J. A. (1995). Studies of individualism-collectivism: Effects on cooperation in groups. *Academy of Management Journal, 38*, 152–172.

Wated, G., & Sanchez, J. I. (2005). The effects of attitudes, subjective norms, attributions, and individualism–collectivism on managers' responses to bribery in organizations: Evidence from a developing nation. *Journal of Business Ethics, 61*, 111–127. DOI: 10.1007/s10551-005-8712-y.

Weick, K. E. (1995). *Sensemaking in organizations*. Thousand Oaks, CA: Sage.

Weiner, B. (1986). *An attribution theory of motivation and emotion*. New York: Springer-Verlag.

Welch, J., & Welch, S. (2006, August 21). The nitty-gritty on nepotism. *Business Week*, p. 144. Retrieved from http://www.businessweek.com/perm/content/06_34/b3998070.htm.

Werbel, J. D., & Hames, D. S. (1996). Anti-nepotism reconsidered. *Group and Organization Management, 21*, 365–379. DOI: 10.1177/1059601196213006.

Wines, W. A., & Napier, N. K. (1992). Toward an understanding of cross-cultural ethics: A tentative model. *Journal of Business Ethics, 11*, 831–841. DOI: 10.1007/BF00872361.

10

A Model of Organizational Nepotism

Bridgette K. Mulder
De Paul University

The purpose of this chapter[1] is to present a model of organizational nepotism that integrates the limited research on nepotism with more robust research findings from closely related areas (e.g., organizational justice, affirmative action, family-owned businesses). Many of the constructs and relationships presented in the model have already been addressed in the previous chapters and the objective here is to provide a clear rationale while minimizing repetition. To begin, the underlying assumptions of the model are discussed first, followed by the presentation of the model, and concluding with some preliminary research findings and implications. If a reader has not yet been convinced of the importance of increasing research efforts toward nepotism by the contents of the preceding chapters, it is hoped that one would, at minimum, have a more thorough understanding of the practice after considering the massive scope, scale, and impact this practice can have on individuals, families, organizations, and even societies.

UNDERLYING MODEL ASSUMPTIONS

There are three primary assumptions underlying the model of nepotism presented in this chapter. The first assumption is based on what may be best described as the neutrality principle. Similar to the humanitarian principles of neutrality (see, for example, the International Federation of Red Cross and Red Crescent Societies, n.d., neutrality principle), nepotism is a practice that must be considered and researched from an unbiased, or *neutral* perspective. This perspective allows researchers to obtain accurate findings and make sound recommendations to organizations regarding practices. Bellow's (2003) main assertion is that, despite its negative connotations and the common emphasis on its negative consequences, we should assume that nepotism itself is neither good nor bad. Rather, it is the way nepotism is practiced that determines its positive or negative characteristics. Although much of what currently exists in the nepotism literature has focused on its negative aspects, the model itself is presented as an impartial organizing framework potential relationships and their associated outcomes.

Second, it is assumed that nepotism is practiced in a variety of ways among family members and may include anything from hiring to promotion, or from inflated performance appraisals to avoidance of disciplinary practices. Although much of the following discussion refers to hiring practices or promotions, it is still assumed that nepotism is any form of (preferential) treatment provided to one or more family members but not granted to others within the same organization. It is understood that this type of (preferential) treatment may occur within an organization among nonfamily members as well. However, the emphasis and basis for this model relies heavily on kinship, a factor unique to nepotism that differentiates it from other organizational practices. Kinship is expected to substantially influence the predictors and outcomes of nepotism in a way that may not exist in other circumstances.

The third assumption underlying the model is that economic, industry, cultural, and organizational factors are all intertwined (Jones, 2004; Katz & Kahn, 1978; Senge, 1990). In other words, it is assumed that nepotism arises from, operates under, and is affected by economic, industry, cultural, and organizational conditions. Economic and industry conditions are important precursors of any opportunity for employment and may affect the ultimate success of a decision to engage in nepotism. Culture can be viewed similarly to economic and industry conditions, and several authors in the previous chapters have already noted the important role culture may have in determining the frequency and outcomes of nepotism (for example, Dickson, Nieminen, & Biermeier-Hanson, this volume, Chapter 5; Van Hooft & Stout, this volume, Chapter 4; Wated & Sanchez, this volume, Chapter 9). From an organizational perspective, numerous factors may impact the decision to utilize nepotism and how successful that decision will prove. These factors include the organization's history, culture, and norms, as well as characteristics such as its size, location, and family-owned versus nonfamily-owned status.

Based on these underlying assumptions, the model is, therefore, presented next, with the neutrality principle and the unique factor of kinship at its core, and the recognition of the importance of contextual and systemic dynamics at play in these situations.

A MODEL OF ORGANIZATIONAL NEPOTISM

The model is displayed in Figure 10.1 and is based on the most current (albeit limited) nepotism survey and research findings. Findings from organizational justice research, economics, and evolutionary psychology were also important to the model's development. Two bodies of literature were particularly influential and warrant further elaboration before providing a detailed discussion of the model. These are the research pertaining to family-owned businesses (FOBs) and research pertaining to affirmative action (AA).

As Muchinsky (this volume, Chapter 3) notes, the research surrounding FOBs has obvious potential for overlap with nepotism, given that family members are employed within the same organization and nepotism is a fact of life. Two particularly relevant topics are (a) the FOB subsystems at work in the FOB research; and (b) decision-making abilities and processes in the organization.

Tagiuri and Davis (1996) identify three overlapping FOB subsystems: business, ownership, and family. They argue that these three subsystems and their overlapping components explain how individuals in a family business make strategic decisions and how they interact with one another depending upon where an individual falls within the overlapping subsystems. Parker (2004) puts forth a prescriptive decision-making model with the purpose of providing guidance to decision makers in a family business when a business opportunity arises (Figure 10.2). Taking the unique interactions of FOBs into consideration, Parker designed her model to progress through four levels of questioning, with the goal of leading the decision-maker to a more objective final conclusion—one based less on family matters and more on the consideration of all relevant perspectives and options.

Like much of the FOB research, Parker's (2004) model does not directly address nepotism. However, applying key features of her model makes sense because of the potential factors that both family-owned and nonfamily-owned firms may need to acknowledge regarding a decision to utilize nepotism, as well as decisions that must be made once nepotism occurs

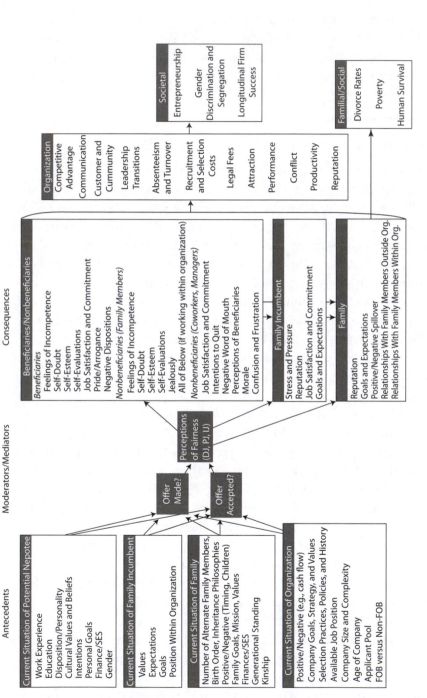

FIGURE 10.1
Model of organizational nepotism.

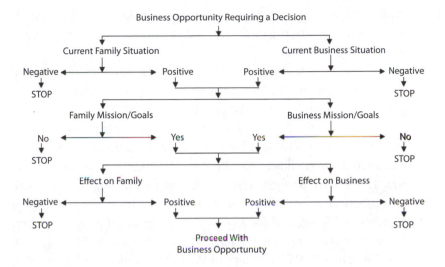

FIGURE 10.2
Parker's (2004) multilevel family business choice model.

(e.g., reporting relationships between family members, business decisions that may impact the family, and vice versa). Parker's concept of a business opportunity arising is the first step in the process, followed by an analysis of the current family and business situations. These are incorporated into the model of nepotism with two minor modifications.

First, the goals and mission of the family and business are extended in the model under the "individual nepotee's current situation" and the "current situation of the family incumbent." Thus, the business, family, family incumbent, and nepotee are all believed to have goals and missions that impact decisions to extend and accept offers of nepotism. Second and similarly, the "current situations of the family and organization" are extended to the nepotee and family incumbent. This means that the nepotee's and incumbent's current situations are as important to decisions of nepotism as the current situations of the family and business.

The result of the modifications to Parker's (2004) model is four major categories of antecedents: (1) the current situation of the nepotee; (2) the current situation of the family incumbent (both considered at the individual level in the model); (3) the current situation of the family; and, (4) the current situation of the organization (both considered at the group level in the model). A similar distinction between individual- and group-level variables is made regarding the consequences of the model: Beneficiaries, nonbeneficiaries, and the family incumbent are considered at the individual level, with the family, organization, social, and societal consequences presented at the group level.

Similar to the FOB research, the AA literature provides meaningful examples of variables to consider when researching and modeling nepotism, given the parallels between the two. One of the most frequently cited negative aspects in both AA and nepotism is the idea of preferential treatment and the debate regarding an individual being hired based upon factors other than merit (Bellow, 2003; Ford & McLaughlin, 1986; Kravitz et al., 1997). This debate provides the foundation for the stigma associated with both practices as well. The AA stigma results from the assumption that an individual is selected for a position as a result of group membership rather than qualifications (Golden, Hinkle, & Crosby, 2001; Harris, Lievens, & Van Hoye, 2004; Heilman, 1994; Heilman, Block, & Lucas, 1992; Heilman, Simon, & Repper, 1987; Kluegel & Smith, 1983). Similarly, the stigma associated with nepotism arises from the belief that nepotism is not just favoring a relative, but also favoring someone who is unqualified or incompetent compared to other applicants (Bellow, 2003). Although the basis of preferential treatment may differ between the two situations (e.g., race or gender versus familial ties), negative reactions and consequences, specifically for beneficiaries (discussed in more detail later), are common to both (Welle, 2004). Last, both AA and nepotism have a history of discrimination, which could provide meaningful insights not only in practice but also in research (for example, see Gutman, this volume, Chapter 2).

With these parallels in mind, perceptions of fairness are at the heart of the proposed nepotism model, as they are in much of the AA research (Kravitz et al., 1997). In addition, numerous other variables from AA research are incorporated as predictors and consequences in the nepotism model (e.g., beneficiary feelings of incompetence and self-doubt). The specific factors under each of the four antecedent categories in the model are described next, followed by a discussion of the consequences, moderators, and mediators, respectively.

ANTECEDENTS

In general, it is proposed that the extension and acceptance of an offer of nepotism depends upon the current situation of the nepotee, the current situation of the family incumbent, the current situation of the family, and the current situation of the organization. For example, the current situation of the nepotee may affect whether an offer is made or when an incumbent family member, the family as a whole, or the organization agree to extend an offer. If the potential nepotee possesses the appropriate education, work experience, or demonstrates motivation to do the job, then an offer may be more readily extended and accepted. This same thought process is the basis for each of the antecedent categories and their corresponding variables.

CURRENT SITUATION OF THE NEPOTEE
Work Experience, Education, Disposition, and Personality

Van Hooft and Stout (this volume, Chapter 4) have sufficiently elaborated on the concepts of modern nepotism, opportunism; and an individual's work experience, education, and personality (i.e., self-determination). Welle (2004) identified additional personality traits through a study in which students were asked to list descriptors that came to mind when they thought of a recently hired organizational member who was their boss's son. The descriptors mainly related to two categories: work-related attributes and nonwork-related attributes. The work-related attributes had to do with the nepotee's competence and qualifications (included in the model as work experience and education) and also dispositional work-related qualities, such as intelligence. The nonwork-related attributes described by participants included descriptors regarding the dispositional qualities of the nepotee, such as "arrogant," "spoiled," "unapproachable," "unfriendly," and "condescending."

With these findings in mind, researchers should address the possibility that individual nepotees may, in fact, possess these negative traits at some level. That is, perhaps nepotees are viewed as arrogant or unfriendly because they are actually more arrogant or unfriendly than others. To account for this possibility, both work-related and nonwork-related (primarily negative) dispositions are included in the model as antecedents, consequences, or both where appropriate.

Cultural Values and Beliefs

The likelihood of nepotism occurring and the resulting consequences are expected to be related to the culture under which it occurs. Although culture was originally conceptualized as a group-level construct (Hofstede, 1980), it has been argued that culture also can be thought of as an individual's tendency toward behaving in certain ways across a variety of conditions based on how the individual was raised in a certain type of cultural setting (Robert & Wasti, 2002; Triandis, 1996; Triandis, Chan, Bhawuk, Iwao, & Sinha, 1995; Triandis, Leung, Villareal, & Clack, 1985). In terms of family living arrangements, for example, cultural values place immense pressure on the behavior of individual family members, as well as the family as a whole, in dictating the conformity or resistance to prevalent cultural norms (He, 2005). The same or similar pressures likely exist in certain cultures for situations of nepotism in organizational settings. For brevity purposes, culture is only discussed here at the individual level, but is assumed to be a factor at multiple levels (e.g., family, organizational) affecting multiple outcomes (e.g., offers of nepotism extended and accepted, perceptions of beneficiaries).

Intentions

For years, employee turnover researchers have emphasized the role of intentions as a strong predictor of actual behavior. A number of models and studies have shown that turnover intentions not only mediate the relationship between work attitudes and actual turnover but also are found to be one of the best predictors of turnover in general (Griffeth, Hom, & Gaertner, 2000; Tett & Meyer, 1993). Intentions are expected to play a similar critical role in influencing whether nepotism takes place.

Welle (2004) argues that a potential nepotee's intentions to take advantage of a hiring situation may affect whether an offer is made or accepted, as well as perceptions of fairness and ultimate perceptions of the nepotee (i.e., the beneficiary). As Welle points out, there may be occasions when a nepotee attempts to conceal his identity when applying to an organization or for a specific job to ensure that a selection decision is based on merit alone. If a job is offered without the organization recognizing a family connection, the potential nepotee may be more likely to accept this offer, particularly if the individual is high on self-determination (Stout, Levesque, & Jones, 2007). Other times, nepotees may unabashedly identify their familial connection within the organization and their intention to utilize that relationship to help them obtain the desired position. In this situation, so long as the offer is extended, the nepotee is likely to accept, assuming the use of the family connection is a source of intended advantage to ensure the job offer.

Although Welle's (2004) focus is on the consequences of a nepotee concealing or claiming familial ties in a selection situation, it could be seen how purposeful intentions to utilize a family connection could heavily influence whether an opportunity is offered. Referrals (e.g., from a family member) are one of the best ways to obtain a job (Rynes, 1991). Furthermore, selecting people who have been referred by someone inside the organization has been shown to be a highly beneficial recruitment strategy, leading to lower turnover and better job performance when compared to the selection of employees using sources outside the organization (e.g., agencies, newspaper ads) (Zottoli & Wanous, 2000). Thus, so long as no selection rules are broken (e.g., anti-nepotism policies), an organization may be more inclined to offer an open position to a family member as compared to another applicant with no internal connections, given the long-term advantages stemming from this sort of recruitment tactic. Moreover, the nepotee may be more likely to accept the offer compared to an average applicant with no internal ties, because the nepotee may have greatest knowledge of the business and a potentially more realistic job preview compared to the average applicant (Bellow, 2003; Zottoli & Wanous, 2000).

In sum, the intentions to purposefully reveal and utilize family connections in a selection situation are expected to influence the likelihood of a job being offered and accepted, and may impact a number of long-term outcomes as well.

Personal Goals, Finances, and Socioeconomic Status

Parker (2004) includes goals and finances under the current family and business situations in her decision-making model, and they are extended to the individual-level variables in the model of nepotism. Consistent with the concepts discussed concerning career choice and job search strategies (Van Hooft & Stout, this volume, Chapter 4), an individual's personal goals and mission, as influenced by their personality and personal choices, play a role in determining whether they would take advantage of an opportunity, as well as what kind of opportunity they might accept or aim to obtain (i.e., type of job, company, industry).

The potential nepotee's current personal financial situation may also determine whether a person chooses to take advantage of an opportunity and what kind. If the potential nepotee is doing well financially and is not in need of a job, he or she may be more likely to decline an opportunity of nepotism than someone who is financially struggling or actively seeking a job. Closely related to one's financial situation is one's socioeconomic status (SES). This too is considered an important individual- and group-level predictor and is explained in more detail in the section "Current Situation of Family."

Gender

Historically, the practice of leaving the family estate, including the family business, in the hands of the firstborn son is known as primogeniture (Flandrin, 1979). Bellow (2003) discusses numerous examples of the firstborn son receiving all or most familial privileges, including those from biblical and colonial times. Throughout the 19th and 20th centuries, feminist movements and the focus on women's rights and equality in the workforce, specifically in the 1960s and 1970s (see Bellow, 2003; Friedan, 1963, 1981), contributed to making the use of primogeniture less likely and less favorably viewed. Today, there is evidence that families more commonly support the principle of equal inheritance or the splitting up of familial assets equally among all children, including daughters (Gilding, 2005). However, evidence suggests that gender segregation and wage inequality continue to exist in modern-day organizations (Ferraro, 1984; Figart, 2000; Gibelman, 2003; Levin, 1986). Given this, it may not be surprising to find that the gender of a potential nepotee may still impact a decision to engage in nepotism depending upon the type of job or industry. In a heavily male-dominated field, for example, a female nepotee may not be offered a position within the organization, particularly if other potential (male) nepotees are available alternatives.

CURRENT SITUATION OF FAMILY INCUMBENT

The family incumbent is the person currently employed by the organization who may be contemplating whether to extend a job offer or make a job opening known to a family member. It is recognized that more than one family incumbent may play a role in such a decision, particularly if the business is family owned. For the sake of simplicity, the following discussion refers to the family incumbent as one individual with the recognition that it often involves multiple incumbents and family members.

Values, Goals, and Expectations

Similar to the nepotee's current situation, the values, goals, and expectations of a family incumbent may influence whether an offer of nepotism is extended, as well as whether it is accepted. As Dickson, Nieminen, and Biermeier-Hanson (this volume, Chapter 5) discussed, the attraction–selection–attrition (ASA) model applies well to the proposed nepotism model and even the congruency between a family incumbent and potential nepotee. A family incumbent, for example, may extend an offer of nepotism to another family member only if the potential nepotee's values and goals match the organization's as well as the incumbent's. Likewise, a potential nepotee may only accept an offer from a family incumbent when the incumbent's values and goals match the nepotee's. Expectations could also be interchanged with values and goals. If an incumbent does not believe the nepotee will meet his or her expectations, the likelihood of extending an offer of nepotism may be low. If the nepotee perceives the incumbent's expectations as unrealistic, the likelihood of accepting the offer may be low. The reciprocal nature of this relationship is extended to the family's and organization's values, goals, and mission as well.

Position Within Organization

The family incumbent's position within the organization may influence who is selected and for what job. If the family incumbent holds a leadership position in an organization, the likelihood of an offer being extended to a family member may be greater than if the incumbent holds a job lower in the organization. The incumbent who holds a powerful organizational position may only have to request that the nepotee be hired or may even have the authority to hire him or her personally. Additionally, the family incumbent's position within the organization could also affect how likely it is that nepotism would occur at all. For example, if the family incumbent holds a powerful position, the company's selection policies and practices may have been created or even modified according to this incumbent's wishes. Perhaps, at the command of a powerful family incumbent, the organization would make its anti-nepotism policies more lenient, should strict policies presently exist in the organization. Thus, a powerful incumbent may have the authority to ensure that nepotism can occur more (or less) often.

On the other hand, a powerful incumbent's position might dissuade nepotism from happening because an act of nepotism may be much more visible across the organization. Evidence supports the idea that the organization is ultimately held responsible for an unfair selection outcome (Welle, 2004). If this is the case, an organization may be extremely hesitant to allow high-ranking incumbents' family members to work in the organization and may have a policy (or norm) prohibiting it due to the increased potential for perceived unfairness spanning broadly across the organization. Furthermore, from a manager's perspective, it may be much easier and much less awkward supervising a family member of a lower level employee compared to supervising the relative of someone higher up in the organization (Ford & McLaughlin, 1986). This provides another reason for a company to discourage nepotism at the upper levels of the organizational hierarchy. Bellow (2003) argues, however, that nepotism is not isolated at any level in the social hierarchy, and it may be that nepotism is not predicated by the level of the family incumbent in the organizational hierarchy.

CURRENT SITUATION OF FAMILY

Number of Family Members, Birth Order, and Inheritance Philosophies

The number of family members with the potential or willingness to take advantage of nepotistic opportunities should have a direct impact on when, how, and to whom an offer of nepotism is extended and accepted. Historically, the birth order of children within the family has played a role in the determination of who receives benefits and of what kind (Bellow, 2003; Flandrin, 1979). However, familial philosophies of equal inheritance (Gilding, 2005) as well as the number of potential nepotees may affect a family's decisions in modern times. In the case of multiple children from one family, the philosophy of equal inheritance may make a decision of nepotism increasingly difficult; a family may actually choose not to utilize nepotism for a particular opportunity. In situations involving multiple family members who are not siblings, the level of kinship may play a more influential role than birth order or inheritance philosophies, as elaborated in the discussion of "Kinship Level."

Positive or Negative Situation

In accordance with Parker's (2004) decision-making model, the positive or negative situation of the family should affect the decisions that are made regarding nepotism. In the model of nepotism, a positive situation is any situation that facilitates a decision to engage in nepotism. As one example, high levels of trust between the family and the potential nepotee might lead to an increased likelihood of a family incumbent extending a job offer to the nepotee. A negative family situation is one that discourages the family from engaging in nepotism. An example of a negative family situation might be one in which the family and potential nepotee have had a turbulent history that may actually lead the family to not extend an offer of nepotism. The same positive or negative situation could also lead the nepotee to accept or decline an offer of nepotism, as well.

Family Goals, Mission, and Values

As mentioned at the individual level, the family's goals, mission, and values are included in the model based on Schneider's (1987) ASA model. At the group level (i.e., family level), Parker (2004) discusses one family's goal of keeping the family located within close proximity of one another to accommodate their family values, one of which involves spending quality time together. Because of this family goal and value, an offer of nepotism may not be extended or accepted if it means that a family member would have to travel a great deal or live significant distances apart for the job.

Finances and Socioeconomic Status

In a family business context, Parker (2004) argues that, if the amount of risk involved with a decision is too high for a family financially, then the current family situation should be deemed negative and the decision-making process should go no further. The same could hold true in any organizational setting. For example, a family incumbent could attempt to persuade a potential nepotee to join an organization that is not firmly established, presenting possible financial and job security risks. Or, perhaps the family does not view the potential nepotism opportunity as one that would help the individual or the family achieve certain financial goals, so the opportunity is declined until a better one arises. The amount of financial risk involved with the opportunity could be expected to impact a decision to engage in nepotism, as it would affect any individual considering employment within any organization.

Similarly, a family's SES is also expected to play an influential role in situations of nepotism; however, SES is often not as straightforward as the family's finances. There are many methodological flaws and theoretical complications in defining social class (see Ming Liu et al., 2004, for review; see also Gryczynski, 2005). Some define social class by income, others define it by education or occupation, and yet others define it as one's wealth or total resources (Gryczynski, 2005). Moreover, social class may be indicative of one's familial resources and background, or it may be characterized by the person's own individual situation in life (for example, Miller, 2007; Ross, 1995). Despite the problems affiliated with its definition, social class is still widely considered in a variety of research areas as a significant predictor of important outcomes (e.g., mental illness, physical health, negative affect), and is proposed to be an important predictor of nepotism as well.

Bellow (2003) argues that nepotism occurs at all levels of the social hierarchy and does not contain itself solely to one group of people (e.g., upper class). Bellow firmly holds that nepotism has, in fact, been a phenomenon most popular among the middle classes. In a study involving college students, Harder (2006) found no significant relationship between SES and perceptions of fairness. In line with Bellow's premise, it might be that perceptions of fairness are not related to SES because it is not class specific. Perhaps, regardless of class, people have similar fairness perceptions of nepotism because, presented with the opportunity, they too would also want to help out or be helped by a family member in an organizational setting. Anthropological theories suggest similar arguments (Hamilton, 1964; Maynard Smith, 1964; Spranger, 2005).

At the same time, however, Harder (2006) found evidence that suggests individuals are likely able to recognize the discrepancies involved when nepotism occurs at different SES levels, which may be manifested in their attitudinal responses toward the practice. Self-reported upper-class students held more positive attitudes toward nepotism than those individuals who reported being in the middle or lower classes. Harder reasoned that people in the upper classes may have more positive opinions of the practice because they may be more familiar with nepotism, benefit from it more often, or even benefit more profitably than individuals in lower classes. That is, families higher in SES are likely able to provide more lucrative opportunities for their family members over lower SES families, which may contribute to the more positive attitudes.

Whether based upon Bellow's (2003) arguments or Harder's (2006) findings, SES appears to be associated with nepotism either in the form of attitudinal reactions or in the type of opportunities that can be offered as a result. Given its multifaceted definition, SES appears in the model as both a group-level (family) and individual-level (potential nepotee) predictor.

Generational Status

Most small- and medium-sized family businesses have a short lifecycle, and a surprisingly small proportion get passed to second-generation family members, with an even smaller proportion making it to third, fourth, or fifth generations (Gilding, 2005). This finding is incorporated two ways in the model of nepotism. First, the generational standing of the potential nepotee may affect his or her choice to join or to continue in the family business. Second, the age of the family business (included under the section "Current Situation of Organization") may dictate which generation is appropriate to target as employees for the business and whether that generation will accept the opportunity.

Kinship Level

Level of kinship is based upon kin selection theory and pertains to the level or degree of relatedness between two family members (e.g., first-degree relative, second-degree relative, third-degree relative). Kin selection theory was substantiated in primate research and asserts that the preferential treatment of kin degrades by the degree of genetic relatedness (Hamilton, 1964; Maynard Smith, 1964). Spranger (2005) describes kin selection theory as demonstrated when individuals act less competitively, and even assist and favor their relatives over nonrelatives because of the shared proportion of genes (e.g., .50 for siblings, .25 for grandchildren, .125 for cousins). Moreover, it is the theory of inclusive fitness (see Hamilton, 1964) that explains one's preferential treatment of kin as a way to continue one's genes through successive generations. This is done by assuming an additive function of the individual's own reproduction (direct fitness) plus the effect of his or her actions on the reproductive success of relatives (indirect fitness). Essentially, individuals engage in behaviors such as nepotism to maximize their inclusive fitness rather than their individual fitness by increasing the production of successful offspring through kin selection (Hamilton, 1964; Spranger, 2005).

Applying kin selection theory to an organizational setting translates into nepotism becoming less frequent as degree of relatedness widens (i.e., going from a first-degree to a second-degree relative, or from second- to third-degree relative and so on). From the family's perspective, level of kinship may also play a role in whether a family member is willing to grant the benefits of nepotism to a potential nepotee. In other words, a family member may be less inclined to show favoritism to another family member as level of kinship widens, particularly if closer kin are an option over more distant kin. From a nepotee's perspective, perhaps even expectations of nepotism decrease as level of kinship widens such that a nepotee may not even attempt to obtain an offer from a more distant relative. In some cases, this may lead to a decrease in the actual occurrence of nepotism as well.

CURRENT SITUATION OF ORGANIZATION

Positive or Negative Situation

Similar to the current family situation, Parker (2004) argues that family businesses must also carefully consider the current business situation. Parker defines a positive or negative business situation in terms of cash flow. An example of a positive business situation is when more money is coming into the business than is going out. Positive business situations may be a good time for an organization to consider engaging in nepotism, as more opportunities may be available or there may be more openness to risk taking. Due to the potential for negative consequences (for example,

Pérez-González, 2006), some may indeed consider nepotism a risky business decision.

Company Goals, Strategy, and Values

Parker (2004) recognized the importance of considering the company goals, values, mission, and strategy prior to making a decision in an FOB. Here again, Parker's logic is extended to include any company, not solely family firms. Therefore, within any organization, choosing to engage in nepotism is a decision that is only successful when it is a decision that follows the company's goals, strategy, and values, so long as those match the family's or the individual's.

Human Resources Selection Practices, Policies, and Norms

Exactly how far kinship takes a person in an organizational selection process likely depends upon the company's selection practices, policies, and history with nepotism. Moreover, the norms under which a company is accustomed to operating are expected to impact nepotism. Ultimately, how a company chooses to recruit, what policies and methods are used in the selection process, and the norms under which nepotism is operating should predict several outcomes, including which applicants choose to apply, which applicants are hired, and even future job performance and turnover (Hausknecht, Day, & Thomas, 2004; Ryan, Horvath, & Kriska, 2005; Rynes, 1991; Zottoli & Wanous, 2000).

Available Position or Opportunity

It has been proposed that a potential nepotee may choose whether to take a position when one is made available (Van Hooft & Stout, this volume, Chapter 4). Part of this individual's decision will likely involve considering what type of opportunity or position is being offered. A more lucrative opportunity or high-level organizational position may be more difficult to pass up from an individual standpoint and potentially more difficult to offer from the organization's perspective. Pérez-González (2006), for example, found that, when a firm replaces the outgoing CEO with a family member of the departing CEO or a large shareholder, the firm tends to underperform in terms of operating profitability and market-to-book ratios relative to firms that promote nonfamily members to a CEO position. This knowledge alone may make an organization less willing or at least more cautious when promoting family members to higher levels within an organization.

Company Size and Complexity

Evidence pertaining to the relationship between company size and nepotism is mixed. Gilding (2005) discovered that, as FOBs become larger and more complex, there is a tendency for the business to pass out of family hands. Thus, nepotism becomes less likely as the size and complexity of the business increases. Holding complexity constant, others have argued that the "larger the organization, the less nepotism," because "large organizations won't put up with it" (Bratches, 1986, as cited in Barmash, 1986, p. 5). In contrast, Hayajenh, Maghrabi, and Al-Dabbagh (1994) conducted a study where several hundred human resource managers completed questionnaires and found that large organizations "lend themselves to being a theatre for nepotism more than smaller enterprises" (p. 66). In contrast, De Paola and Scoppa (2003) found that small firms use informal referrals as a selection tool twice as often as other selection practices or techniques, paving the way for more opportunities of nepotism. Inconsistencies aside, the findings that are available support organizational size and complexity as two factors that may impact the likelihood of nepotism occurring within an organization.

Company Age

As noted previously, Gilding (2005) found that the older a business becomes the less likely it is to remain in family hands. Her findings led her to conclude that family ownership becomes less likely beyond the second generation.

Applicant Pool

It is well known that the characteristics of the company's applicant pool affect hiring decisions (see Boudreau & Rynes, 1985; Rynes, 1991; Zottoli & Wanous, 2000). Whether a nepotee is selected for an opportunity in an organization may be as simple as who is in a company's applicant pool and how the potential nepotee compares to others at different phases in a selection process. Similar to other selection situations, if there are other, more qualified applicants, the potential nepotee may not be selected based upon a more qualified applicant alone. On the other hand, organizations that have a limited supply of applicants may embrace nepotism with open arms and encourage family members to apply. Assuming one of the organization's goals is to hire the most qualified applicant, consideration of other qualified applicants should take place in their selection process. Thus, the applicant pool should affect the likelihood of nepotism occurring, particularly if the nepotee is unqualified for the position.

FOB Versus Non-FOB

Although an exact definition of FOB is not consistently agreed upon (Spranger, 2005), Tagiuri and Davis (1996) concisely defined a family business as one in which (a) ownership is controlled by one family, (b) includes at least two family members in its management, and (c) has non-family employees as well (see also Muchinsky, this volume, Chapter 3). FOBs are important to consider in a model of nepotism because it may be that nepotism occurs more frequently in FOBs relative to non-FOBs. Thus, opportunities for nepotism may be greater or more lucrative in FOBs as compared to non-FOBs, and nepotees may be more likely to accept an offer if nepotism is common in the organization.

CONSEQUENCES

Throughout this book, we have addressed numerous positive and negative outcomes of nepotism. To avoid duplication, many of these outcomes are not elaborated upon further in this chapter. However, in the following I provide a few noteworthy examples of research specifically pertaining to the variables and relationships put forth in the model. Similar to the antecedent categories, the consequences included in the model are grouped into individual- and group-level outcomes.

Individual-Level Consequences

Aligned with AA terminology, individuals who are involved in or who witness an act of nepotism can be thought of as beneficiaries (i.e., those who receive the benefits of nepotism) or nonbeneficiaries (i.e., those who do not benefit from nepotism). Beneficiaries and nonbeneficiaries experience the effects of nepotism, both positive and negative, when nepotism is utilized and even when it is not. For example, perceptions of fairness may be higher for beneficiaries if nepotism is utilized and lower for nonbeneficiaries; however, if nepotism is not used, perceptions of fairness may be lower for the would-be beneficiary and higher for nonbeneficiaries. Additionally, it is important to consider the possibility that nonbeneficiaries may be either nonfamily members (e.g., unrelated incumbents, coworkers) or family members (i.e., those potential nepotees who either did not accept or were not offered a job), and the consequences may vary for each group.

Given the parallels between affirmative action and nepotism, the outcomes resulting from the perceived preferential treatment and stigma associated with AA are included in the model of nepotism. For beneficiaries, these outcomes might include lower self-esteem, increased self-doubt and feelings of incompetence, and lower self-evaluations (Heilman et al., 1987; Kluegel & Smith, 1983). For nonbeneficiaries, these outcomes may include decreased perceptions of fairness (Harris et al., 2004; Kluegel & Smith, 1983; Kravitz et al., 1997; Nacoste, 1985, 1987; Slaughter, Sinar, & Bachiochi, 2002), decreased satisfaction (James, Brief, Dietz, & Cohen, 2001), and decreased perceptions of beneficiaries' competence or dispositions (Heilman et al., 1987; Sowell, 1978; Welle, 2004).

As mentioned, the most important differentiator between nepotism and AA is kinship. Laker and Williams (2003) found evidence that level of kinship does, indeed, affect perceptions of nepotism in a positive manner in organizational settings. The study's findings supported the conclusion that the more "nepotized" the employee (e.g., employees working in an organization with multiple, closely related family members), the more likely one was to have higher levels of satisfaction and commitment to the organization compared to employees with no relatives (or fewer relatives) employed in the organization (see also Becker, this volume, Chapter 6).

Research on romantic couples in the workforce has also provided evidence that could extend to a situation of nepotism, particularly with regard to married couples in the workplace. Based on their review of the literature on this topic, Pierce, Byrne, and Aguinis (1996) developed a model of workplace romance in which they found that romance in the workplace can result in increased productivity, increased employee morale, increased job satisfaction, and even increases in overall life satisfaction.

The same body of research has also demonstrated that many of these positive findings could easily become negative, particularly if the relationship takes a turn for the worse (see Pierce et al., 1996, for a review).

In their survey research, Ford and McLaughlin (1986) found more evidence to support the negative side of nepotism over the positive, concluding that the disadvantages of nepotism strongly outweigh its advantages. Other findings suggest a negative impact on employee morale, confusion, and frustration among supervisors of nepotees related to high-level executives, including decreased satisfaction and organizational commitment (Vinton, 1998), though Laker and Williams's (2003) findings suggest otherwise. More recent research suggests that nepotism can lead to an increased likelihood of nonbeneficiaries quitting the organization (i.e., quitting intentions) and negatively talking about the organization to others within and outside of the organization (Arasli, Bavik, & Ekiz, 2006).

Group-Level Consequences

Proponents advocating nepotism's positive characteristics (for example, Bellow, 2003) argue that nepotism, for the most part, is a beneficial business strategy—a strategy that when practiced appropriately creates a potentially powerful advantage, such that all that is required to profit from an opportunity involving nepotism is the willingness to take advantage of it. Nepotism could also be viewed as a competitive strategy, with efficient and prosperous business resulting from the transferred knowledge and contacts imparted to close kin who have been involved with the family business since a very young age (Bellow, 2003). From a group-level perspective, Bellow (2003) argues the family, the organization, and even society all experience the outcomes of this powerful business practice.

Family

Nepotism has been described as a "conflict of interest" and an "unprofessional phenomenon" (Arasli et al., 2006, pp. 296, 305) due to the combination of family and business. It has been a common argument that, with nepotism, family problems become business problems and can improperly influence the corporate decision-making processes (Abdalla, Maghrabi, & Raggad, 1998; Arasli et al., 2006; Becker, this volume, Chapter 6; Ford & McLaughlin, 1986; Ichniowski, 1988). Research has shown that family problems can spill over into an employee's performance at work, and business problems can spill over and affect employees and their family (see Frone, Yardley, & Markel, 1997; Greenhaus & Beutell, 1985; Masuda & Visio, this volume, Chapter 7; Staines, 1980). Sibling rivalry and family fighting, for example, have been tied to nepotism (Ichniowski, 1988). Furthermore, work-related stressors can translate into increased stress and conflict at home (Eby, Casper, Lockwood, Bordeaux, & Brinley, 2005; Greenhaus & Beutell, 1985). Common stressors, such as a family's financial difficulties, have been found to contribute to a significant source of stress and strain between husbands and wives (Westman & Vinokur, 1998), and reduced family functioning, including problems with family cohesion and increased familial conflicts (see Eby et al., 2005).

On the positive side, family members exposed to the same stress caused within one organization may cope better together due to an increased understanding of the other's stressful situation. Crossfield, Kinman, and Jones (2005) have found that dual-career couples who expressed an understanding and were helpful to the other in work-related discussions contributed to reduced stress levels for their partners. Moreover, the findings in this study showed women to have increased levels of well-being because of this type of communication and rapport regarding work-related stress.

When nepotism has been found to result in problems at work, however, the familial problems are brought on site and may affect more than just the family members' work performance. Tension and discomfort among nonfamily members within the organization have been reported (Abdalla et al., 1998; Arasli et al., 2006; Ford & McLaughlin, 1986; Ichniowski, 1988). Confusion and frustration, as well as fear, were also reported by managerial survey respondents concerned about having to supervise the boss's child (Ford & McLaughlin, 1986). Masuda and Visio (this volume, Chapter 7) devote their entire chapter to exploring these concepts and research findings in greater depth, an indication of how important this area of research is in studying nepotism.

Departmental and Organizational Factors

Survey respondents have cited numerous advantages to using nepotism as a selection process (for example, Allerton, 1994; Ford & McLaughlin, 1986). Individuals employed in FOBs, for example, claim that nepotism has improved communications, increased organizational acceptance by their customers and community, and led to more consistent policies and smoother transitions of leadership positions (Ford & McLaughlin, 1986). Others have concluded that nepotism creates an increased ability to attract more committed, satisfied, and loyal employees (Bellow, 2003; Dailey & Reuschling, 1980; Lentz & Laband, 1989; see also Dickson, Nieminen, and Biermeier-Hanson, this volume, Chapter 5). Allerton (1994) surveyed members of the Society for Human Resource Management and found reports of increased productivity in organizations utilizing pro-nepotism policies. When a recruitment source is a family incumbent, organizations may also save on recruitment and selection costs when nepotism is utilized (Abdalla et al., 1998; Dickson, Nieminen, and Biermeier-Hanson, this volume, Chapter 5).

Disadvantages reported in the literature often conflict with the advantages and include the inability to attract nonfamily managers for fear of being surpassed by family members in the promotion process (Laker & Williams, 2003; Toy, Brown, & Miles, 1988). In contrast to Allerton's (1994) findings, Hayajenh et al. (1994) concluded that organizations practicing nepotism are less effective than those that do not utilize nepotism. Inequity and discrimination as a result of real or imagined favoritism have also been reported disadvantages (Laker & Williams, 2003; Wexler, 1982). Companies that use nepotism may also suffer reputation problems due to increased levels of employees speaking poorly of the company (Arasli et al., 2006). Dickson, Nieminen, and Biermeier-Hanson (this volume, Chapter 5) note several other possible consequences that speak more toward the dangers of internal recruitment tactics (i.e., nepotism), such as increased homogeneity, slower socialization for nonfamily members, and the development of subcultures as a result of increased group salience.

Societal-Level Consequences

Conway (2004) describes Bellow's (2003) definition of new nepotism as involving the promotion of high ideals, such that the outcomes serve more than private interests alone; new nepotism is beneficial to many rather than beneficial to only one individual, family, or organization. Similar to AA's positive effects on minority's and women's employment rates and income attainment levels (Kravitz et al., 1997), practicing nepotism may affect society as whole. In fact, Bellow argues that society would face extreme negative consequences should nepotism cease to exist, including effects on the survival of organizational enterprises and even humankind.

To provide an example, entrepreneurship is an important economic activity that creates competition, jobs, and improves overall quality of life (Baumol, 1968; Beugelsdijk, 2007; Leibenstein, 1968; Schumpeter, 1934, 1951; "Searching for the Invisible Man," 2006). Barmash (1986) recognized nepotism as having the potential to provide sustained entrepreneurialism in an age of corporate takeovers. Though estimates vary, the powerful presence of FOBs across a number of countries is recognized by most (for example, Conway, 2004; Muchinsky, this volume, Chapter 3; Pérez-González, 2006; Tagiuri & Davis, 1996), and speaks to the significance of nepotism as an entrepreneurial force in society today. Families not only start businesses together, they also sustain success by bringing in more family members who have the preestablished knowledge and networks available to them upon entry, creating a greater likelihood for longevity and sustainability (Barmash, 1986; Bellow, 2003). Bellow (2003) argues that nepotism provides a solid foundation from which a company can grow and succeed. This suggests that long-term firm success may be affected by nepotism, not only in FOBs but in other organizations as well.

Social Factors

Families have been referred to as the "fundamental unit of American society" (Fagan & Rector, 2000), and the societal effects of familial conflict and problems are well documented. Conflict within the family can lead to financial problems, which in turn contribute to problems such as divorce (for example, Amato & Rogers, 1997; Poortman, 2005; Stanley, Markman, & Whitton, 2002; Terling-Watt, 2001). Divorce, in turn, has been shown to negatively affect not only children, but adults and society as a whole (Espenshade, 1979; Fagan & Rector, 2000). Divorce has been linked to increased college dropout rates, drug usage, suicide rates, and even increased likelihood of poverty as a result of significant income reductions (Fagan & Rector, 2000). Family problems are, therefore, society's problem, and the negative effects of nepotism could have a direct effect on society as well.

MEDIATORS AND MODERATORS

Offer Extended, Offer Accepted

Offer extension is the point at which favoritism may first be perceived in a situation of nepotism. It is, therefore, reasonable to expect that perceptions of fairness are impacted if an offer is extended, regardless of whether it is accepted. Offer extension is a proposed mediator between the antecedents of nepotism and perceptions of fairness (Frazier, Tix, & Baron, 2004). Offer acceptance is the point at which nepotism has officially occurred. An extension of an offer of nepotism will precede acceptance (or nonacceptance) of the offer. It is expected that perceptions of fairness would be lowest in the presence of nepotism when it has actually occurred as compared to when nepotism is only a possibility (e.g., when it has only been offered) or when it does not occur at all (i.e., when it has not been offered, or when it has been offered and not accepted). Offer acceptance is, therefore, proposed to moderate the relationship between offer extension and perceptions of fairness in the nepotism model.

Fairness

Fairness has been linked to affective and attitudinal outcomes in both applicant reactions (Gilliland, 1993; Hausknecht et al., 2004; Ryan & Ployhart, 2000) and affirmative action (Kravitz et al., 1997; Nacoste, 1985, 1987). In the applicant reactions literature, fairness plays a significant role at every stage of the selection process, and perceived fairness can have both short-term and long-term effects that influence job acceptance intentions, decisions, and future job performance (Hausknecht et al., 2004). In the AA literature, fairness has been shown to fully mediate the relationship between affirmative action programs and subsequent attitudes, resulting in more favorable attitudes when higher levels of fairness are perceived (Heilman, McCullough, & Gilbert, 1996; Kravitz et al., 1997). Kravitz et al. (1997) conclude that people often think of AA in terms of fairness. With the limited research to date, empirical findings suggest fairness plays a similarly critical role between nepotism and potential outcomes (Spranger, 2005; Welle, 2004).

Welle (2004), for example, found that hiring a family member may be viewed as violating several procedural justice principles (Leventhal, 1980), including those of consistency, freedom from bias, and consideration of job-relevant characteristics in the decision. Welle argues that the violation of these norms leads to a discounting process in which nonbeneficiaries view the beneficiary of nepotism as less competent and willing to violate the moral norms of a selection process in order to further their own interests. One of the most powerful findings in this study is that a hiring decision based on nepotism was viewed as less fair than an AA hire.

Spranger (2005) found that nepotism had a negative relationship with procedural, distributive, and interactional justice among nonfamily beneficiaries. Ironically, however, family members within FOBs apparently did not regard acts of nepotism as a fairness issue. Spranger suggests a possible reason for this finding could be that family members may view preferential treatment as an inherent part of a family business culture. In other words, family members in FOBs expect nepotism (Spranger, 2005). Given the preliminary evidence pertaining to nepotism and the important role fairness plays in related research, fairness is a proposed mediator between the occurrence of nepotism and the outcomes in the model.

Family-Owned Business

As mentioned, FOBs are important to consider because it may be that nepotism occurs more frequently in FOBs compared to non-FOBs. FOBs have been included as an organizational antecedent in the model, but are also proposed to have moderating effects on perceptions of fairness and the potential outcomes, particularly at the individual, nonbeneficiary level. For example, Spranger (2005) found that family members and nonfamily members within FOBs have come to expect nepotism, which may mitigate some of the potential negative consequences, particularly for nonfamily members.

In Figure 10.1, FOB is not currently depicted as a moderator, but included only as an antecedent despite the recognition that it may also have moderating effects. Several other moderators (e.g., personality, gender, marital status) are proposed in previous chapters (e.g., Dickson, Nieminen, and Biermeier-Hanson, this volume, Chapter 5; Masuda & Visio, this volume, Chapter 7) that are also not included in the current model. These moderators are recognized as potentially important considerations for future research and model revisions.

Empirical Test of the Model

In a study involving 557 participants made up of students ($n = 416$) and nonstudent working adults ($n = 141$), Mulder (2008) tested several components of the model using both surveys and vignettes. Overall, the research showed that nepotism is regularly practiced and that most people have some form of experience with nepotism in organizational settings.

More than one-third of participants in the study had attempted, received, or accepted offers of nepotism. That said, however, participants had more experience as nonbeneficiaries of nepotism than as a beneficiaries. Additionally, participants were found to have more experience as both nonbeneficiaries and beneficiaries of nepotism than as family incumbents, which may be confounded by the ages of most participants in the study (i.e., 35 or under).

A number of the model's individual-level variables were hypothesized to be related to offers of nepotism received and accepted, and their subsequent impact on perceptions of fairness. Support for the hypotheses was mixed. Contrary to predictions, gender and education were not significantly related to whether offers of nepotism were received or accepted. An individual's cultural characteristics (i.e., allocentrism or idiocentrism) were also not significantly related to offer extension or acceptance. Similarly, neither number of siblings nor birth order was related to offers or acceptance of nepotism.

Contrary to Bellow's (2003) core argument that nepotism occurs equally at all levels of the social hierarchy, Mulder's (2008) findings show that nepotism occurs most frequently among families higher in SES. However, given the differences between student and nonstudent populations, further empirical investigations of SES, social class, and nepotism would be worthwhile, particularly if more objective indices of family and individual SES can be used (e.g., family income levels, education levels). Recognizing that nepotism occurs most frequently in the upper classes is important because it could result in a less diversified workforce, particularly in the upper levels of an organization.

Mulder's (2008) study is one of the only empirical estimations of the prevalence of nepotism in the 21st century. Given the previous suspicions and findings on nepotism's historical prevalence (for example, Bellow, 2003), one can feel confident in concluding that nepotism is an important factor in organizations today and is alive and well in America (Abdalla et al., 1998; Bellow, 2003; Kiechel, 1984). Furthermore, this study's findings show that people may experience nepotism in a variety of ways through different stages in their careers. With varying experiences, individual attitudes and perceptions of fairness may likely differ regarding the practice, which also substantiates previous research (Laker & Williams, 2003;

Spranger, 2005). Overall, the results suggest that nepotism is easily recognizable from a young age, and one's role in, experiences with, and perceptions toward nepotism may differ depending on a number of factors identified in the model.

CONCLUSIONS

The purpose of this chapter was to present a model of organizational nepotism that integrates several established areas of research with the limited nepotism findings available to date. It is hoped that the model will provide a more thorough appreciation for the practice and lead to more rigorous nepotism research and model revisions. Nepotism researchers should consider the myriad of variables that may influence the decision to utilize nepotism as well as the possibility for widespread consequences (both positive and negative). Practitioners must recognize the impact nepotism can have on an organization, its employees, and their families, and be prepared to discuss the pros and cons with organizational decision makers prior to recommending its use. The preceding chapters in this volume coupled with the model and the preliminary findings should equip researchers and practitioners to do just that.

ENDNOTE

1. Portions of this chapter were written for the author's master's thesis (Harder, 2006) and doctoral dissertation (Mulder, 2008).

REFERENCES

Abdalla, H. F., Maghrabi, A. S., & Raggad, B. G. (1998). Assess the perceptions of human resource managers toward nepotism: A cross-cultural study. *International Journal of Manpower, 19*, 554–570.

Allerton, H. (1994, March). Work and family. *Training & Development*, 79–80.

Amato, P. R., & Rogers, S. J. (1997). A longitudinal study of marital problems and subsequent divorce. *Journal of Marriage & the Family, 59*, 612–624.

Arasli, H., Bavik, A., & Ekiz, E. H. (2006). The effects of nepotism on human resource management: The case of three-, four-, and five-star hotels in Northern Cyprus. *The International Journal of Sociology and Social Policy, 26*, 295–308.

Barmash, I. (1986). A defense of nepotism. *Across the Board, 1*, 5–8.

Baumol, W. (1968). Entrepreneurship in economic theory. *American Economic Review, 58*, 64–71.

Bellow, A. (2003). *In praise of nepotism: A natural history*. New York: Doubleday.

Beugelsdijk, S. (2007). Entrepreneurial culture, regional innovativeness, and economic growth. *Journal of Evolutionary Economics, 17*, 187–210.

Boudreau, J. W., & Rynes, S. L. (1985). Role of recruitment in staffing utility analysis. *Journal of Applied Psychology, 70*, 354–366.

Conway, B. (2004). The new nepotism [Review of the book *In praise of nepotism: A natural history*, by Adam Bellow]. *Public Interest, 154*, 130–135.

Crossfield, S., Kinman, G., & Jones, F. (2005). Cross-over of occupational stress in dual-career couples: The role of work demands and supports, job commitment and marital communication. *Community, Work and Family, 8*, 211–232.

Dailey, R. C., & Reuschling, L. T. (1980). Managing continuity in the family-owned company. *Journal of General Management, 5*, 49–56.

De Paola, M., & Scoppa, V. (2003). Family ties and training provision in an insider-outsider framework. *Journal of Socio-Economics, 32*, 197–217.

Eby, L. T., Casper, W. J., Lockwood, A., Bordeaux, C., & Brinley, A. (2005). Work and family research in IO/OB: Content analysis and review of the literature (1980–2002). *Journal of Vocational Behavior, 66*, 124–197.

Espenshade, T. J. (1979). The economic consequences of divorce. *Journal of Marriage and the Family, 41*, 615–625.

Fagan, P. F., & Rector, R. E. (2000, June 5). *The effects of divorce on America*. Retrieved April 19, 2007, from http://www.heritage.org/Research/Family/BG1373.cfm.

Ferraro, G. A. (1984). Bridging the wage gap: Pay equity and job evaluations. *American Psychologist, 39*(10), 1166–1170.

Figart, D. M. (2000). Equal pay for equal work: The role of job evaluation in an evolving social norm. *Journal of Economic Issues, 34*, 1–19.

Flandrin, J. F. (1979). *Families in former times: Kinship, household and sexuality*. Cambridge, UK: Cambridge University Press.

Ford, R., & McLaughlin, F. (1986). Nepotism: Boon or bane. *Personnel Administrator, 31*(11), 78–89.

Frazier, P. A., Tix, A. P., & Baron, K. E. (2004). Testing moderator and mediator effects in counseling psychology research. *Journal of Counseling Psychology, 51*, 115–134.

Friedan, B. (1963). *The feminine mystique*. New York: W. W. Norton & Company.

Friedan, B. (1981). *The second stage*. New York: Summit Books.

Frone, M. R., Yardley, J. K., & Markel, K. S. (1997). Developing and testing an integrative model of the work-family interface. *Journal of Vocational Behavior, 50*, 145–167.

Gibelman, M. (2003). So how far have we come? Pestilent and persistent gender gap in pay. *Social Work, 48*, 22–32.

Gilding, M. (2005). Families and fortunes: Accumulation, management succession, and inheritance in wealthy families. *Journal of Sociology, 41*, 29–45.

Gilliland, S. W. (1993). The perceived fairness of selection systems: An organizational justice perspective. *Academy of Management Review, 18,* 694–734.

Golden, H., Hinkle, S., & Crosby, F. (2001). Reactions to affirmative action: Substance and semantics. *Journal of Applied Social Psychology, 31,* 73–88.

Greenhaus, J. H., & Beutell, N. J. (1985). Sources of conflict between work and family roles. *Academy of Management Review, 10,* 76–88.

Griffeth, R. W., Hom, P. W., & Gaertner, S. (2000). A meta-analysis of antecedents and correlates of employee turnover: Update, moderator tests, and research implications for the next millennium. *Journal of Management, 26,* 463–488.

Gryczynski, J. (April, 2005). *Measuring the concept of social class: The Interdependency of class, race, and gender in American Society.* Paper presented at the annual meeting of the Southern Sociological Society, Charlotte, NC.

Hamilton, W. D. (1964). The genetic evolution of social behavior. I and II. *Journal of Theoretical Biology, 7,* 1–52.

Harder, B. K. (2006). *On nepotism: An examination of kinship, merit, and perceptions of fairness.* Unpublished master's thesis, DePaul University, Chicago, Illinois.

Harris, M. M., Lievens, F., & Van Hoye, G. (2004). "I think they discriminated against me": Using prototype theory and organizational justice theory for understanding perceived discrimination in selection and promotion situations. *International Journal of Selection and Assessment, 12,* 54–65.

Hausknecht, J. P., Day, D. V., & Thomas, S. C. (2004). Applicant reactions to selection procedures: An updated model and meta-analysis. *Personnel Psychology, 57,* 639–683.

Hayajenh, A. F., Maghrabi, A. S., & Al-Dabbagh, T. H. (1994). Research note: Assessing the effect of nepotism on human resource managers. *International Journal of Manpower, 15,* 60–67.

He, W. (2005). Introduction: Kinship and family in international context. *International Journal of Sociology and Social Policy, 25,* 1–8.

Heilman, M. E. (1994). Affirmative action: Some unintended consequences for working women. In B. M. Staw & L. L. Cummings (Eds.), Research in organizational behavior (Vol. 16, pp. 125–169). Greenwich, CT: JAI.

Heilman, M. E., Block, C. J., & Lucas, J. A. (1992). Presumed incompetent? Stigmatization and affirmative action efforts. *Journal of Applied Psychology, 77,* 536–544.

Heilman, M. E., McCullough, W. F., & Gilbert, D. (1996). The other side of affirmative action: Reactions of non-beneficiaries to sex-based preferential selection. *Journal of Applied Psychology, 81,* 346–357.

Heilman, M. E., Simon, M. C., & Repper, D. P. (1987). Intentionally favored, unintentionally harmed? Impact of sex-based preferential selection on self-perception and self-evaluation. *Journal of Applied Psychology, 72,* 62–68.

Hofstede, G. (1980). *Culture's consequences.* Beverly Hills, CA: Sage.

Ichniowski, T. (1988). The new nepotism: Why dynasties are making a comeback. *Business Week, 31,* 106–109.

International Federation of Red Cross and Red Crescent Societies. (n.d.). Principles and values: Neutrality. Retrieved December 22, 2009, from http://www.ifrc.org/what/values/principles/neutrality.asp.

James, E. H., Brief, A. P., Dietz, J., & Cohen, R. R. (2001). Prejudice matters: Understanding the reactions of Whites to affirmative action programs targeted to benefit Blacks. *Journal of Applied Psychology, 86,* 1120–1128.

Jones, R. G. (2004). [Review of the book *In praise of nepotism: A natural history*, by A. Bellow]. *Personnel Psychology, 57*, 550–553.

Katz, D., & Kahn, R. L. (1978). *The social psychology of organizations* (2nd ed.). New York: John Wiley & Sons.

Kiechel, W. (1984). How to relate to nepotism. *Fortune, 119*, 143–144.

Kluegel, J. R., & Smith, E. R. (1983). Affirmative action attitudes: Effects of self-interest, racial affect, and stratification beliefs on Whites' views. *Social Forces, 61*, 797–824.

Kravitz, D. A., Harrison, D. A., Turner, M. E., Levine, E. L., Chaves, W., Brannick, M. T., … Conard, M. A. (1997). *Affirmative action: A review of psychological and behavioral research*. Bowling Green, OH: Society for Industrial and Organizational Psychology.

Laker, D. R., & Williams, M. L. (2003). Nepotism's effect on employee satisfaction and organizational commitment: An empirical study. *International Journal of Human Resources Development and Management, 3*, 191–202.

Leibenstein, H. (1968). Entrepreneurship and development. *American Economic Review, 58*, 72–83.

Lentz, B. F., & Laband, D. N. (1989). Why so many children of doctors become doctors: Nepotism versus human capital transfers. *The Journal of Human Resources, 24*, 396–408.

Leventhal, G. S. (1980). What should be done with equity theory? New approaches to the study of fairness in social relationships. In K. Gergen, M. Greenberg, & R. Willis (Eds.), *Social Exchange* (pp. 27–55). New York: Plenum.

Levin, M. (1986). Comparable worth: The feminist road to socialism. *Commentary, 74*, 13–19.

Marin, C. (2008, August 20). State politics smitten with incurable plague. *Chicago Sun Times*, pp. 1, 27.

Maynard Smith, J. (1964). Group selection and kin selection. *Nature, 201*, 1145–1147.

Ming Liu, W., Rasheed Ali, S., Soleck, G., Hopps, J., Dunston, K., & Pickett, T., Jr. (2004). Using social class in counseling psychology research. *Journal of Counseling Psychology, 51*, 3–18.

Miller, T. (2007). Can you go home again? The impact of social class mobility via graduate education on identity and family relationships. *Dissertation Abstracts International, 67*(08), 4761.

Mulder, B. K. (2008). Risking the business or reaping the benefits: The antecedents and consequences of nepotism. *Dissertation Abstracts International, 70*(12).

Nacoste, R. W. (1985). Selection procedure and responses to affirmative action. *Law and Human Behavior, 9*, 225–242.

Nacoste, R. W. (1987). But do they care about fairness? The dynamics of preferential treatment and minority interest. *Basic and Applied Social Psychology, 8*, 177–191.

Parker, T. (2004). A multi-level family business choice model: A dichotomous approach. *The Coastal Business Journal, 3*, 56–60.

Pérez-González, F. (2006). Inherited control and firm performance. *The American Economic Review, 96*(5), 1559–1588.

Pierce, C. A., Byrne, D., & Aguinis, H. (1996). Attraction in organizations: A model of workplace romance. *Journal of Organizational Behavior, 17*, 5–32.

Poortman, A. (2005). How work affects divorce: The mediating role of financial and time pressures. *Journal of Family Issues, 26*, 168–195.

Robert, C., & Wasti, S. A. (2002). Organizational individualism and collectivism: Theoretical development and an empirical test of a measure. *Journal of Management, 28*, 544–566.

Ross, J. L. (1995). Social class tensions within families. *The American Journal of Family Therapy, 23*, 338–350.

Ryan, A. M., Horvath, M., & Kriska, S. D. (2005). The role of recruiting source informativeness and organizational perceptions in decisions to apply. *International Journal of Selection and Assessment, 13*, 235–249.

Ryan, A. M., & Ployhart, R. (2000). Applicants' perceptions of selection procedures and decisions: A critical review and agenda for the future. *Journal of Management, 26*, 565–606.

Rynes, S. L. (1991). Recruitment, job choice, and posthire consequences. In M. D. Dunnette & L. M. Hough (Eds.), *Handbook of industrial and organizational psychology* (2nd ed., pp. 399–444). Palo Alto, CA: Consulting Psychologists Press.

Schneider, B. (1987). The people make the place. *Personnel Psychology, 40*, 437–453.

Schumpeter, J. A. (1934). *The theory of economic development*. Cambridge, MA: Harvard University Press.

Schumpeter, J. (1951). Change and the entrepreneur. In R. V. Clemence (Ed.), *Essays of JA Schumpeter*. Reading, MA: Addison-Wesley.

Searching for the invisible man. (2006, March 11). *The Economist, 378*(8468), 68.

Senge, P. (1990). *The fifth discipline: The art and practice of the learning organization*. New York: Doubleday

Slaughter, J. E., Sinar, E. F., & Bachiochi, P. D. (2002). Black applicants' reactions to affirmative action plans: Effects of plan content and previous experience with discrimination. *Journal of Applied Psychology, 87*, 333–344.

Sowell, T. (1978). Are quotas good for blacks? *Commentary, 65*, 39–43.

Spranger, J. S. (2005, April). *Genetic density as a predictor of nepotism in the family firm*. Paper presented at the Society for Industrial and Organizational Psychology conference, Los Angeles, CA.

Staines, G. I. (1980). Spillover versus compensation: A review of the literature between work and nonwork. *Human Relations, 33*, 111–129.

Stanley, S. M., Markman, H. J., & Whitton, S. W. (2002). Communication, conflict and commitment: Insights on the foundations of relationship success from a national survey. *Family Process, 41*, 659–675.

Stout, T., Levesque, C., & Jones, R. G. (2007). *Nepotism, self determination, and career choice*. Paper presented at the Society for Industrial and Organizational Psychology conference, New York.

Tagiuri, R., & Davis, J. A. (1996). Bivalent attributes of the family firm. *Family Business Review, 9*, 199–208.

Terling-Watt, T. (2001). Explaining divorce: An examination of the relationship between marital characteristics and divorce. *Journal of Divorce & Remarriage, 35*, 125–145.

Tett, R. P., & Meyer, J. P. (1993). Job satisfaction, organizational commitment, turnover intention, and turnover: Path analyses based on meta-analytic findings. *Personnel Psychology, 46*, 259–293.

Toy, S., Brown, C., & Miles, L. G. (1988). The new nepotism: Why dynasties are making a comeback. *Business Week, 31*, 106–109.

Triandis, H. C. (1996). The psychological measurement of cultural syndromes. *American Psychologist, 51*, 407–415.

Triandis, H. C., Chan, D. K. S., Bhawuk, D. P. S., Iwao, S., & Sinha, J. B. P. (1995). Multimethod probes of allocentrism and idiocentrism. *International Journal of Psychology, 30*, 461–480.

Triandis, H. C., Leung, K., Villareal, M., & Clack, F. L. (1985). Allocentric versus idiocentric tendencies: Convergent and discriminant validation. *Journal of Research in Personality, 19,* 395–415.

Vinton, K. L. (1998). Nepotism: An interdisciplinary model. *Family Business Review, 11,* 297–303.

Welle, B. (2004). The price of privilege: The derogation of the work and personal characteristics of favored employees. *Dissertation Abstracts International, 65 (03),* 1588B.

Westman, M., & Vinokur, A. D. (1998). Unraveling the relationship of distress levels within couples: Common stressors, empathic reactions, or crossover via social interaction? *Human Relations, 51,* 137–156.

Wexler, J. G. (1982). Husbands and wives: The uneasy case for antinepotism rules. *Boston University Law Review, 62,* 75–142.

Zottoli, M. A., & Wanous, J. P. (2000). Recruitment source research: Current status and future directions. *Human Resource Management Review, 10,* 353–382.

11

Toward a New Understanding of Nepotistic Organizational Behavior

Robert G. Jones
Missouri State University

Nepotistic organizational behavior (NOB) is a pervasive phenomenon. The authors of this book give graphic and sometimes impassioned examples of its existence and its potential effects in organizations. What every author says in some way is that we have missed this essential research topic.

Every author also provides very well-considered and actionable ideas for starting to break new ground. In this final chapter, following from the promises made to readers in the first chapter, I provide a broad summary of what the authors suggest. This is organized according to the definition of NOB, its probable consequences, practical ethics, and predictors. Although every chapter provides meaningful next steps in the NOB frontier, a few more will be developed at the end of this chapter, with particular emphasis on issues for practice.

THE PHENOMENON OF NEPOTISTIC ORGANIZATIONAL BEHAVIOR

In the interest of psychological definition, it is often illustrative to ask about the internal phenomenology of a problem. In the case of NOB, it seems appropriate to ask why nepotistic stories from organizations are typically treated as embarrassing gossip, something to be kept secret or disapproved. What about nepotistic behavior makes it seem unsociable or private? Like most emotive responses, this "embarrassed" emotional response to NOB suggests that there is a social motive at work (Russell,

1994). If most emotive displays provide information about whether people are group members, then this embarrassment may signal people's realization that there are members and nonmembers in an important social group. Three chapters in this volume (those by Muchinsky; Mhatre, Riggio, and Riggio; and Wated and Sanchez) deal explicitly with this defining characteristic of NOB by referring to in-group and out-group (using Muchinsky's terminology, nepot and non-nepot) dynamics. By extension, the embarrassment may be part of the reason for the negative response people have to NOB more generally. People really do not like being excluded from attractive opportunities, and many do not like to exclude others from such opportunities either. So, the emotional response gives rise to the social evaluation of NOB.

Another defining characteristic of nepotism is its apparent adaptive power. For most human phenomena that, like NOB, cross cultural and temporal boundaries, the explanation is that the phenomenon is "hardwired," a fundamental part of our endowment that has been associated with survival and success as a species. Examples of these hardwired phenomena from introductory psychology texts include language and emotional displays; nepotistic organization appears to be such a hardwired part of our endowment, given its long history and pervasiveness across cultures. Furthermore, like the mental abilities that help us to survive and thrive, the social psychological organizing accomplished by familial work relationships appears to have provided some sort of adaptive value to us as well. Being part of a working family group gives us some advantages that have been touched on in several chapters (Dickson, Niemenin, & Biermeier-Hanson; Mhatre, Riggio, & Riggio; Muchinsky; Van Hooft & Stout). An essential question for industrial and organizational psychology is to what extent this organizing structure remains adaptive in modern, complex organizations, where it is regularly applied.

In light of this, eradication of NOB is probably a futile goal. Like trying to eliminate language and emotional display, it would be more than a little counterproductive. Instead, understanding how individuals make nepotistic decisions (Mhatre, Riggio, & Riggio, this volume) and how organizations adapt structures around this essential urge are likely to prove very helpful. Our definition should therefore take into account the pervasive, emotionally charged, and potentially adaptive power of NOB phenomena.

A DEFINITION

After reviewing the chapter definitions, it seems most appropriate to refer to the phenomena originally framed as *nepotism* as a set of phenomena that are referred to here as *nepotistic organizational behaviors*. Although NOB appears to be a definable and even singular phenomenon, it is clearly multidimensional, involving individual, group, and organizational variables. Most of these are actual or perceived behaviors (especially decisions) and outcomes of these behaviors, rather than precursor or moderator variables. As such, NOB might be thought of at least as a mediating behavior with respect to numerous organizational outcomes, as Mulder illustrates in the previous chapter.

Individually, it includes organizational decision makers providing special treatment to familial relations (including cronies and friends of the family), as well as potential and actual job incumbents deciding to accept the largesse provided by familial relations. The person in power choosing to behave preferentially toward a family member or crony is the core of the classic definition. The person given opportunities for largesse (or being coerced by family) may be more or less likely to choose to take largesse (or succumb to coercion), which is consistent with Bellow's "new nepotism" (Van Hooft & Stout, this volume).

At the group level, NOB involves both the apparent behaviors of nepots and the perceptions of these behaviors by other members of both the in-group (thus, work–family issues; Masuda & Visio, this volume) and the out-group members (the perception of nepotism variables, cited in Mulder, this volume, and elsewhere). It also relates to behaviors and responses with respect to people in leadership positions (Mhatre, Riggio, & Riggio, this volume).

Finally, at the organizational level, NOB encompasses broader leadership issues (Mhatre, Riggio, & Riggio, this volume) and questions about organizational structure (Dickson, Nieminen, & Biermeier-Hanson, this volume; Muchinsky, this volume), change (Becker, this volume; Dickson, Nieminen, & Biermeier-Hanson, this volume; Muchinsky, this volume; Wated & Sanchez, this volume), and development (Dickson, Nieminen, & Biermeier-Hanson, this volume; Mulder, this volume). The perception and reality of leadership succession, with its influences on culture, are perhaps the most obvious of these. However, organizational structures may be altered by the creation of new jobs, developmental experiences of

FIGURE 11.1
A mapping sentence for defining nepotistic organizational behavior.

nepotees, and deliberate attempts to change NOB (e.g., through anti-nepotism policies, structured decision-making processes, and so forth).

The following definition of nepotistic organizational behaviors is based on an integration of the definitions discussed in the book, and organized according to a facet analysis (Guttman, Epstein, Amir, & Guttman, 1990). Figure 11.1 provides a mapping sentence to describe the definitions offered so far.

ORGANIZATIONALLY EFFECTIVE NOB?

A vital question for practice is whether nepotistic behaviors relate meaningfully (for better or worse) to organizational effectiveness. Put in terms of equal employment opportunity (EEO) law, how can we make the case for or against the business necessity of NOB? Can an organization's decision makers make a business case for using family relationships as a basis for employment decisions? It is clear that we are nowhere near having a definitive answer to this question, but plenty of research questions are posed in this volume to lead policy and research well into the future. Based on authors' propositions and by various criteria (individual performance, commitment, satisfaction, justice perceptions, conflict and litigation, broader organizational performance), the answer is, "it depends."

Certainly, in terms of perceptions of nepotism, there are both procedural and distributive components of the fairness criterion. Most popular discussions of NOB appear to focus on distributive components. However, the ideas here suggest a closer consideration of the procedural components. For a start, Gutman (this volume) suggests that the process through which we make decisions in the presence of NOB may have important legal consequences. Additionally, policies against NOB may reduce problems with perceptions of unfairness, thus increasing commitment among non-nepots. Mhatre, Riggio, & Riggio (this volume) suggest that formal, transparent decision processes will reduce actual NOB as well. The idea here is that the perception of NOB can be changed along with its actual occurrence. On the flip side, can transparent processes move perceivers toward an understanding that NOB, though apparent, is not directly influencing outcomes? Put differently, *perceived* NOB may actually be fair, and an understanding of procedures should help to make this clear.

TOWARD AN ETHICS OF NOB

Related to this, and accentuated by the issue of multiple definitions, are the ethical questions that arise from nepotistic practices. It is quite illustrative that several authors in this volume followed the negative response most people have to nepotism, and tried to find ways to reduce it, or at least its apparently negative consequences, in organizations. This engineering approach (trying to provide a "solution" to this "problem") was juxtaposed with other authors' more neutral attempts to describe how familial relationships are manifest in workplaces. It remains to each of us to decide whether the circumstances we address in the workplace are made better or worse by the presence of familial relationships. In most cases, the more descriptive approach seems to me to have advantages over the engineering approach, but the engineering approach provides potential means for managing problems encountered by clients.

Let me elaborate. One could argue that management practices and policies regarding nepotism are good or bad, depending on whether they avoid the appearance of preferential treatment. But, we should remember that current industrial–organizational (I–O) psychology practices, while attempting to provide the appearance of preference based on defensible, job-related grounds, may still have the effect of being inappropriately preferential (e.g., weighing false-positives disproportionately against false-negatives) or may violate perceptions of fairness (e.g., not have face validity or have adverse impact). Extending the same benefit of a doubt to apparently nepotistic practices and policies should allow scientist–practitioners to understand and more directly address the motivations underlying apparently nepotistic outcomes.

This amounts to a redefinition of the "criterion problem" (Austin & Villanova, 1992). Instead of defining outcomes of importance in terms of relatively short-term job performance and (more recently) retention (Higgs, Papper, & Carr, 2000; Ployhart & Weekley, 2010), we might ask organizational decision makers what outcomes they hope to achieve through hiring of family members. Their answers might surprise us. For example, Masuda and Visio (this volume) suggest that life enrichment (work–family integration) or avoidance of work–family conflict might be meaningful criteria for evaluating staffing practices that integrate family hiring. Similarly, being able to attract top-tier applicants may rely to some extent on trailing-spouse policies, affecting recruitment practices. Time required for training and acculturation may be important factors as well as bringing political capital to a work unit through hiring the offspring of important organizational decision makers.

In terms of organizational costs, it may be that family members are less expensive to hire and compensate (Dickson, Nieminen, & Biermeier-Hanson, this volume). Given the substantial stake many family members have in the continuance of a family firm as a resource (Mhatre, Riggio, & Riggio, this volume), lower current wages may be offset by eventual benefits for family employees. Also, it may be that there is relatively better pay for family members compared to other opportunities with the same qualifications. So, it is a good deal for both the organization and the individual under these circumstances. This low cost, coupled with a longer term view may help to explain the tendency toward nepotism and the success of nepotistic firms.

Other values gained by NOB are also suggested in the chapters. Dickson, Nieminen, & Biermeier-Hanson (this volume) and Mhatre, Riggio, & Riggio (this volume) argue that the amount of time taken to establish trust and value congruence (Judge & Cable, 1997) may be substantially reduced through NOB. Van Hooft and Stout (this volume), and Dickson, Nieminen, & Biermeier-Hanson suggest that nepotees have a more realistic preview of the workplace and are therefore likely to be more committed and satisfied. Nepots may be more likely to have a good idea of those with whom they will be dealing, as well (Muchinsky, this volume).

All such positive outcomes are likely to be balanced by difficult trade-offs, which have been more common foci of NOB discussions here. Unfairness, dissatisfaction, work–family conflict, and poor leadership have all been important concerns. The difficulty leading to these problems for many observers may be the apparent violation of "all else equal" rules in NOB. That is, if all other sources of information do not provide a clear distinction between two courses of action (e.g., choosing between two job candidates), would NOB be an appropriate source of further information for decision making? However, by each of the criteria for system effectiveness, arguments have been made in this book that all else is simply not equal when family ties are involved. So, attempts to empirically answer questions around the complex and multifaceted phenomena described in this book will almost certainly wind up being equivocal and complex themselves. What we think of as good and bad are more likely some blend of trade-offs, with net effects of NOB and the practices being used to manage it.

Methodologically, evaluating effectiveness at the work unit level (Kehoe, Mol, & Anderson, 2010) presents significant challenges, even if the problem being dealt with is fairly straightforward. Thus, I urge the reader to try to understand nepotistic behavior on its own terms first (Mulder, this volume), then seek solutions. This is consistent with the inquiry-based approach that is a central ethos of our field (i.e., being empirically informed before acting).

Nevertheless, managing NOB appropriately will rely on many ethical decisions. Wated and Sanchez (this volume) discussed multiple stakeholder theory as one way to accomplish this. This theory relies on (a) identifying legitimate stakeholders in a decision and (b) getting representation of their interests in the procedure through which decisions are made (Phillips, 2003). The potential for conflict where nepotistic behavior is suspected makes getting stakeholders together a pretty daunting task. Nevertheless, a recurring theme in this book is that dealing with nepotistic behavior will almost certainly require active conflict management. As mentioned earlier, focusing on the procedures through which decisions are accomplished is likely to help with this.

PREDICTING NOB

Avoiding conflict in the first place is also one way to manage it. This turns our inquiry to understanding precursors that predict nepotistic decisions by employers and employees. The fundamental question here is why NOB happens. This volume's authors have shed considerable light on this. Mulder's chapter in particular covered a long list of likely precursors. Other authors have proposed additional possibilities. At the broadest sociocultural level of analysis, Wated and Sanchez suggest that cultural differences (collectivist–individualist) make it more or less likely that family members will be made offers and accept them. At the organizational level, there may be cost-savings accrued by hiring and compensating family members (Dickson et al., this volume), particularly as socialization (especially realistic job previews) and trust building are accomplished more quickly by nepotistic staffing. Along these same lines of "expedient decision making," Van Hooft and Stout, Muchinsky, Becker, and Mhatre, Riggio, and Riggio (all this volume) suggest similar expedient decision-making effects arising from a readily available and deeply attractive labor pool (family). Again, it is important to note that there are potential benefits to the individual and the organization accrued through some of these predictors.

On the darker side of prediction, Van Hooft and Stout (this volume), and Muchinsky (this volume) also argue that there may be coercive pressures on both the nepot (a spouse who demands that the nepot hire a nephew) and the nepotee (your parent will disown you if you do not take this job). Ironically, to avoid familial conflict, people expediently make and accept nepotistic offers that may, in turn, create greater organizational conflict. Such is the nature of trade-offs.

NEXT STEPS: A GREEN FIELD

As Mulder's chapter makes quite explicit, the number of research questions concerning nepotism is exceptionally large. Nevertheless, the chapter authors focus attention on questions that will do much to advance our understanding of the field as well as the practice of I–O psychology. I will rely on these, in chapter order, but will expand on them as well.

Among the revelations in Gutman's chapter, three cases stand out as requiring empirical attention. In *Yuhas v. Libbey-Owens-Ford Co.* (1977), *Wright v. Metrohealth*, and *Thorne v. City of El Segundo* (1983), "morale" was cited as the courts' reason for allowing no-spouse rules. But, there is very little evidence about the relationship between such no-spouse rules and climate, commitment, satisfaction, fairness perceptions, or other morale variables. Arasli and Tumer (2008), and Laker and Williams (2003) do show relationships between satisfaction and perceived nepotism, which would tend to support the courts' decisions. However, following from Werbel and Hames's (1996) look at the potential effects of anti-nepotism rules, a study comparing morale for companies with such rules and those without might be instructive. Similarly, at the individual level, morale for people with nepotistic relationships in the organization (i.e., where both spouses work in the organization) versus those without may be worth pursuing. This is a question that is also addressed by Masuda and Visio (this volume) and Cleveland and Colella (2010).

Similarly, other organizational and individual effectiveness outcomes as they relate to nepotism and nepotistic policies are worth evaluating. Following from EEO law, job relatedness of nepotism policies might also be evaluated in other ways. One interesting possibility, taken from observation of families in the arts and sports, is the possibility that work involving intricate, real-time coordination and anticipatory action is better accomplished by family groups, on average. This would certainly build a job-related case for nepotism in these sorts of work. It also highlights the reciprocal nature of nepotistic relationships, emphasized in Mulder's, and Van Hooft and Stout's chapters.

Muchinsky (this volume) developed a long list of important research questions in the area where many would firmly place NOB: personnel decision making. I will not belabor this already daunting list of questions. There are, however, a couple of very innovative questions that deserve highlighting. First, Muchinsky tackles the difficult, underresearched issue of succession, suggesting this as a primary function in family organizations. The potential benefits of this as a primary organizational mission, and the far-reaching component variables involved (e.g., the knowledge their continued employment with the business is not in jeopardy and the mitigation of the sense of territoriality that is inherent in assigned job titles) provide for a shifting of the way we think of personnel decision making in the context of organizational effectiveness. In a way, it is perhaps fortunate that we have done very little research about the broader evaluation of human resource practices (Kehoe et al., 2010), given this fundamental change in viewpoint.

The analysis of degrees of nepotistic organization in this chapter is also potentially valuable. Some have argued that such an analysis of context (Pearlman & Sanchez, 2010) is an essential next step in developing organizational psychology. Might analyses around different degrees and stages of nepotistic organization be used as this sort of "contextual" analytic tool?

Muchinsky also provides one of the clearest descriptions of a trade-off faced in nepotistic decisions. He suggests that, with the greater benefits received there are greater obligations created for nepots. This foreshadows the coerciveness of nepotistic relationships described by Van Hooft and Stout.

Perhaps even more interesting in Van Hooft and Stout's work (this volume) is the idea that, in emerging economies and oppressive circumstances, where trust and family connection and long-term commitment are essential, integrating of family and work settings may be an extremely adaptive approach. The Jews in 17th–18th century Europe and the clans of Scotland and Ireland during English oppression found some advantages by relying on these sorts of relationships. One might wonder whether the negative reaction to nepotism in the powerful is based on the fear that the less powerful will successfully compete using the same means (NOB) that was used to gain their own position of privilege. Mulder's (this volume) fine-grained analysis of this provides some important direction for pursuing this question.

Van Hooft and Stout (this volume) also reiterate the powerful influence of families in forming career identities and attendant KSAOs (knowledge, skills, abilities, and other characteristics). In terms of preferences developed early in life, one might suppose that willingness to learn and commitment to the firm may be the bases for hiring relatives over others. One empirical question is whether relatives are inherently more motivated to develop necessary skills in anticipation of the organization being passed along to them.

Given this, it is hard to see why there would not be a disproportionate number of successful candidates and high performers coming from families, with all else equal. In light of this, the idea that it is unfair or preferential to hire family members prima facie seems misguided. In fact, and given the possibility that privileged people dislike NOB, one could argue that anti-nepotism policies are based on prejudice rather than firm evidence of job-related factors. Following from the logic of other employment laws, these policies might be outlawed.

Dickson, Nieminen, & Biermeier-Hanson (this volume) give us even more reason to pause about the blanket condemnation of NOB. They suggest a number of possibilities, including start-up costs being lower in nepotistic firms (which may help to explain the longer survival of family firms), enhanced trust in functional families (also discussed by Mhatre, Riggio, & Riggio, this volume), and some very interesting variations on the attraction–selection–attrition model. In particular, the organizational level of analysis here suggests a developmental model, where new family firms are more likely to succeed but struggle with such things as socialization of nonfamily (also discussed by Wated and Sanchez, this volume), succession decisions, and change issues as they mature. These latter issues of succession and change in nepotistic organizations deserve considerably more attention, and are treated by Mhatre, Riggio, & Riggio and Muchinsky as well.

Perhaps most troubling of these is the possibility that nepots actually create positions for family members. Mulder and Muchinsky both suggest that this may be one of the most obvious cases of NOB. However, even this may follow from Snow and Snell's (1993) "staffing as strategy" model, where a "best player" is hired in order to make strategy. In particular, rather than having staffing decisions follow from a predefined strategy, organizational succession in leadership roles may follow from this approach. Given likely "real" advantages of nepotistic succession in terms of commitment, social capital, and legitimate knowledge and abilities, the implication is that, even in this situation, it may be premature to assume purely selfish motives.

By dissecting the components of commitment, Becker (this volume) gives a finely grained insight into the psychology of NOB. His propositions deal with the values associated with norm violation, the fit between commitments and nepotistic relationships, the consistency between values of the nepot and the larger organization, and the potential conflicts that may arise from NOB. His research questions address many of the ethical concerns that can be addressed through our research, and thus provides the basis for "testing" of philosophical constructs, consistent with psychology since (at least) William James. Taking this broader approach further will no doubt stimulate considerable debate and fruitful, empirically testable, and practical dialectics.

Like Muchinsky, Mhatre, Riggio, & Riggio (this volume) provide a long list of potential questions worthy of further research. Their distinctions regarding "all else equal" decisions and "perceived versus actual" nepotism seem particularly important. How would we define and demonstrate that all else is equal when hiring relatives over other applicants? This is consistent with the focus on fairness versus perceived or actual "preferential" treatment in decisions pointed to in several chapters. This suggests the need to manage both the actual fairness (my nephew is likely to be a better performer based on standardized tests and accepted selection indicators) and the perceived fairness (how do I let the rest of the people who are watching me hire my nephew know about their test scores without breeching confidentiality?) of decisions. A major challenge that may arise from this important distinction is the ease of measuring perceived nepotism (fairness breeches) versus identifying unequivocally actual acts of nepotism, where all else is not equal. To further complicate matters, practice may show a distinction between managing the perceptions of the nepot versus those of the nepotee.

These authors, as well as Mulder, also call up the problem of distinguishing different sorts of familial relationships. So, paramours and spouses versus parents and siblings may differ in terms of closeness. Relative wealth of the family, the size of the family, and the degree of dysfunction in the family's members may also be potentially important contingent relationships that suggest again how decisions about familial exclusion and inclusion in the workplace are fraught with complex trade-offs. This provides perhaps the strongest recommendation for practitioners at this point: Be careful to think through these sorts of variables as decisions are made.

It is also comforting to practitioners to know that work–family research has dealt with some of the individual and group variables relating to NOB. Not surprisingly, Masuda and Visio (this volume) provide a rich set of questions for incipient research. In fact, by incorporating NOB into our research, work–family research should become far more central to our understandings of such things as effectiveness criteria (Cleveland & Colella, 2010), citizenship and commitment (as seen in Dickson, Nieminen, & Biermeier-Hanson; Becker, both this volume), performance and prediction (as seen in Van Hooft & Stout; Muchinsky, both this volume). Masudo and Visio illustrate this at a deep level, and many research questions emerged. Among their more counterintuitive findings to conventional views of nepotism is that the social support of family members appears to reduce conflict, depending on segmentation and integration strategies. Understanding the precursors of these strategies, including traits associated with effective boundary management, is a key area for study. The chapters by Mulder, Mhatre, Riggio, and Riggio, and Becker provide some starting points for understanding these decisions.

Wated and Sanchez (this volume) suggest a broad, culturally defined example of such a trait: tolerance for nepotism. Combining this with Mhatre et al.'s chapter suggests another possible individual difference predictor as well. These authors suggest that we rely on heuristics, which are famously more likely to be activated under threats of time pressure and limited information. Some people are more likely to see the world in a threatening, nonmunificent way: Higher neuroticism may predispose people to see the world in terms of crisis. Does this make them more likely to fall back on a nepotistic heuristic? At the organizational level, are nepotistic organizations more often characterized by higher neuroticism?

Finally, Mulder's (this volume) carefully integrated framework provides for many specific topics to pursue. Two questions deserve special attention. First, Mulder's own research suggests that people's perceptions of nepotism are alterable. A large set of research questions about the management of such perceptions follows from this important insight. For example, such research could help organizations with historical NOB to change such perceptions, with some expectation that perceptual changes would be followed by changes in culture and future NOB. Such research ideas again underline the importance of understanding NOB on its own terms, without prejudice, in the interest of organizational change.

Second, the organizational context that breeds nepotistic decisions is treated by Mulder's (and Mhatre, Riggio, & Riggio, this volume) conceptualizations. In particular, the munificence of the organizational context may affect whether there is a need to rely on heuristic NOB in order to make "quick decisions." If there is a way to reduce the likelihood of NOB, this seems a particularly powerful lever. Helping decision makers to stop and think through contingencies carefully, even in the face of enormous pressures, may be particularly good advice in many circumstances. It is also very consistent with the sort of decision-making assistance that I–O psychologists provide in many other circumstances.

SUMMARY

Nepotistic organizational behavior is a complex set of phenomena, involving decisions made by multiple actors and having potential effects at the individual, group, organizational, and societal levels. It is not what most popular characterizations would suggest, however: an unmitigated evil. In fact, a closer examination strongly suggests multiple trade-offs, intricate management problems, and a strong adaptive tendency in human organizations. Eradication is almost certainly not an option. I–O psychologists have the opportunity to apply our carefully considered, ethically informed, inquiry-based decision aids to help organizations adapt to this reality in a way that enhances their effectiveness.

This volume provides some strong initial directions for deeper inquiry into what is currently a very broad topic area. Although suggestions for practice and change—engineering—await these deeper inquiries into NOB phenomena, much of the volume provides a clear call for inquiry *before* definitive action, consistent with the scientist–practitioner ethos. Using the frontier analogy, the authors in this volume suggest some careful mapping and respectful contact with current NOB practices before attempting invasion and conquest.

REFERENCES

Arasli, H., & Tumer, M. (2008). Nepotism, favoritism, and Cronyism: A study of their effects on job stress and job satisfaction in the banking industry of north Cyprus. *Social Behavior and Personality, 36*(9), 1237–1250.

Austin, J. T., & Villanova, P. (1992). The criterion problem: 1917–1992. *Journal of Applied Psychology, 77*(6), 836–874.

Cleveland, J. M., & Colella, A. (2010). Criterion validity and criterion deficiency: What we measure well and what we ignore. In J. L. Farr & N. T. Tippins (Eds.), *Handbook of employee selection* (Chap. 26). New York: Routledge.

Guttman, R., Epstein, E. E., Amir, M., & Guttman, L. (1990). A structural theory of spatial abilities. *Applied Psychological Measurement, 14*(3), 217–236.

Higgs, A. C., Papper, E. M., & Carr, L. S. (2000). Integrating selection with other organizational processes and systems. In J. F. Kehoe (Ed.), *Managing selection in changing organizations* (Chap. 2). San Francisco, CA: Jossey-Bass.

Judge, T. A., & Cable, D. M. (1997). Applicant personality, organizational culture, and organization attraction. *Personnel Psychology, 50*, 359–394.

Kehoe, J. F., Mol, S. T., & Anderson, N. R. (2010). Managing sustainable selection programs. In J. L. Farr & N. T. Tippins (Eds.), *Handbook of employee selection* (Chap. 10). New York: Routledge.

Laker, D. R., & Williams, M. L. (2003). Nepotism's effect on employee satisfaction and organizational commitment: An empirical study. *International Journal of Human Resources Development and Management, 3,* 191–202.

Pearlman, K., & Sanchez, J. I. (2010). Work analysis. In J. L. Farr & N. T. Tippins (Eds.), *Handbook of employee selection* (Chap. 4). New York: Routledge.

Phillips, R. 2003. *Stakeholder theory and organizational ethics.* San Francisco, CA: Berrett-Koehler.

Ployhart, R. E., & Weekley, J. A. (2010). Strategy, selection, and sustained competitive advantage. In J. L. Farr & N. T. Tippins (Eds.), *Handbook of employee selection* (Chap. 9). New York: Routledge.

Russell, J. A. (1994). Is there universal recognition of emotion from facial expression? A review of the cross-cultural studies. *Psychological Bulletin, 115,* 102–141.

Snow, C. C., & Snell, S. A. (1993). Staffing as strategy. In N. Schmitt, W. C. Borman, & Associates (Eds.), *Personnel selection in organizations.* San Francisco: Jossey-Bass.

Werbel, J. D., & Hames, D. S. (1996). Anti-nepotism reconsidered: The case of husband and wife employment. *Group and Organization Management, 21*(3), 365–379.

Index